Blanket of Stars

Thru-Hiking the Camino de Santiago

C.W. Lockhart

Labrador & Lockhart

a small press

Seabeck, Washington

 Lockhart, C.W., 1967- author.
Blanket of Stars: Thru-Hiking the Camino de Santiago / C.W. Lockhart

Trade Paperback ISBN-13: 978-0692072073
(Labrador & Lockhart Press, LLC)
ISBN-10: 0692072071
E-book ISBN: 978-0692072073

First Edition

CONTENTS

Introduction: Notes from a Peregrina   *1*

PART 1: Basque Country
Seattle to Pamplona   *5*

PART 2: Navarre
Pamplona to Logroño   *17*

PART 3: La Rioja
Logroño to Viloria de la Rioja   *93*

PART 4: Castilla y León
Viloria de la Rioja to Herrerias   *131*

PART 5: Galicia
Herrerias to Santiago de Compostela   *223*

Acknowledgments   *277*

About the Author   *279*

INTRODUCTION

Notes from a Peregrina

Archeological evidence suggests prehistoric peregrination. The study of early pilgrims lends incalculable heritage value in cataloging our ancestral origins. Historical and ongoing acts of faith aid in our quest to understand one another through the complex matrix of mystical beliefs encompassing the infinite spiritual dimensions of humankind.

Worldwide pilgrimage methods vary; however, the act usually requires a pilgrim, a path, and a shrine. I am a *Peregrina*, the Spanish translation for lady-pilgrim. My path is the Camino de Santiago de Compostela. My shrine is the actual *Way*, the living Camino in all her magnetic glory.

The *Way* may be interpreted as an allegory illuminating oneness of sacred journey and human purpose. Physical elements of peregrination, combined with emotional and spiritual obstacles, sacrifice and heartache, injury and illness, and aloneness are metaphorical fodder narrating daily life.

The Camino is traditionally a Catholic pilgrimage. I am not Catholic. I am without a formal religion. When it comes to rites and traditions, I like a buffet-approach, take what works and leave the rest. For me, pilgrimage works.

Following the path beneath a blanket of stars offers an experience to embrace the earthly and the celestial. Peregrination is the transcendence of a human being on a spiritual quest to a spiritual being on a human quest. The journey is sacred and deeply personal. To ensure the privacy of fellow *peregrinos*, pseudonyms are used throughout this book.

¡Buen Camino!

Part 1
Basque Country

Blanket of Stars: Thru-Hiking the Camino de Santiago

Seattle to Pamplona

I was born a perfect bundle of energy and light. My home was beneath a blanket of stars. I grew fearless and intuitively connected to nature. I held a childlike faith in God and a trust in human kindness. I nurtured my wanderlust and owned a pilgrim's heart. But that was then. And now? Now, I want it back.

The plane touches down in Madrid, my shoulders relax, and I send up a *hallelujah*. I used to love flying, but not so much anymore. The flight from Seattle was unremarkable, just how I like it. Now safely in Madrid, my next goal is to catch a train to Pamplona. In the morning, I'll grab a shuttle to the Basque village of St. Jean Pied de Port, on the French side of the Pyrenees.

I hope to explore St. Jean before setting off to hike the *Camino de Santiago*. The ancient pilgrimage is about 500 miles, or 800 kilometers, up and over the French Pyrenees, across northern Spain, and to the famous cathedral holding the relics of Saint James the Apostle in *Santiago de Compostela*.

I'm a bundle of emotion, sad and afraid and excited. Going on pilgrimage should be a joyful adventure, but I intend to undergo an emotional overhaul and life tune-up. I expect to change. Walking the Camino is the first step in leaving behind my old life, but there are parts of my old life I will dearly miss, and I can only hope what is pure and right in my universe now will follow me and continue to be mine. I'm afraid because I am always afraid. *Fear* is my constant companion, and I'm sick to death of her shit.

When my husband, Jim, dropped me curbside at SeaTac airport I cried. I cried a little more on the flight, but not much. I clutch the balled-up, brown handkerchief in my right hand. Jim pulled it from his jeans pocket and handed it to me in the car. His gift added levity to our sad goodbye. The hanky is a relic. It is a military-issued item from the 1980s. I don't think you can even buy brown handkerchiefs anymore. The sight of it cracks me up. The hanky represents all that is right and wrong with Jim and our relationship. Apart from frugality-to-a-fault, he is dependable. Jim is the man with a hanky to offer the damsel in distress. This is charming, but the 1980s handkerchief also symbolizes adversity to change. Jim has a drawerful of brown handkerchiefs, green woolen socks, and Army T-shirts from a lifetime ago. More than three years have passed since we both retired from the military. Jim is holding on, but I must move forward.

I unfasten my seatbelt, grab my carry-on from beneath the seat in front of me, and edge my way into the aisle. Fellow passengers rush from the rear of the aircraft, clogging the aisles and pushing toward the exit. The disarray and failure to follow the usual, zipper-like pattern rattle me. I would never classify myself as the anal-retentive type. I don't mind breaking a few rules; however, I'm a stickler for manners and rather fond of logical order. I blame the military for the latter.

I am unprepared for the assertiveness and the close physical proximity of travelers on this flight. I hate when people I do not know touch me. And right now, far too many people I do not know are touching me. I inhale deeply three times, trying to stave off panic. When panic prepares to visit, I feel this peculiar ticking. It's like I've swallowed a cheap watch that winds up faster and faster until I do something about it. In the old days, I smoked, but now I ride it out and try to breathe.

I haven't smoked in years. I dabbled with the filthy habit in high school, sneaking into the parking lot before a test to ease anxiety. I perfected the craft during Army Basic Training; however, boot camp smoking was never about squelching the tick because the tick never went away during my entire first enlistment. Ever-present, I got used to it and adopted it as part of my usual self.

Smoke 'em if you got 'em. Boot camp cigarettes were about shirking duty. The equation was simple. Smoking equaled a break. No smoking equaled no break. I did the math and lit up. The habit didn't last. I gave up the smokes while pregnant with Nicholas, my firstborn. Instead of nicotine, I pacified panic with food – great gobs of it and mostly sweet. During my younger years, I could really clear a pantry. As life grew more complex, binge eating gave way to binge drinking, and I drowned my fears in vodka. I'm mostly over that part now. But every now and again, I slip.

I should have ordered a dirty martini or three before landing. That would have numbed me to the current chaos, but it's too late for cocktails as my body is flushed from the plane and carried in a crashing wave of passengers gushing through passport control and flooding the baggage claim area. I can't breathe.

Drowning in a sea of bodies, I find a tiny bubble of space against a pillar and wait for my red backpack to appear. Bags are claimed, and the crowd dissipates. My lungs fill with air again, and I try to relax. I'm thrilled to see my pack vomited from a steel mouth to the black conveyer belt. My backpack's name is *Little Agnus*. I snatch her up and cinch her tightly to my back. I feel much better now, not so alone.

It takes me a long while, but I finally make my way toward the airport train station. The crowd has regained its density, and Agnus and I seek shelter in the entrance of the ladies' restroom. The din in the ground-transportation terminal makes me dizzy, and I struggle for equilibrium. I try to cross over to the other side of the terminal, where I can see a long cue of passengers waiting to purchase train tickets, but I can't do it. My feet won't move. To kill time and future need, I duck in a stall. When I exit, I wash my hands, splash water on my face, give my reflection a little pep-talk, and try again. But, it's no use. I can't cross over.

I don't know how or why this little phenomenon happens, but it's the same shit that happened almost every time I tried to go into the *YMCA* during the past nine months of Camino training. I dressed in my gym clothes, pulled my dark hair into a high ponytail, drove twenty minutes to the gym, parked in the lot, and then sat there. Sometimes I played a little game on my phone or perused social media. On good days, I coached myself free from the safety of my Subaru wagon within minutes. On bad days, it took a full hour. On particularly bad days, I drove back home. If Jim bothered to ask about my workout, I'd lie. "It was okay." I'd shrug it off and then make up a story about how the gym was super busy or how the yoga instructor was late again or grumble about how swim lessons took over the adult lap lanes. It didn't matter which lie I told because Jim never heard me. He stopped listening years ago. He typically replied with a grunt and went back to watching television. He remained clueless to my crazy.

Our wedding anniversary is two days away. Instead of delaying my trip to celebrate with Jim, I am here – All alone in Madrid, and I'm too scared to board a stupid train to Pamplona. If Jim were here, I'd be dragging him across the terminal, probably scolding him for moving slowly. I'm stronger in his presence, bossy, and taking charge because someone's got to do it. I hate the roles we play, but I don't hate our marriage. I miss him already. Perhaps he feels ignored and taken for granted too.

Fifteen years ago, I was over-the-moon in love with that boy. I still am, but it's so different now. I cannot definitively say we will last another year. I'm making decisions and taking actions against his will – and often against my own will. But, I can't not. I'm in a severe funk. I can't sit on the sofa and let *it*, whatever *it* is, get me. I must move or rot in place, but mental-paralysis fights me every step of the way. Not all agoraphobia is alike. I do not fear wide-open spaces like classic agoraphobes. Instead, I fear the people in those spaces. Agoraphobia is an ugly souvenir with an even uglier war story, and I intend to ditch the story and the fear on my way to Santiago. It's the prayer contained in the smooth, white rock tucked in the secret compartment of my rucksack.

It's the rock that according to *El Camino Francés* tradition I will lay down at the *Cruz de Ferro*, or the Iron Cross, in a few weeks. Drop the rock, drop my fear – or at least that's the plan.

I leave the safety of the ladies' room, hugging the wall toward an airport bar. A quiet table in the rear helps me chill out and wait for the ticket line to clear. I order a beer, and it works like liquid courage. When I exit the bar and cross the terminal to the train station, I'm proud of my accomplishment.

Victory is short lived. I am too late. The last train to Pamplona departed twenty-five minutes ago. The next train to Pamplona isn't until 0645, tomorrow morning.

I'm pacing and cursing and pacing and cursing. Now what? I'm not panicking, but I'm angry and frustrated with my stupid self. While I do have a sleeping bag and mat, I do not want to spend the night in the Madrid airport. I am supposed to sleep in Pamplona. "I'll be damned if you think I'm staying in Madrid!" I whisper this to myself and waltz over to the *Hertz* counter. I negotiate a one-way rental car with navigation, and within minutes, I'm on the road and back on track.

Inside the rental-car, a silvery-blue economy model with a lightning-bolt logo, I feel as safe and secure as I do in my Subaru Outback. Driving helps me participate and belong to the outside world, all while staying segregated in a bubble of glass and steel. I love driving, and it's a good thing because I've got about 250 miles to go to make Pamplona.

My feet are hot and cramped, so I wiggle out of my hiking boots and toss them in the back seat. Something strange has happened. My feet do not look like my feet at all. The toes and the ankles are swollen and red. This is probably caused by the flight, but I've never had this problem in the past. I opt to drive barefoot and flip the air conditioner to the floor vent.

The drive, like the flight, is rather uneventful. I do get off to a rough start because I haven't driven a manual transmission for a couple of decades. And to be honest, I wasn't any good at it twenty years ago. Despite troubles with the stick, I make Pamplona in five hours.

I pull into the airport car-rental lot, and as predicted by the *Hertz* agent in Madrid, the Pamplona rental office is closed. I grab my boots from the back seat, but my swollen feet won't fit back inside. Instead, I slip on a pair of rubber gardening clogs, unattractive but comfortable, and clip my boots to my pack. I pull Little Agnus from the car, cinch her up, and lock the doors. On the outside wall of the *Hertz* kiosk, I find the nighttime drop box and deposit my key. That was so easy!

It's after midnight, and the airport parking lot is a ghost town. I make my way to the concrete apron spanning the entrance in hopes of finding a cab, but I am out of luck. Everything is dark and eerie. I'm sure a taxi will be along soon, so I open the door and enter.

Once inside, I'm surprised to find the place so dimly lit. I had heard it was a small airport, but this is crazy. I make my way to the bathroom, totally creeped out because there is nobody behind the counters and not a soul in the lobby. It's as if I am utterly alone. I slide a travel-sized canister of pepper spray from my purse into the palm of my hand before entering the stall.

It's impossible to keep my cool and remain calm enough to hover an inch off the public-toilet seat and take a pee. I breathe deeply and relax my tensed-up torso just enough to release. Panic peeing never works out well, but I succeed and avoid collateral damage.

I exit the bathroom with my finger on the trigger of the pepper spray. I have goosebumps as hypervigilance calls the hairs on my arms to attention. My steps into the foyer are slow and methodical. It's a *Scooby-Doo* kind of moment, and I know I must look like an ass. I hang a right, making my way back to the entrance when I'm hit by a beam of light. I catch a few words of harshly commanded Spanish. It takes me a moment, but I stutter a reply, "No hablo." I can speak a little Spanish, but I can't right now.

Blinded by the beam, I squint to watch what I hope is a security guard drawing near. "Passport!" he demands. My heart is in my throat, and I'm ready to puke, but I act cool as a cucumber. I casually tuck the pepper spray, considered an illegal weapon in most of Europe, into a line of sweaty cleavage and unzip my shoulder bag to search for my passport. After producing my passport, the guard informs me the airport is closed, and I must get out. I had assumed as much.

Speaking *Spanglish*, Spanish with English fillers, I manage to explain I am a Peregrina-Americana who flew into Madrid, missed her train to Pamplona, rented a car with a stick shift, drove five hours to get here, needs help finding a cab, and is ready to cry. I can fight the tears. But why? Tears are weapons. I blink hard and release two huge drops. The tears don't hit my cheeks before his demeanor softens.

"Come with me," he says in heavily-accented English.

I follow the man to his office and listen while he calls three different cab companies. He is growing frustrated on the phone and asks the person on the other line to hold a moment.

"No one wants to come for you," he says. "It's too late."

"What?" I'm shocked. "How far away is Pamplona?"

"Too far to walk and too dangerous."

I now regret the ease and efficiency in which I found the nighttime drop box for the rental car key. Although damn compact, I could have slept in that car. Or I could have driven it to a hotel. At least with the car I had something, some shelter. But now I'm totally screwed. Not even I can squeeze out enough tears to convince this man to let me set up camp in his office. Two more drops slide down my cheeks.

"Don't cry, Peregrina," he coos.

He called me a *Peregrina,* a lady pilgrim, and now it is all so surreal. It's really happening. I'm on pilgrimage! I blow my nose on Jim's brown hanky and cry harder.

"No. Don't cry. Please peregrina," the guard speaks softly and apologetically now. "This man on the phone will come but demands one hundred euros."

I'm stammering from sticker shock, but I don't have much choice. "Okay, I will pay."

"He wants me to see the money first."

"Are you kidding me?" My eyes have run bone dry now. Secretly, I only have seventy euros on me. I was hoping to use a credit card or strike a bargain. Thank God there is a cash machine inside the terminal. I go over to withdraw the money while the security guard waits on the phone, but then I pause. Wait. What if this is a scam? What if there isn't anyone on the other end of the phone.

I curse my cell phone company for not offering an international plan and for refusing to unlock my phone, so I could insert a European SIM card. I am at the mercy of this security guard. What if he knocks me over the head with his flashlight and steals my money? What if he kills me. Or worse?

I fumble with my banking pin number and eventually get it right. "It's only a hundred bucks," I coach. "He's not going to kill you for chump change." Feeling foolish, yet still apprehensive, I make my way back to his office. Once the guard sees the cash, he utters a few words into the phone, and the deal is done. He escorts me out of the airport and stands on the sidewalk to wait with me on the cab. His kind gesture of waiting with me on the curb makes me feel like a total jerk.

In less than five minutes, a cab screeches up, and a thin man with dark hair hops out. The driver helps me ease Agnus from my back and toss her into the trunk. I climb into the passenger seat and buckle up. "Please take me to a hotel on the Camino de Santiago."

"*Lo siento*…," he says before switching to English. "I'm sorry, Señora. I did not know you were a peregrina."

There's that word again! *Peregrina.* Hearing it aloud makes my head tingle. We ride in silence for a much shorter distance than I had anticipated. When we arrive at a hotel, he retrieves Agnus, and I reluctantly pass two fifty-euro notes.

"No, no." He shakes his head and refuses my money. "When you get to Santiago, say a prayer for me. Give old Saint James a hug and say a big prayer for *Rafael.*"

I'm stunned. I shake his outstretched hand, holding the cash in my other. "I will, Rafael. Gracias. Muchas gracias!"

"Buen Camino, Peregrina."

I'm touched by Rafael's change of heart. I turn to avoid dropping more tears. I'm worn out with today's misadventures, and crying has become too easy. I hop up the short flight of steps to the hotel lobby and trade one of the euro notes for a room. I'm so thankful to have found a bed.

Part 2

Navarre

Pamplona to Puente La Reina

I wake refreshed and surprised. I don't usually sleep well in strange places. Surrendering to exhaustion, I can't remember brushing my teeth before hitting the rack. Hygiene aside, I do remember fretting over bed bugs. Having read horror stories in online Camino forums, I let my imagination get the best of me. I stripped away blankets and spread a nylon barrier sheet, permeated with *permethrin*, over the mattress and used my treated sleeping bag as a coverlet.

The nylon barrier is the footprint belonging to a tiny tent I contemplated carrying but decided against. There is no need for portable shelter on the Camino de Santiago unless you're into that sort of thing. I am not. Permethrin, belonging to the *pyrethroid* family of synthetic insecticides, is the toxic stunt double of the chrysanthemum flower. The chrysanthemum is naturally pest-repellent against fleas, mosquitoes, ticks, head lice, and bed bugs. But a chrysanthemum corsage would never last on the Camino, and I had no luck finding it's pure essential oil. Instead, I sprayed everything down with poison and hoped for the best. Reckless. Totally reckless.

I've never had the misfortune of hosting bed bugs, ticks or lice, and I don't plan on starting now. The permethrin is only one layer in my creepy-crawly defense. I also have a fragrant bar of my homemade cedar and citronella soap. Both essential oils are potent bug deterrents. Conveniently, the soap is gentle enough to double as shampoo. As for hair conditioner, I made my own concoction with the essential oils of cedar, clove, cinnamon, sandalwood, and patchouli – heavy on the patchouli. I smell like an old hippie, but my hair is beautiful and will remain, with any luck, bug-free.

I love the smell of patchouli. I wore it all the time during my Army years. The scent, associated with counter-culture, was in sharp contrast to my crisp uniform and clipper-cut hair. It threw people off, but they didn't exactly know why. The scent is a powerful weapon.

My mother hates patchouli and makes a ridiculous deal about it anytime she smells it. I never visit without dabbing a little here and there. Her reactions amuse me.

"Have you been smoking pot?"

"No, Mother."

"Bullshit. You've been smoking pot."

Mom has probably never smoked, seen, nor smelled pot, but these factoids mean little to her. I don't care about the counter-culture affiliation with the scent. It's a damn good bug repellent. However, I am concerned about annoying fellow peregrinos because not everyone likes patchouli. I will be sleeping, eating, and showering in close-proximity to others. I don't want to detract from the joy and experiences of another by causing an olfactory assault or an allergy attack.

One of my goals during this adventure is to be kinder and more thoughtful. I practice my little mantra: *I will greet each pilgrim with love and kindness in my heart.* It's corny, but I need to remind myself to be a better human being. I plan to repeat this mantra every morning, and I'll use it when I'm particularly frustrated or afraid. Working on my social game is essential.

I've spent the past few years acting self-centered, consumed with my illness and feeling sorry for myself. I've grown impatient. I don't talk to my sons anymore; instead, I issue orders. I stopped hosting dinner parties and backyard bar-b-ques because I can't stand the din of small-talk. I've weeded out the superficial friends who want to go shopping or get pedicures together. I've gone from extroverted and fun-loving to recluse and almost bitter. While I do like being more reserved and reflective, I've taken it too far. I need balance – a social-life equilibrium.

I psych myself up for the day's challenge with a few positive affirmations. "I am a good peregrina. I help others. I listen carefully and cheerfully return chitchat." I'm warming up now. "I love making new friends. I am funny and generous, and people like me." I'm so ready to be liked again, and the first step to being likable includes proper dental hygiene. I grab my toothbrush and prepare to greet the world.

Last night, when I asked the cab driver to drop me at a hotel on the Camino de Santiago, I hadn't realized I was making a crucial decision about my trek. But this morning, it is apparent. *I am here now*, a few hundred feet from the path. I am literally moments from starting the journey I've dreamt about and prepared for over the past nine months. I'm ready to roll, but there's one problem. My guidebook, *A Practical & Mystical Manual for the Modern-Day Pilgrim*, written by John Brierly, suggests otherwise. The Brierley guide, considered by many to be the gold standard of all guidebooks, breaks the journey into thirty-three stages, some more daunting than others. The first phase begins in *St. Jean Pied de Port*. Starting in St. Jean has been the plan all along. Crossing over the French Pyrenees is all part of the struggle and glory of walking El Camino Francés. This is how it should be done. Or is it?

Do Spanish pilgrims cross the border into France, so they can then backtrack across their own country to Santiago? I wouldn't think so. If they live somewhere along the Camino, do they go backward to go forward? No. That doesn't make any sense. Medieval pilgrims started their journeys to Santiago at the thresholds of their own front doors. If this is the case, I have already begun. My Camino started in Seabeck, Washington.

I wrestle with the idea: *What would a real pilgrim do?* Before that question can be answered, I must decide on the qualifications of a *real pilgrim*. I haven't a clue, but the idea of finding and paying a shuttle bus to drive more than 60K backward and drop me off, so I can turn around and walk right back to where I am now, sounds ridiculous. It's time to do what I came here to do. And just like that, I make my first break from the nagging need to maintain a logical order. I break the rules, or at least what I once misinterpreted as the rules and the correct way to walk El Camino Francés. This is my first Camino success!

Outside of my hotel, I am surprisingly disoriented. I don't know exactly what I expected, but all around me is the hustle and bustle of Pamplona and not the peaceful trail I envisioned. It's not like I thought there would be fanfare or balloons or ribbons roping off the route and redirecting traffic as you might see in a marathon. But I did expect to see a directional street sign or the iconic seashell or the yellow arrow that marks the route.

And then I see her. She is an old lady with silver hair cascading beyond her shoulders. She is wearing a pastel, plaid button-up shirt that clashes with her red stretch pants. She carries a pink backpack, no larger than a child's bookbag, slung low on her shoulders. On her feet are silver sneakers. Her left arm swings back and forth along her side, and her left hand holds the handle of a gilded birdcage. I do a doubletake. Perched smartly on a wooden dowel is a blue-green parakeet. I don't know exactly why, but I follow her.

The curious bird-lady leads me out of town, winding through streets and cutting across the grassy parks. She takes me toward the university, and I stumble over my first seashell sunk into the concrete sidewalk. I stop to take a picture of the shell, a metal marker with the hinge of the shell pointing toward Santiago de Compostela. With my head down, I can see the sidewalk is studded with markers. Giddy, I hop from one to the next. When I glance up, my bird-lady is gone.

With the throb of Pamplona behind me and the bird-lady nowhere in sight, I find myself happily alone. As I step on a footbridge to cross over a gentle stream, I feel the rush of a bicyclist fly by. The rider lifts an arm in the air yelling, "Buen Camino!"

"Buen Camino!" I call out, but I'm sure my voice is lost in the expanse of the open fields. I'm too thrilled to be startled by the speedy intruder. It's my first peregrino-to-peregrina greeting. This is really happening. I'm really in Spain. I'm doing it. I'm off the sofa! High on life, I pump my purple hiking poles in the air and march through the sun-drenched haze of blowing wheat and dancing red poppies.

I feel so alive – manic even. I'm walking steeply uphill, but I hardly notice until my thighs scream out near the 750-meter summit of *Alto del Perdón*. Geez, that was quick. I turn around to view my progress, and the panorama leaves me breathless. The golds and the greens and the bright blue sky are too much to take in all at once. I cut the scene up in the viewfinder of my camera, snapping shots as I pan from right to left.

I've never been this close to windmills before. I listen to the whoosh-whoosh of the giant blades. They are massive, mechanical angels hacking away at blue fields of sky with their white machetes.

I ascend the summit and behold the *Monumento Peregrino*, a metal cutout sculpture of peregrinos on horseback and on foot. There are donkeys and a cut-out of a dog. Of course, I immediately recognize the scene from Emilio Estevez's 2010 film, *The Way*, starring his father, Martin Sheen. I follow the line of metal peregrinos to the last one. I reach out and wrap my hands around the sculpture's rusty but trim waistline, just as the overweight character, *Yost,* had done in the movie. Apart from conquering my demons, I am a little like Yost in my hopes of dropping a few pounds too.

I wish my introduction to the Camino de Santiago rang with a mystical tone, like a visit from a dead grandmother or ancient goddess interrupting my dreams. Over the past few months, I have read several accounts of angelic guidance, ghostly whispers, mysterious messages passed in a collection plate during mass, and goddesses penetrating dreams and meditations. If not supernatural, I would have settled for a religious or an academic approach; instead, I owe my discovery and much of my physical and future emotional recovery to my couch-potato ways. It wasn't therapy, or yoga, or prescription meds that lifted me from my agoraphobic funk and placed me here today, on the summit of Alto del Perdón. It was binge-watching movies on the sofa. To be precise, it was Emilio Estevez's film, *The Way*. I bought the film, watched it a couple of times, and then moved to online forums and blogs. I kept asking myself, "Why do I not already know about this?" I collected guidebooks, maps, and memoirs written by peregrinos before me. Of course, how we learn is not as important as the knowledge itself, but I still wish for ghostly conscription demanding peregrination. It would make for a better story.

I wasn't always a couch potato or an agoraphobe, but I spent a sad couple of years glued to the sofa, suffering from chronic migraines and Meniere's Disease, a debilitating inner-ear disorder. The migraines, complete with blinding aura and projectile vomiting, worked in tandem with vertigo, tinnitus, and staggered gait to make the idea of leaving the house and walking anywhere almost out of the question. And yet, here I am.

Life before my illness was a grand adventure. After serving nearly nineteen years in the Army, I left the enlisted ranks and earned a commission in the United States Coast Guard. As an officer, I spent my days rolling along the seas in command of armed-escorts for Navy submarines. The responsibility was gigantic and thrilling, and I was surrounded by a crew of gunners I dearly loved, and together we accomplished a mission we believed in. Life had such purpose until illness forced me to trade it all in for a cognac leather sofa and solitude. The separation was crushing. The loss of command and control, combined with the loss of my comrades, made me question everything, particularly my identity. Wallowing in solitude and lost self-esteem, the darkest of memories worked their way to the surface and pierced the skin.

I cannot recall precisely when the flashbacks started. These flashes, souvenirs from a long stint in the military, rattled me to the core. In truth, I had probably been flashing for years, but life's hectic pace and vodka kept the demons at bay. But in the still of forced retirement, there wasn't enough vodka in the world to drown my boogeymen. And they raged.

I kept myself busy. I wrote essays and stories and completed a low-residency degree – A master's in fine arts, no less. I cultivated heirloom tomatoes, tended the garden, threw pottery, and maintained a tidy house. I home-schooled the youngest child, forcing him to earn a high-school diploma against his will. I gathered blueberries and huckleberries and wild mushrooms that grew on our wooded-property. I made beer and cider and wine. I pickled hot-peppers and cucumbers and green beans. I canned peaches and made jars and jars of blackberry jelly. But it wasn't enough.

Once I learned about the Camino, I couldn't unlearn it and thought about it constantly. Without the guidance and direction of an angel or a ghost or a goddess, and without the support of my husband, I decided to make the pilgrimage. It was my inner-voice – my gut, my instinct. I don't know the difference between gut and instinct, but I do know I told myself to walk. *I had to walk.* It was crystal clear. If I ever wanted to regain my vitality or to reclaim a shred of plummeting self-esteem, I had to get my ass off the couch.

I depart the summit of Alto del Perdón, saying goodbye to the wind angels and to the *Monumento Peregrino.* The trail down is bloody brutal. More than a few times, I slip on loose gravel and tumbling rocks. I can barely keep my feet under me. My equilibrium is shot, and I'm relying on my trusty, purple hiking poles to save my ass. So excited about the scenery, I had hardly noticed the climb up the mountain, but now my head is down, and all I see is the rocky trail. My knees snap and pop like a bowl of crispy rice cereal, and my ankles are pools of jelly.

I pass a crying Korean girl sitting on a boulder. It takes me a moment to register the scene. I stop, rethink, and recite my mantra in my head. *I will greet each peregrino with love and kindness in my heart.* I turn around and ask if there is something I can do to help. My inquiry turns her gentle whimpers into loud sobs. Her name is Mi Sun, and she has fallen twice, scraped her knee, and is afraid to go any further. My heart overrides my brain, and I lend her a hiking pole. I grab her free arm to provide extra support. "Come on, now. Easy does it. I've got you." Despite the steep incline, the trail becomes less daunting. Holding tight to Mi Sun, I find my feet.

The rocks slowly disappear, and she and I are left on a soft dirt path. We stay together until we find her boyfriend napping beneath a tree. He barely acknowledges Mi Sun as we plop down on a wooden bench beside him. When he finally does speak, it doesn't sound kind. Since I don't speak Korean, I can't know exactly what he said. But he glanced at his watch and rolled his eyes. I imagine it was something like, "What took you so long?"

Mi Sun is probably seventeen or eighteen. The boyfriend looks older, possibly twenty, the same age as my middle son, Garret. Luckily, her dirt-bag of a boyfriend is not my son, or I would snatch him up by the ear and scold his unthoughtful behavior.

Mi Sun thanks me and returns my hiking pole. She reaches into her backpack and brings out two small gifts. I try to refuse, but secretly, I want what she is holding in her right hand. In her left hand, she has a bon-bon wrapped in a green and white paper – a piece of candy, I assume. But in her right hand, she holds a perfect reddish-brown orb with a green stem. It's a *Black Krim* heirloom tomato, one of my favorite varieties I've grown for years.

With little convincing, I accept both gifts and hug her goodbye. I choose to ignore the boyfriend. With the Black Krim safely riding in the top of my pack, I unwrap the bon-bon from a wrapper printed in a font I cannot read. The bon-bon is some sort of boiled molasses confection, a dark-brown lollipop without a stick. I pop it into my mouth. It is uncomfortably large, so I move it to my cheek. Apart from the molasses, I'm unable to identify the flavor. Star anise, clove, fenugreek? Maybe a hint of cinnamon?

I pop the candy out of my mouth, pinching it between thumb and forefinger, for further inspection. My mouth is polluted with sticky sweetness. I spit a thick, brown strand, like the juice of a squished grasshopper. I don't hate the candy, but I don't love it either. I toss it in the bushes for the ants and rinse my mouth. The candy is long gone, but after several sucks from the blue tube of my hydration water bladder, I continue to spit brown juice. This is what it must be like to chew tobacco.

I stop in at a lovely café with a busy outdoor patio in Uterga. Happy peregrinos are eating plates of fried squid and drinking frosty beers. I want to be one of those happy peregrinos, so I walk in. I order my beer and squid, and notice a *sello*, or stamp, on the counter. I pull out my pilgrim passport and add my second stamp for the day. My first stamp, while unorthodox, came from the desk clerk at my hotel this morning.

The pilgrim passport, or peregrino credentials, is required to stay in the pilgrim hostels, called *albergues* or *refugios*. The passport is an accordion-folded booklet made of cardstock with grid squares to collect sellos, or stamps, just like a travel passport. Typically, the first stamp is issued at an official peregrino office, like the one I didn't go to in St. Jean Pied de Port. While I did want the traditional stamp, the hotel clerk did fine in a pinch. I must collect two stamps per day to prove I have walked. When I'm finished with my journey, my passport book will be full of the stamps from the places I have visited. When I arrive in Santiago, I will take the passport to the pilgrim office and receive my *Compostela*. Peregrinos must walk at least a hundred kilometers to qualify for a coveted Compostela. Horseback riders and bicyclist have different requirements.

In the simplest form, the Compostela can be thought of as a diploma or as a certificate of completion. However, it holds much higher value to others. Some peregrinos of Catholic faith earn the Compostela to satisfy familial or religious expectations. The document proves the deed of pilgrimage and is believed to reduce time in purgatory. I'm not a Catholic, and I'm on the fence when it comes to purgatory. For me, the Compostela is a *Get-out-of-hell-free-card*. It's not my intent to mock faith, but on judgment day I'll have some explaining to do, and I like the idea of insurance. A little padding never hurt a girl like me.

After stamping my credential at the counter, I collect my beer and fried squid and join a table of peregrinos outside. Everyone is talking to everyone, except me. I don't mind. I don't need conversation. I'm enjoying the volley of different languages ping-ponging across the table and over my head. I hear German, Korean, French, Spanish, and maybe Italian, but I'm not positive. I also hear English, spoken with a lovely Australian accent. The world has gathered in Uterga today to drink beer and eat plates of squid together. The atmosphere is electric. I feel amazing. I've walked about 12K, and there is still a tiger in my tank. The beer loosens my shoulders first and then works down to my thighs. My legs grow warm and flexi. My whole body feels good, even my feet.

Before leaving home, I carefully studied each of Brierley's thirty-three stages, several times over. I researched towns, churches, and sites rich in historical and cultural value. On stage four, the section I am walking today, Pamplona to Puente La Reina, there is an alternative route leading to the secluded and mysterious *Church of Saint Mary Eunate*.

Built in the 12th century, the Romanesque, octagonal structure was inspired by the *Church of the Holy Sepulchre of Jerusalem*. The eight-sided, unadorned design is associated with the *Knights Templar*, although firm evidence of the church as a Templar location has yet to surface. The seclusion of the church supports the secrecy shrouding the Templar order. Most historic churches along the Camino are surrounded by a medieval village. But the Eunate stands alone with nothing but windswept fields, a sparse fringe of pines, and underbrush.

Speculation regarding the church's origin and purpose abound. I've read everything from a family chapel to a secret worship site, and from a hospital and a morgue to a cemetery. Archaeological digs in the churchyard have unearthed burial sites containing the familiar scallop shell worn by peregrinos.

So, it is likely the location was used as a peregrino hospital and cemetery.

There is another church of similar design about 50K west and directly on the Camino, in the village of Torres del Río. I first read about this church in Father Kevin Codd's, *To the Field of Stars: A Pilgrim's Journey to Santiago de Compostela.* I love what he writes about Romanesque style. According to Father Codd, "Gothic proclaims God is *up there* while Romanesque murmurs that God is *down here* on the earth with its wheat fields and vineyards and dusty roads, and of course, all its fleshy joy and bloody pain. Both are right and beautiful, but at this stage in my life, I must say, I gawk at the Gothic but I pray in Romanesque."

The Eunate is off the beaten path and will add a few extra kilometers to my day's journey. I make the decision to bypass Eunate, for now, and visit the sister-church in a few days. It's a wise choice because the swelling in my feet, from yesterday's flight and the long drive, is making my boots too tight. My feet are suffering from a few hot spots I suspect will blister before reaching Puente La Reina. Besides, 24K is plenty for my first day on the trail.

I stop in *Muruzábal* to pop my head into the Church of *San Esteban* and to admire a statue of St. James. While inside, I send up a few prayers and praises. I'm filled with joy and gratitude. I light three candles: one for my boys, one for my granny, and one for my marriage.

I poke around town for a *farmacia*, thinking it might be wise to have ibuprofen for later tonight. But it is siesta time, and the hamlet is asleep. I mosey about in a beer-and-sunshine induced daydream. Once I emerge from my daydream, I find myself on a graveled road without a yellow arrow or a seashell to guide me. I must have taken a wrong turn in *Muruzábal.* Up ahead, I see a group of peregrinos, so I keep walking. "Trust yourself," I coach.

Confident I am headed in the right direction, I whistle the opening to Mozart's *Serenade No. 13 in G Major.* My lips only take me through the first few stanzas before the tempo speeds up and I lose my place. I try again, but now the wind interferes, whipping my hair in my mouth and my eyes. I pull a ponytail holder from the cork handle of a hiking pole and secure the dark mop in a knot atop my head. The wind is relentless, howling across the open fields, collecting bits of grit and dust to pepper my skin. It is so loud I do not hear the farm tractor until it is right behind me. I step off the road into a ditch, and the tractor passes by, kicking up more dust and grit. It is said the Camino provides what a peregrino might need. Evidently, I need full-body exfoliation. I keep walking with my head down into the wind.

When I come to a strand of straggly pine, I glance up. I am delighted and stunned to be standing right before Eunate! There is no need to consult Brierley for verification. The structure is unmistakable. Like a magnet to steel, *Santa Maria de Eunate* drew me into the safety of her charming, double-arched cloister and into the glowing sanctuary of her cool, alabaster-lit vault. The light filtering through the sheets of alabaster window pane emits a creamy, golden glow. Father Codd was right. I pause to meditate in the church's earthy dampness and send up a prayer. I had a part in this, in losing my way out of town, but I can't help but think I was led to Eunate by a delicious touch of the divine.

The path from Eunate ends at the arched gateway of *Albergue Jakue*, on the outskirts of Puente La Reina. I don't consider exploring the village or comparing accommodations. I'm in need of refuge, and right before my eyes, a refugio materializes. Who can argue with that kind of corner-store convenience?

Over the past few years, I've grown accustomed to four and five-star hotels. I'm almost looking forward to roughing it, but I've never stayed in a hostel or a refugio or an albergue. When it's my turn in the cue, I don't know what to request. I should have paid more attention to the others before me. The young man working the check-in desk is surly and a bit of a smart ass. He demands my peregrino credential and my travel passport. He makes some notes in his ledger, stamps my credentials, and stares at me. "Well?" He drums his fingers on the desk.

"Do you have space for me?" I sound meek and ridiculous. "Sleeping space. A bed?"

"Oh. You want a bed? Yes. I have." He runs his finger down a column in the ledger. "Seven euro." He holds out a demanding palm.

"Boots off!" he barks and points to a shelf as he leads me down a corridor to the dormitory. I remove my boots in a hurry and catch up with him standing in front of a 4-bed cubical arranged in two sets of bunks. The cube is for ladies only and near the showers. He points to a top bed, and I shake my head.

"Do you have anything on the bottom? I have chronic vertigo." I also want to tell him I'm too tired to heft my old ass up to a top bunk. But I keep that part to myself.

"No, no. So, so, sorry." He says he is sorry, but I know he is not. With a smirk, he turns and leaves me standing in front of the daunting climb to the top bunk.

One bottom bunk is occupied by a sleeping young woman with long, black hair. Her skin is deeply-tanned. The lump of her body beneath the blanket tells me she is built short and squatty. The other bottom bunk is occupied by a lanky and pale girl with a hedge of closely-shorn pink hair and dazzling blue eyes. Sprawled across her bed, the girl gives me a smile and goes back to bobbing her head to the rhythm leaking from her headphones.

I fish around for a towel, toiletries, shower shoes, and a change of clothes before stuffing Agnus in a locker. When I return from the shower, the dark-haired girl is still asleep, but the other girl removes her headphones. Her name is Krystal. She's from Germany, and she invites me to supper.

We settle on an Irish pub, but the only thing remotely Irish about this Irish pub set in a medieval, Spanish village, is it serves Guinness on tap. This is good enough for me. Krystal is happy because the bar is showing the football game. I don't follow soccer at home, but it is a huge deal

here. Krystal catches me up on the latest details and explains
how Germany will dominate the *World Cup* this year. The
bartender and his son give her thumbs-down signals and let
out a boo. Krystal and the bartender banter back and forth in
English and Spanish. I read over my guide-book and make
plans for tomorrow. The atmosphere is cozy and familiar.

Krystal and I agree to walk together to Estella tomorrow
morning. I'm happy to have made a new friend. I'm especially
interested in meeting German hikers because if all goes well,
I'll be living in Germany shortly after returning home from
Santiago. The Camino is my proving ground for a recent job
offer abroad. The job, a full professorship, is a dream. But I
question if I'll be brave enough to live and work, all alone, in
a new country. Having a few contacts will certainly help.

The kids are grown, and the nest is newly emptied. I'll
miss them, but they won't necessarily miss me. I invited Jim
to join, but he refused. Do I go anyway? Will absence make
the heart grow fonder? Does it really matter anymore? Jim
has been more of a roommate and less of a husband for
years. Family matters aside, the truth is I am afraid. I am
afraid to move, but I am more afraid to stand still.

The job offer is one of a windfall of blessings dropped in
my lap since training for the Camino. Pre-Camino, I wouldn't
have applied, no matter if it was my dream job. I wasn't brave
or strong enough. I first saw the announcement in January. I
was in training, walking every day, and walking gave me time
to think. Two days before the application deadline, I worked
up the guts and hastily filled out the online application and
submitted the required documents. And then I waited.

I continued training for my Camino, purchased gear, and
arranged flights. Less than six weeks ago, the offer came
through, a full professorship based in Germany. Nearly thirty
years ago, as a young soldier, I was stationed in Germany. I
have always wanted to return to Europe, and teaching is my
God-given talent. I am whole and alive when I'm helping
adult students learn. This is my dream job, but life isn't always
about following dreams, or is it?

Puente La Reina to Estella

After a fitful night's sleep on the top of a squeaky bunk bed, I lie awake for what must be an hour or better. Finally, I surrender and crawl down. The ladder serves as a torture device on my hamburger-feet. Gasps of agony slip out, but I try not to disturb the peaceful pattern of Krystal's breathing. She sounds so comfortable. I am happy for her and envious all at the same time.

I slip on my shower shoes, grab my phone from the charger, and pad off to the bathroom. In the darkness of a white-tiled stall, I check my phone. It's two hours too early. Krystal and I agreed to walk together today, but we decided on a much later start. Shining the light on my feet, it's apparent the night's rest did little to alleviate the swelling. My pigs are fat sausages ready to explode. *Water.* I need more water. I'm far too stubborn to accept the truth. Water will help, but what I need is time. I need time off my feet to let the swelling subside, but that's not going to happen. Not today.

I dress and pack my bag in the dark, hoping not to leave anything behind. No matter how careful I try to be, the crinkle of my nylon stuff-sack and the metallic stutter of a slowly drawn zipper shatter the silence. Thankfully, Krystal doesn't stir, and neither does the girl with the long, black hair. Bending down to Krystal's bunk, I make out the sharp angle of her jaw illuminated in the green light of the exit sign. I whisper, "See you in Estella." She doesn't respond. I don't feel guilty about leaving her. Each peregrina must walk her own Camino. We shared a couple of beers, a bowl of olives, and friendly conversation. Sometimes, this is enough. My farewell to Krystal is the first in a series of Camino-*resets*, where I will break company to go my own way. However, at my turtle-speed, she'll probably catch up later today.

Toward the exit, a row of bookshelves holds the hiking boots of resting peregrinos. Scanning the shelves for mine, I

secretly hope someone stole them away in the night. No such
luck. My boots, with purple laces and menacing orange
tongues, are easy to spot. The barrel full of hiking poles is a
little daunting, but there are only a few with cork handles. I
find mine and move outdoors to a bench. To my surprise, it
is still dark.

The boots are entirely too small for my swollen feet, but I
stuff into them anyway and leave the garden of the Albergue
Jakue to make my way through the village. Although it is
dark, I don't need my headlamp because I walked this same
path last night to the Irish pub and back with Krystal. And
there is just enough morning glow to find my way.

The air is cool and fresh, and the cobblestones are wet. It
must have just stopped raining because I can smell and feel
the heaviness in the morning air. I pass beneath the arch of
the *Iglesia del Crucifijo*, with its Y-shaped crucifixion, and
beyond the *Padres Reparadores* before slipping into the
shadows of Puente La Reina's hauntingly beautiful, medieval
village. I realize how alone I am. But I am not afraid.

The clack of my poles threatens to wake sleeping
villagers. Embarrassed, I stop clacking and tuck the sticks
under my arm. It is better this way. I don't need hiking poles
to negotiate sidewalks and cobblestone. I step gingerly
around puddles without a sound. My shoulders relax, and my
leg muscles grow loose and elastic. For now, I forget to fixate
on my feet. Everything is bliss. I could stay in this peaceful
moment forever.

A stone archway leads out of the village, but I am
reluctant to go. I would like to enjoy a coffee and maybe a
breakfast here, but I am way too early. A yellow arrow
painted in the center of the portal marks the route, and I snap
a quick picture with my phone. The shot is too dark and
doesn't begin to do justice to what I see. The contrasts of a
bright arrow and the dark portal are stunning. The tunnel is
awash in deep indigo, like blue jeans before they begin to
fade. I take a few steps in and the darkness envelopes around
me. My heart skips a beat as the thud of fear plummets into

the pit of my stomach. My feet try to run, but I resist. I fight for control and force myself to slow down, to relax, to enjoy the stillness – to be brave.

I exit the tunnel feeling satisfied with my performance. I am again at ease. In the dim light, I recognize the iconic Romanesque bridge I've seen online in peregrino forums. It is highly speculated that among many famous pilgrims to cross this bridge, *Saint Francis of Assisi* passed over these six arches while on his pilgrimage in 1214. To think I am following in the footsteps of the patron saint of animals and nature delights me. Now typically, I'm all about Mary. But St. Francis runs a close second, especially in this subdued morning light in full witness of the lush flora and kitchen gardens lining the banks of the muddy-green river.

The 12th-century bridge, built on command of *Dona Mayor*, the wife of *King Sancho III*, has ensured the safe passage for peregrinos crossing the río Arga over the past thousand years. So significant was the building of this bridge, the entire village was renamed. Puente La Reina roughly translates to *Bridge of the Queen.*

In the movie, *The Way*, Tom loses his backpack when the pack falls from the bridge railing. The bag, complete with his son's cremated remains, floats downstream. But something doesn't look right. In the film, the river is swift, dotted with jagged rocks, and capped in the gush of white rapids. The real-life river, or at least this section of the río Arga, is a bloated ribbon of beach glass – smooth, opaque, and tumbled into submission.

A backpack dropped into this calm water would be a total pain in the ass, but not overly dramatic. My guess is the movie scene was shot in another section of río Arga or on an entirely different river. It doesn't matter because it isn't a factual story, but I'll probably obsess on this point until I'm in WIFI range and can look it up. Without roaming data, my cell phone is as useful as a brick.

I'm relieved to be up early enough to avoid traffic as I cross what appears to be a major highway. There is not a car in sight, but I quicken my pace out of habit. I follow an arrow down a path flanking the river to my left and the *Convento Comendadoras del Espiritu Santo* to my right. I'm too early for morning mass, but I'm not overly disappointed. I am excited to attend my first Catholic ceremony, but I'm also intimidated. I've researched the rules about taking communion and what to do while it's going down. Since I'm not Catholic, I am not supposed to drink the blood and eat the body of Christ. And I've got to say, I'm relieved to be excluded. It sounds so weird to me. Instead, I can get in line and ask for a blessing by crossing my chest with each hand on opposite shoulders, or I can just stay in my seat. I'll play it by ear and do whatever feels right at the time.

I have read about the Camino Comendadoras, a female chapter of *The Order of Santiago*. But I can't find the research to make a connection with this convent. The Order of Santiago was a military regiment founded by *King Fernando II* of León in 1170 to provide defense and security for peregrinos. Of course, the original order was strictly for men. The lady Comendadoras were mostly responsible for the education of the knight's children, and some cared for the wounded and infirm. Speculation circulates about the Order's connection to the Knights Templar, just as there are unconfirmed rumors some of the Comendadoras were warriors.

I'd like to think in a past life if such a phenomenon were possible, I would belong to the Comendadoras as a lady warrior. It makes perfect sense to me. I am an old soul and a natural seeker of light. I was born a protector and a guardian. My guardianship mostly concerned farm animals and injured baby birds, but I also spent twenty-four years in the military as a soldier and as a sailor. In my present life, I have served as a warrior. Protecting the safe passage of peregrinos would be a likely occupation for the medieval-me.

I am not sure where I stand with the whole concept of past lives. The idea doesn't jive with my simplistic Christian upbringing at a Methodist church in rural Oregon. I have not

habitually attended church as an adult, but I was quite the
regular in Sunday-School sessions. If I'm to be completely
candid, I found Sunday school way more useful than the adult
church. First, there were my school buddies, Hank and Tony,
and opportunities to play tunnel-tag and red-rover in the
church-yard. Then there was the taboo playdough which was
banished from my household. I cannot whiff a canister of the
briny goodness without visualizing a technicolor Jesus Christ.

Sunday school was an escape, at least for a few hours, an
opportunity to shirk endless chores on my family's farm. It
provided furlough from the unpredictable crankiness of my
father. This was especially true in the wet spring months
when it was commonplace to cut and stack winter firewood
in the pouring Oregon rain. Woodcutting was always dicey.
There were far too many whipping sticks and chunks of
wood readily available to hurl. Punishment, deserved or not,
was imminent. Summer Sunday school equaled escape on hot
days, stuck inside the acrid hog shed, shoveling pig shit from
pens to field spreader. The only highlight to shoveling shit
was my father usually didn't stick around to supervise. Why
would he? I mean, it was just shit.

I love how my shadow stretches out in the morning light.
With the sunrise to my back, I am long and lean, a contrast to
my square and squatty frame. I see another shadow before I
hear it's owner. The dark shape stretches nearer with every
step. He will overtake me soon. His shadow-head rests below
my hip. I try to estimate his distance by gauging the proximity
of his shadow to my own, but I have little experience in this
arena. I pop a hiking pole out to the left, slicing off his
shadow-head with one fatal blow. But he keeps coming. I
sense him on my left side, but I still don't hear the crunch of
gravel beneath his step.

"Buen Camino." His speech is as soft as his step.

"Y usted también." My Spanish is sketchy

"Do you speak English?"

"Yes. Almost exclusively."

"Oh, good!" he says. Because I can't speak Spanish at all."

We are shoulder to shoulder but heads apart. The man must be close to seven feet tall. I can gauge this with confident accuracy because I was once married to a man two inches shy of seven feet. I purposefully make no mention of his height. He probably hears it all the time, "My gosh, you're so tall. How tall are you? How's the weather up there? Do you play basketball..." I imagine the lines are the same regardless of language.

"It's a lovely morning," he offers.

"Yes. Yes, it is."

"Where are you coming from?

"Puente La Reina, the Albergue Jakue."

"No, I mean where did you start your Camino?"

"Pamplona." Oddly, I'm embarrassed about this fact and need to justify. "Well, I had intended on hiking the Pyrenees, but I had trouble with the train in Madrid. I had to rent a car and drive to Pamplona. And then you wouldn't believe this, but by the time I got to Pamplona, the airport was closed. I had a hell of a time getting a cab into the city. So, when I woke the next morning..." I'm rambling like crazy.

"Oh, so this is only your second morning?"

"Yes." My reply is a little too defensive.

He is quiet for a while and stays aligned with my left shoulder. His legs are so long, and I realize he has slowed to talk to me. Reciting my mantra in my head, I am obligated to ask, "So, where did you start?"

"At my doorstep, in Holland!"

"No. I mean where did you actually start walking?"

"In Holland. I've walked from home."

"You got to be shitting me. You've walked from Holland?"

"Yah. And through France, and over the Pyrenees, and now right next to you." I draw out a long whistle, hoping this is an international signal of how truly impressed I am. "My name is Levi."

I shake Levi's hand and tell him my name. Apparently, he wants to talk. And I'm okay with that, but I was enjoying the silence and the meditative rhythm of my hiking poles striking the ground.

"I'm a heroin addict," he whispers.

I try to think of a reply, one that won't express surprise or carry judgment, but I've got nothing. Instead, I nod.

"I'm walking to beat my addiction."

Again, I am without an intelligent or sympathetic reply. I've never met a self-proclaimed heroin addict. My neighbor's son is addicted to heroin, but nobody talks about it. I don't know what to say.

"My wife left me. I've lost my daughter, Eugenia. And I live with my mother, now." He clears his throat and continues. "She's the one who bought me my backpack and boots and encouraged me to walk. My mother is the only one left in the world who still believes in me."

"Yeah," I say. "Mothers are like that."

Our silence is awkward. The poor guy dumped his heart out, and I'm lost for words. I take the easy route with small talk about children. Everybody can find common ground when talking about their kids. "How old is Eugenia?"

"She's ten now, but she was eight the last time I saw her." He is so sad about his lost child. Evidently, Levi has no time for idle chitchat either, and he gets right into it, explaining the gritty details of his fall from fatherhood.

"My wife won't let me see her until I give up the drugs."

"So, is it working – the Camino?"

"I don't know."

"Have you used heroin since you left home?" I'm shocked at my boldness.

"No. Not yet."

"So, you've been clean for how many days now?"

"About seventy-five, I think."

"Wonderful! And how do you feel?"

"Like I want heroin."

"Aw, what a bummer. You'd think it would be out of your system by now."

"I know. I keep hoping I'll walk an entire day without thinking about it."

"So, what keeps you from getting some – a fix?" I try on lingo I've never used.

"It's the nature of the Camino. We keep moving, and I can't afford to stay in a city. I camp, mostly in fields outside of populated areas. I never find a source."

"Wow. I hadn't thought of that."

"Really, it's better than rehab. I have less chance of scoring out here."

His last line makes me laugh, but I know none of this is funny. "I'm sorry you're going through this, but you're on the road to recovery. This is a magical journey, you know, one filled with miracles."

"I'm afraid to reach Santiago."

"You've walked from Holland. Why should you be afraid?"

"What if I get to Santiago, and I want *it*?"

"Keep walking, Babe. Walk your narrow ass out to Finisterre, visit Muxia too, and then head down through Portugal. When you run out of trail in Portugal, turn around and walk back to Santiago. Just keep walking."

He is silent now, ruminating over all the *what-ifs* once he runs out of trail. I do not understand addiction. To truly understand the power of addiction, I think one must be an addict or a former addict. I divorced my second husband after he was unable to give up his excessive drinking and smoking. At the time, I couldn't believe he'd give up on the marriage before the bottle. He'd risk custody of his kids for another drink and smoke. While I indeed abused alcohol during the rougher patches of my life, I was not an alcoholic. I smoked in my youth but tossed the pack when it was time to quit. Losing my children to booze or drugs or any other substance or activity is unfathomable. And for this, I am grateful.

"Look." I point to a yellow scallop shell, "It's facing the wrong way."

"What do you mean?"

"The hinge, it's not pointing to Santiago. If you followed the direction of that shell, you'd end up back in Puente La Reina."

"Wait. It's a shell?"

"Yes, silly. The hinge represents Santiago, and the ridges are all the pilgrim routes to get there." I stare at him sideways, "What did you think it was?"

He laughs and grabs the sleeve of his jacket to show me his patch, sewn with the hinge pointing down. "I thought it was the sunrise."

"How have you made it this far?"

"Luck." He shrugs. "And a collection of maps."

I sense the impatience growing in his gait. I'm walking faster and faster to keep up, and yet I'm slowing him down. He is too polite to leave me, or perhaps he is not ready to be alone. The steep incline of the forest trail takes my breath away, and I can't speak to break the silence or provide comfort.

We exit the tree-lined trail and enter *Mañeru*, another location linked with the Knights Templar. The pinky toe on my right foot is on fire. I know it must be blistered. I hobble to a stone bench and begin unlacing my boot. Levi takes a seat beside me and starts rifling through his backpack.

"I want to give you a gift," he says.

"Oh, it's not necessary."

"Yes. I want you to remember me."

"Seriously, Levi? I'll never forget a man who pours out his heart to me."

"You're the first person I've told, the first on the Camino." I give him a questioning look, but he continues. "Really. It just came out. I needed to talk, and I felt like I could trust you."

"Thank you, Levi. That's the sweetest thing anyone has said to me in a long while."

"You are a kind and understanding lady, and you don't think bad of me. Do you?"

"No, sweetie. I don't think bad. I'm going to light a candle for you and your daughter. I wish you success, and I hope for a speedy recovery and reunion with Eugenia."

He reaches into a cargo pocket and fumbles around before pulling out something very tiny. "Here it is! It's your present!" He smiles down at me and holds a small, green and white plastic tool between this thumb and forefinger - A miniature crowbar, Barbie-doll sized.

"It's a tick-puller. When you use it, will you think of me?"

His gift makes me laugh aloud. "Oh my God, Levi. I hope to never use it! But if I do or do not, I still promise to think of you."

He extends a large palm toward me, and I take it in both hands. We shake and say goodbye. It is another Camino reset, but unlike Krystal, I don't expect to see Levi anywhere again on the way to Santiago. His legs are long, and his mission is critical. He must keep moving.

The tip of my pinky toe is capped with a blister the size of a pencil eraser. I dig out my first-aid kit, drop in my handy-dandy tick extractor, and pull out a silicone toe-condom. The sleeve stretches over the wounded digit, and for the most part, it does as it should – cushions the bubble and keeps it from popping. I put my socks back on and slide into my boots. The toe is fine. I lace up and drive on.

I cross another medieval bridge spanning the río Saldo. According to the *Codex Calixtinus*, the 12th-century peregrino guidebook also known as the book of Saint James, the river is poisonous. Rumor had it that if a pilgrim's horse stopped to take in the waters, it would drop dead on site. The same was said to be true for the peregrino who stopped for a swim or to quench his thirst. A few dishonest villagers from Lorca waited on the river's banks for unsuspecting peregrinos on horseback. And then like vultures, the villagers would set about flaying the pilgrim's fallen horse. I haven't a horse to worry about, and I'm carrying enough water to make Estella.

My current-century guidebook states the water is fine, but I'm not taking chances.

The climb from the river valley to Lorca is steep, but I handle it with ease. The village is tiny, about a hundred residents, but is swarming with peregrinos. I follow the commotion to a children's playground. Pilgrims sleep on park benches in the warm sun. Others claim the swings of the red, metal playset. In the center of the courtyard, an inviting stone fountain burbles jets of frigid water. A group of pilgrims sit hip-to-hip on the fountain's wide ledge and soak their feet.

I can't get my boots off fast enough. I scoot between an American teenager and an exhausted lady. She is slumped over inspecting her toes. Everything about her presence appears to be worn-out. Sitting next to the teen boy doesn't help her case. He is fresh and bright and confident. Even his haircut is new. His left arm is draped around the shoulders of an exotic Brazilian girl. He's so into the girl he doesn't notice my intrusion.

I chitchat with the lady. She has walked from Pamplona this morning, thirty-five kilometers in the heat. She's done for the day. Her name is Elke, and like Levi, she has walked from her home in Holland. This partly explains why she looks so utterly broken.

"Holland? You've walked all the way from Holland?" Regardless of my encounter with Levi, I'll never get used to this idea. Elke just smiles and nods.

"You are the second Dutch pilgrim I've met today." For me, this is amazing. Before today, I had never met a Dutch person. So, meeting two in one day is a big damn deal.

"You must be referring to Levi."

"Yes! We walked into *Mañeru* together."

"He came through here about an hour ago. We walk together sometimes."

"Small Camino."

We sit together with our feet in the fountain until my ankles ache from the cold. I pull them out and rest them on the mossy bevel above the waterline. The swelling is better already.

I hear Elke gasp. "Sorry," I say. "Try not to look."

"Come, sit up here." She motions to a stone wall occupied by her backpack. I do as she asks, and she digs in her pack for a medical kit.

Tears well up in my eyes as Elke gently tends to my feet. I'm so touched by the gesture. We are strangers, but she fusses over me like I'm her little sister. She applies antibiotic salve to the open wounds before placing a cushion of blister-wool she brought from Holland. The synthetic wool is fluffy, like a cotton ball, but it won't stick to the wound. She pads and tapes both feet, and then moves on to massaging my ankles. "You need to slow down, girl." She lectures, and I nod in agreement.

Elke chats while she works, telling me how she cared for her ailing parents for the past ten years, and how her mother died a year ago, and how her father followed six months later. "I'm an orphan now, fifty-two and all alone." She is walking to grieve and to figure out the next chapter of her life.

Once Elke completes her patch job, leaving feels awkward, especially after she has shared the personal details of her pilgrimage and touched my gross feet. I feel like I owe her something, but I'm not sure what I have that might be of use. I consider a hug, but I have no clue if she is the hugging kind. Before I lace up my boots to go, she tears off a clump of the magic wool and holds it out to me. "Thank you. You've been so kind. Levi gave me a little gift too, a tick-puller." I show her my green crowbar. Elke reaches back into in her medical kit. She smiles and pulls out a tiny, pink crowbar and waves it in the air. Evidently, the tick-puller is Levi's calling card.

I extend an open palm to bid her farewell. She takes it in both hands but then moves in. She kisses me three times, once on the right cheek, and on the left, and back again on the right. She bids me, "Buen Camino." And I am on my way.

I rest in Villatuerta, about 4K outside of Estella. I need to quit for the day, but I won't. Part of the problem is my ridiculous goal-orientation. Last night in Puente La Reina, Krystal and I studied our Brierly guides, and I made the proclamation to walk on to Estella. This is how it works for me. Once I proclaim it, I must do it. Puente La Reina to Estella is Brierly's 5th stage, and it is less than 22K. It's what Brierly recommends, and he is my trail guru.

I remove my boots and inspect my feet. Elke's bandage job is holding, but the swelling has returned. I have no ankle definition, and my bulging toes strain against the bloody gauze tape. I contemplate the 4K push to Estella. I could quickly make it up in the morning, get a head start and walk further the next day. Simple, right?

I admire a welcoming albergue, *Casa Magica*. I take in the medieval stone building with its rustic, wrought-iron balconies adorned with hanging baskets of red geraniums. I want so badly to break the threshold, that invisible line separating the dust and the heat and me from the building's interior courtyard. I imagine the occupants, fellow peregrinos, relaxing and drinking cold beers in the shade of umbrellas or flopped on brightly-colored hammocks, limbs dangling, swinging in the breeze of an electric fan. It is so tempting.

My feet are more important than my silly goal-orientation. The real obstacle isn't last night's proclamation, its agoraphobia. Panic sits on my chest and wraps a choke-hold around my neck. I sit and stare at the albergue for a while, thinking this might be a good day – a day where I can coach myself over the threshold in a matter of minutes. I pull out my phone and play a round of solitaire and then another. But it's no use. It's just like the *YMCA* at home and the train station in Madrid. *I just can't cross.*

To make matters worse, I can't cram my feet back into sweaty boots and continue my way to Estella. Strangled by fear and screwed-over by my feet, I must keep moving. I slip a clean pair of thin toe-sock liners on my feet, gingerly working them around each painful digit. I unzip my pack and dig out chocolate-colored, gardening clogs. They are ugly, but not as ugly as the ones popular with other peregrinos. Mine are the *Mary Janes* of rubber clogs, multipurpose foot fashion for showering, lounging, sipping wine, and attending evening mass. And now, my Mary Janes are about to make a hiking debut. Anything has got to be better than boots.

I adjust the strap, the little detail differentiating them from ordinary garden clogs, from the front of my foot to the heel. Unfortunately, the band rests atop a weeping blister on my right ankle. I can't stand it and flip the straps back to the front. I must walk slower than usual to keep the clogs on my feet. It will take longer to reach the day's goal, but the soft rubber is cushiony and provides more relief than predicted.

I try singing, hoping to break my silent bubble before I reach the bustle of Estella. I can only think of Christmas songs. I sing a couple verses of *Winter Wonderland* but trail off. It doesn't work in this heat.

I wouldn't be having this problem if I could have left my companion, *Agoraphobia,* at home, sitting on the couch with my husband. She's such a pain in the ass to travel with, a total stick in the mud. I've read all about her and spent a couple of years in therapy, but nothing has helped me understand why she happens when she happens. She's never truly random, but not predictable either. Sometimes, I'm perfectly fine. The problem occurs more when I try to make the transition from the sanctuary of my quiet car into a noisy environment, like the gym or a shopping mall. Although currently sans car, I am not without my bubble of peace.

I haven't spoken a single word since leaving Elke back in Lorca. That's about five kilometers of silence. "Shit!" I scream. "Screw you, agoraphobia. Go home!" Shouting helps. "You're a piece of dog crap!" Breaking the silence now should help me avoid getting stuck with it later. "Piss off, vertigo! Suck it, migraines!" The swearing makes me laugh and improves my mood. I stomp away the next 3K in rubber gardening clogs, hollering obscenities, telling off ailments, and pumping my hiking poles in the air. To an onlooker, I'm sure it seems I've totally lost my shit. Maybe I have?

I'm surprised how quickly I make it to the outskirts of Estella. Swearing and stomping helped pass the time. To my relief, a spigot of potable water gushes from a stone fountain. I dump out the warm leftovers from inside the water bladder and refill it with fresh. It's delicious. I want to put my feet in the fountain, but Elke's bandages are still intact, and I have a little way to go before finding a bed for the night. Instead, I whip off my hiking blouse and stick my head and shoulders in the frigid gush. I stay in as long as I can, stifling the squeal of a little girl running through a backyard sprinkler. I come out ten years younger and ready to take the hill.

As I'm buttoning back up, I examine a small plaque etched into the façade of the fountain wall. My Spanish is remedial, but I read aloud, "Buen pan, exelente aqua y vino, carne y pescado, llena de toba felicidad." I smile because my Spanish is strong enough to interpret without technological intervention. Basically, the plaque claims Estella has everything required to fill me with joy. Good bread, meat and fish, and excellent water and wine. What a wonderful thought. If the rejuvenating fountain is an indicator of what lies ahead, then I'm in for a treat.

The climb from the fountain isn't steep, but it is steady. I stop to rest and marvel at the 14th-century *Iglesia del Santo Sepulchro*. I count the apostles, each statue tucked in his own little alcove, gracing the upper quadrant of the building. Satisfied to find six per side, I whisper, "The gang's all here." The church is in a sorry state of ruin. There hasn't been a mass held here since 1881, but I still sense a presence and feel the need to whisper. Beyond the crumbling Gothic façade, there is something majestic and holy radiating from the arched portal. I'm dying to peek inside, but the door is locked as it probably has been for a hundred years.

The sanctity of the abandoned church leaves me unprepared for the din of traffic as I enter Estella. I'm not ready for street signs, crosswalks, or the impatient honking of motorists who are sick to death of absentminded peregrinos. I can't blame the drivers. We are a swarm of hungry locust blowing into town, dazed and strung out from the road.

I miss a yellow arrow and consequently miss my turn into the old village. I cross a beautifully constructed stone bridge I should not cross, and I find myself misplaced in front of a bus station. Backtracking, I try to admire the river, but I'm starting to panic. Where is my *flecha amarilla,* my little yellow arrow? A yellow arrow isn't completely necessary to get me back on track but seeing one would be a comfort. I know all I must do is scan the skyline for an old bell tower. The Camino almost always beats a path in front of the most antiquated of churches. I spy the Romanesque tower of what I'll soon learn is the 12th century *Iglesia de San Pedro de la Rúa Estella,* the grandest and oldest church in the old quarter.

It's not long before I'm back on track, staring down the behemoth that is *San Pedro. Panic* has all but left the building. When he's in-house, he takes up the real estate between my heart and lungs, making it hard to breathe. *Fear* favors the pit of my stomach, and she drops in like a rock.

The recommended albergue, *Hospital de Peregrinos,* is full or *completo,* and so is the parish of San Miguel. Albergues typically open their doors to pilgrims at 1400 hours. It's already 1830 and finding a bed may be a challenge, but I'm not worried, and I'm not going to panic. I exit the quaint, old town of Estella and keep a stiff-upper-lip as I pass hotels and pensions with no vacancy. "The Camino will provide. The Camino will provide. The Camino …" I whisper a favorite peregrino mantra as I negotiate a roundabout in the harsh sprawl of urban progress. After another roundabout, I am out of the city and out of options. But in the distance, I spot a giant yellow A painted on the side of a building. A is for *albergue.* I'm in luck!

San Cipriano de Ayegui is a municipal albergue with eighty beds positioned on what appears to be the floor of an old gymnasium. The *hospitalero,* or volunteer host, greets me and shows me to the five remaining bunks. He is apologetic, but I am grateful.

The bunks are hastily set up as overflow and crammed tightly in the passageway leading from the bathrooms to the gymnasium floor. I'm surprised and thrilled to find so much available space near the restroom. Of course, I am naive. In the middle of the night, a flow of walnut-bladdered peregrinos will teach me why this is an unfavorable real estate. I drop my gear and head to the ladies' locker room. I'm now certain this is a recycled sporting facility. I stand in a communal shower room under the annoying mist of a water-conserving showerhead. Typically, I'm all for conservation but not today. It takes forever to soak and lather up my thick curls and even longer to rinse. I'm startled at what looks like brownish-red blood running down my torso and legs, but then I remember. *Chocolate-cherry*, my new hair color. It surprises me this is the first time I've washed my hair since dying it the day before I left home. It's only been four days, but it seems like weeks.

After my shower, I pull a green peasant dress over my head and adjust the sheered bodice. The dress, made from the silk of an upcycled sari, is a girly splurge. I purchased two, one green and one purple, last summer at the *Seattle Folk Life Festival*. The dress doubles as both evening and sleepwear and weighs almost nothing. I couldn't decide on green or purple, so I packed both. Braless and without panties, the silk rests like a cool breeze on my skin.

The gymnasium floor is lousy with snoring pilgrims, most of them male. I'm uncomfortable, but I'm not afraid. Mostly, I am lonely. It has been a long day stuck inside of my own head, and I don't know what to do with myself. I sit on my bunk in the passageway tending to my feet. I peel the last bit of sticky tape from the back of a heel and assess the damage. I've never seen my feet, or any feet, in such sorry shape.

I hear a ruckus at the front desk and get up to investigate. I lock eyes with a gorgeous man ripped from the centerfold of an *L.L. Bean* sporting-goods catalog; that is, of course, if

L.L. Bean included centerfolds. His sandy blonde hair sweeps above a set of intense hazel eyes and frames a strong brow and tanned face. I scan him from head to toe, taking in the washboard abs beneath a sweat-soaked shirt and traveling down to his hiking shorts to admire the tone of his legs. Bea-u-ti-ful. I work my way back up and meet his eyes again. I offer a smile, and he returns a flash of perfectly aligned, white teeth. I'm star struck. He's the best-looking man I've seen in ages. But then I see *her.*

She is his opposite. Young, red-faced, exhausted, and filthy. They are a party of four: The L.L. Bean model, the girl, a tall old man, and a handsome boy. The boy carries two backpacks. I assume one belongs to her. I hear my mantra in my head, and I don't know exactly why, but I move toward her. I smile and open my arms in a shallow hug. She comes to me, and we embrace naturally, like old friends. Her name is Gretchen, and she takes the empty bunk next to mine. Her companions claim the remaining three. She introduces Grandpa, Uncle Drew, and her little brother Jonny. And just like that, we form a Camino family.

I walk Gretchen to the bathroom, and at her request, I stay while she showers. I prop myself on the long vanity and bathe my feet in a sink of cold water. "Wow!" She grimaces. "Your feet are fucked." Standing buck-naked before me, her swearing surprises me less than her lack of modesty. She couldn't be more than sixteen. In all my military years of communal showers, I never grew comfortable with full-frontal nudity amongst strangers.

"I can ask Grandpa to check em out." She gently lifts my big toe and winces. "He's a retired physician." I nod in agreement as she continues to inspect my feet. She pulls another face. It hurts her to look at them. "Gnarly. Totally gnarly."

I reply in 1980s valley girl, "Yeah. Like totally." Gretchen helps me down from the vanity, and we make our way back to the makeshift dorm. Grandpa is sleeping when we pass his bunk. I motion for her not to wake him, but she does. Jonny finds Grandpa's spectacles, and Grandpa draws my feet into his lap.

"Is she going to be able to walk tomorrow, Grandpa?"

"I suppose so, Jonny. She can do as she wishes." He cradles the heel of my right foot in the V of his thumb and forefinger. Tilting my toes toward the beam of Jonny's flashlight, he completes a careful inspection before moving on to the other foot. His touch is clinical, not personal like Elke's.

"Other than the blisters," I say. "Do you see anything wrong?" I'm secretly worried about the swelling. Nothing like this has ever happened to me before.

"Wrong?" Grandpa sounds impatient with me. "No, there's nothing particularly remarkable here. Your feet have walked a long way, and you did not prepare."

I want to protest! I want to lay out the details of my rigorous 9-month training program. I'm not some bimbo who picked up a pack and thought the Camino would be fun. I trained. I read everything. I bought and re-bought the best gear. I practiced in all elements. I was a soldier for God-sakes. I have endured hundreds of miles of ruck marching, keeping up with my male comrades. This *is* my normal. This should be a piece of cake. And it makes me so angry it is not a piece of cake, that I am not who I used to be.

There is no use arguing. Grandpa has dropped my feet to resume his nap. Besides, I know it's all my fault. I should have waited. I should have given my feet a break and allowed the swelling to go down after my long flight to Madrid and my equally long drive to Pamplona. I was too anxious, too competitive, too goal-oriented. What I don't understand is why my feet swelled in the first place. But I also know it's not just the swelling. I did something else stupid I now deeply regret. I switched to a lighter boot, a pair of *Merrells*, days before my departure. I read and re-read numerous online blogs and forums and foolishly questioned my fully-broke-in *Lowas*. I hiked for months in those boots and hadn't suffered a blister beyond the first few weeks. But the *Lowas* are heavy and hot and rigid. Popular opinion indicated the *Lowas* were "too much boot" for Spain. So, like a dummy, I opted for a virtually *break-in-free* pair of *Merrells*. Break-in-free? My ass!

The kids and I are quietly starving while Grandpa and Uncle Drew nap. I rifle through my backpack and dig out a small bag of almonds to share. Gretchen presents a half-eaten bar of chocolate, and Jonny pulls out a giant zucchini. "Cucumber?" he offers me a bite.

"Honey, that is not a cucumber." I continue, "It's a zucchini." He shrugs and inspects the squash before taking a bite. He passes it to Gretchen, and she gives it a nibble. It makes its rounds to me, and I take an obligatory chomp into its thick, green skin. I grow zucchini at home in the greenhouse, and this monster is past prime. It's still usable in zucchini bread or fritters, but the overgrown squash is ill-suited as a crudité. Jonny gives it another try before tossing it on his bunk.

The kids make themselves comfy on my single bed. We are whispering, so as not to wake Grandpa, Drew, and seventy-five of our new best friends. I learn Grandpa is walking his fifth and final Camino. It's his farewell tour. He walked with his children and wanted to walk one more time with his grandchildren. They are part of a very Catholic family where pilgrimage-making is an expectation. Unfortunately, Grandpa suffers early-onset dementia; therefore, Uncle Drew has come along to help. I probe a little to learn more about their handsome uncle, but I'm met with mixed emotions. They don't act particularly crazy about him, at least not tonight. Drew manages one of those adventure camps for troubled youth in Michigan. He has apparently brought along his camp wisdom, counseling skills, and disciplinary techniques to the benefit of Gretchen and Jonny. The kids are unimpressed.

Uncle Drew and Grandpa finally wake, and much to my dismay, we are walking back into Estella to find supper. Reluctantly, I accepted Drew's invitation to join them. I don't want to walk anymore, but today is Grandpa's 55th wedding anniversary, and we are off to find the perfect restaurant for such a festive occasion. I'm honored to be invited.

Drew and Grandpa walk ahead. Grandpa is seventy-nine, and he's walking me into the ground. I am embarrassed I cannot keep up with this little, old billy goat; however, I'm not alone. The kids hobble behind with me and cuss like sailors. Apparently, I'm not the only one who thinks hiking and obscenities go together. Unlike me, Jonny and Gretchen lack the freedom to shout out; instead, Jonny spews creatively constructed expletives in a low murmur. "Where in the fuck are they fucking going?" I raise an eyebrow, but it only eggs him on. "Fuck my already reamed and fucked asshole."

I shoot him my infamous *mom-look*. I'm shocked he is so comfortable cursing in my presence. My sons are several years older, and while they might drop the occasional F-bomb in my company, it never flows freely, nor does the prose contain a reference to body parts or the actual act of copulation. *Fuck* is never a literal term. "Jonny," I chide. "Aren't you a Catholic schoolboy." He grins and gears up for another spew. I'm not offended, but I am surprised.

Over a meal of *Arroz Negro*, or squid ink rice, we toast Grandpa's fifty-five years of marital bliss. I hesitate to share the stage, but the wine makes me warm and romantic. "And here's to Jim, my hubby. Today is our 15th anniversary." Grandpa is delighted at the happy coincidence, and we clink our glasses.

"To marriage!" says Grandpa.

When I glance up over my glass, I see Drew is crestfallen. He can't hide his disappointment. Had he not noticed my wedding ring? Although understated, it's visible on the ring finger of my left hand. A little rush of heat floods my cheeks. *He was interested.* He was thinking about it. Ha! I'm inflated in the knowing, the sheer delight he contemplated. Now, it's true, I did undress him with my eyes when he walked into the albergue, and I owned the thoughts of a woman on the prowl. It seems I sent the wrong message, but I'm not sorry.

It's been a long while, too long since anyone – Jim included – reminded me I am still an attractive woman.

We lose track of time and return to our albergue after curfew. We are locked out! Missing curfew, because I was hanging out with an old man and his grandkids, is hilarious. Grandpa is chuckling, and this makes the kids laugh. Our unified jolliness is fueled by entirely too much wine. Drew is sober, and the only responsible adult among us. He beats on the gymnasium door. In a few moments, an irritated hospitalero opens the door. The host chastises our tardiness. The scolding sobers up the kids and me, but Grandpa breaks into a howling belly laugh. He climbs into his sleeping bag, and his laugh turns to hiccups. Gretchen and I can hear him gulping from down in the basement bathroom as we brush our teeth.

Gretchen grabs my arm as we fumble out of the bathroom light into the dark of the gymnasium. She gives me a quick peck on the cheek and slides into her sleeping bag. I'm tucking into mine when something cold and long and hard brushes against my thigh. I leap out of bed with a scream. Jonny hits me with a beam of his flashlight, and in the chorus of angry hushes, I see it – *The Zucchini.*

Estella to Los Arcos

I wake to the crinkle of plastic bags and the rush of
zippers. Grandpa and Drew stand wholly dressed, and Jonny
is lacing up his boots. Gretchen is still bleary-eyed but
dressed in flowing blue and white pants and a sports bra. She
fumbles around in her rucksack for a fresh t-shirt.

"Young lady," Grandpa addresses me sternly. "You better
get a move on it."

Last night over dinner, we agreed on a wake-up time. I set
my phone alarm to vibrate at 0630, but I must have failed to
notice the buzz. Apologetic and startled by my tardiness, I
grab my phone to check the time. Ugh. What a crazy little
family. It's not quite 0600. What are they doing awake?

I can be ready in a flash. This is the beauty of pilgrimage.
The Camino is free from the mundane decisions and
expectations that take up time in ordinary life. It doesn't
matter if I wash my face, style my hair, or brush my teeth in
the morning. No one cares. I have two choices of bottoms, a
hiking skirt or leggings. I have two tank tops with built-in
support, one blue and one coral. I can choose a red hoodie
over a tank top when it's cold or toss a white hiking blouse
on to shield me from the sun when it's hot. I have three
identical pairs of purple wool socks and two pairs of toe-sock
liners. It is all the clothing I own. I am without razor or
makeup, not even tinted lip balm. I packed no bra and only
one pair of undies. I have a preference of going commando
anyway; it's an anti-candida technique tested along many
miles of military ruck-marches. The undies are for swimming,
sleeping, and attending mass. Jesus wants me to wear panties
under my dress when I enter his house.

I'm ready to roll before Gretchen loads her bag. Her
backpack must have exploded in the night, leaving a sea of
gear adrift all over the floor. I snatch up wayward socks, a
bra, and her plaid shorts from beneath her bed and stuff
them in her bag. She isn't well, and she's moving slow.
Cramps. Poor little thing.

Grandpa and Drew are waiting outside the albergue door. Grandpa taps his hiking poles on the blacktop in irritation but says nothing when we join them. Our first destination is the *Bodegas Irache* with its famous *Fuente de Vino*. It's near the ancient Benedictine *Monasterio Irache*, the monastery Grandpa spoke about over dinner. He is a fountain of wisdom and as unique and delightful as the *Irache* fountain of wine.

The fountain of wine, graciously provided by local wine-makers, is a fortification-must for peregrinos. Perhaps it's just me, but wine for breakfast sounds terrible. What I need is coffee. I am nursing a little headache from last night's indulgence. I mixed dehydration with three glasses of deep-ruby *Tempranillo* of the Navarra region. The wine was spectacular, but I ought to know better.

We start the morning hike by reciting the rosary. Drew divides up the parts, strategically assigning me the *Our Fathers*. I don't know how to say the rosary, but I can recite the *Lord's Prayer*. The prayer was a Sunday school requirement to graduate from our basement classroom to the adult church upstairs. Had I realized graduation meant no more playdough, cookies, and games of tag in the churchyard, I would have thrown the match.

Gretchen and Jonny recite their parts. Drew taps my shoulder when it's my turn. I give it my best and Grandpa nods in approval. And this goes on for a few rounds, this game of religious *duck-duck-goose* until we find the fountain of wine.

The idea here is to tap the barrel and catch a mouthful of wine in the seashell peregrinos wear or carry along the route. The shell, an ordinary sea scallop, is the ancient symbol used to identify pilgrims and the pilgrimage route moving toward Santiago. However, the medieval pilgrim wouldn't have obtained a shell until reaching the coast in Muxia, where the legendary boat returning St. James' body to Spain is believed to have washed ashore.

Modern pilgrims purchase shells at starting points all over Spain and France, and the ultra-modern buy shells online.

Opting for an old-school approach, I did neither. I won't claim a scallop shell until I reach Santiago. I like to think of the seashell as a finisher's trophy. I must earn it. Consequently, I have nothing to catch wine. Drew comes to the rescue with a disposable water bottle. This is a perfect solution, better than a shell because while I do want to experience peregrino fortification, I won't be ready for a drink until long after my first café con leche.

Satisfied with our cache of wine, we continue 5K up a gently sloping path and into the hamlet of Azqueta. We stop to appreciate the medieval, parish church of *San Pedro,* rebuilt in the 16ᵗʰ century. Grandpa points out the mixture of Gothic and Renaissance elements and then draws our attention to the newly built tower. His art history lecture is fascinating, but we are not sorry when he stops midsentence, forgetting his train of thought and declaring his hunger.

Grandpa and Drew take off their boots outside the café to settle in and stay a while, but I grab a quick coffee and croissant. Reluctant to eat and run, it is the only solution to keep up with their collective pace. The threatening heat of new blister prickles on the ball of my left foot. Overextension of my short stride creates hotspots and eventually, blisters. I need to walk ahead at my own pace and let them catch up to me after they eat breakfast.

Gretchen and Jonny are dear to me, and I want to stay with them tonight in Los Arcos. They need me, or at least that is my excuse. Truthfully, I'm a bit embarrassed to be clinging so tightly to my newfound family. After being in their company last night, I realize how lonely I have felt since leaving home. I thought I'd love being alone. It's what I wanted and what I still want, but I need to work up to it. *Comfortably alone* is more elusive than I assumed.

I miss the hubby and my kids, but I really miss Jasper. Jasper, a black Labrador, is no ordinary mutt. He is a service dog. Trained to provide mobility assistance, he was instrumental in getting me back on my feet. Before Jasper, illness had not only ended my military career, but it squashed my confidence, glued me to the sofa, wrecked my cardio, and fattened my body. Jasper served not only as my physical therapist, but he was also my trainer. I wouldn't be here now if not for him.

For now, this set of purple hiking poles replaces Jasper's physical support, but the poles are a poor substitute for the emotional strength and companionship he provides. I am braver when I am with him, just as I am braver when I am with my children. I don't expect Jasper or my kids to protect me. In fact, the opposite is true. When I am with them, I am the protector. I am in charge, and I keep them safe. When I am alone, I have no role, no real purpose, not even as my own protector. It's stupid, but I don't know what to do with myself anymore.

I'm lost in thought when Jonny sneaks up and pulls my ponytail. I scream and spin around, brandishing a hiking pole like a sword. He doubles over in laughter and rolls on the dusty trail until Gretchen catches up. My heart is still in my throat, but I'm trying to laugh it off. "Oh, my God! I'm. So. Sorry! I didn't mean..." He carries on. He is pleased with himself but also sorry he scared the shit out of me. He had intended to surprise me but wasn't expecting to evoke a panic-stricken reaction. It's not his fault I am such an easy target.

Gretchen tells me Drew and Grandpa are going to be awhile, and we are to head toward Los Arcos without them. Suddenly very serious, Jonny tells me Grandpa has had a bathroom accident. I'm glad he doesn't find this funny. "It was everywhere," gasps Jonny. "I feel bad for him." He tears-up, and I look away to give him privacy.

"Come here, you little brat." Fully recovered from fright, I grab Jonny and loop my arm into his and give a gentle squeeze. We walk arm in arm, and he confesses how hard it has been to watch Grandpa's decline. He tells me about Grandpa's dementia and the grim prognosis, and I listen and nod and bear witness to Jonny's heartbreak. This is a different kid from yesterday. This isn't the foul-mouthed schoolboy who hid a zucchini in my bed last night. Today, Jonny is a caring little human and loving grandson.

"Don't worry," I try to lighten the mood. "That little billy goat will be along any moment now, and he'll pass us up before we hit the next village. We'll be eating his dust all the way to Los Arcos." I say this without much doubt. The man is a five-time peregrino. A bathroom accident won't cramp his style.

The climb into *Villamayor de Monjardín* is steep. The elevation gain is a mere 150 meters, but it is happening all at once. My tummy is grumbling. The croissant, less than two kilometers old, was like eating nothing but flakey layers of buttery air. It isn't enough to keep me going. I need something real.

We spread a makeshift picnic on a stone bench in the churchyard opposite the *tienda,* a little shop, where we gathered provisions. Gretchen purchased a stubby baguette and a bar of chocolate. I bought a sheep's cheese shaped like a gourd and tied in string netting. Jonny claimed the longest chorizo any of us have seen. He draped it like a scarf around his neck to carry it out of the shop.

Gretchen breaks the bread into three hunks, and I cut fat slices of dense, ivory cheese with my Swiss Army knife. Jonny peels a white fiber casing from the chorizo and borrows my knife. He eats the first few slices and then offers me one still resting on the blade. "None for me." I hold up my hands.

"Me neither," says Gretchen.

"What?" says Jonny. "Oh, come on. It's *Chorizo!*"

"I don't eat pork."

"Like for religious reasons?"

"No, I just don't like it." This statement is true, but not the whole truth.

"One bite," he coaxes. "It's real Spanish Chorizo, from Spain!"

It's been a long time since I've eaten pork. Maybe things have changed. And Jonny's logic is solid because whenever I travel, I know a huge part of the experience is eating like a local. So, I open my mouth, and Jonny slides the wafer of chorizo from the blade of the knife to my tongue. It's a carnivore's communion in the 12th-century churchyard of *San Andrés.*

My gag reflex hits before I can swallow. I try one more time to get it down but nearly vomit before spitting in my hand and tossing it to a fortunate stray cat looming near. "I'm sorry, Jonny. That shit's just nasty." Undaunted by my revulsion, Jonny slices and unceremoniously eats about eight inches of the monster sausage.

Gretchen spies Drew and Grandpa cresting the hill. Jonny is the first to jump up and offer Grandpa a hug. "How do you feel?" Jonny asks.

"Grateful." Grandpa pats Drew's shoulder. "I am grateful to have a son who deeply cares for me and who also wears the same size of shorts." He offers an authentic chuckle, and we gawk at his knobby knees peeking out from Hawaiian flower board shorts.

"You look awesome!" says Gretchen. And he does. I admired his grace. He is indeed undaunted.

We agree to split up into two groups, and Grandpa and Drew push on to Los Arcos before the heat becomes unbearable. Heat or no heat, and with ten kilometers to go, my feet cannot afford to be in a hurry. So, as predicted, Grandpa and Drew leave the kids and me eating dust.

The graveled path leaving *Monjardín* is refreshingly downhill, and I take it at a near jog. Jonny and Gretchen follow behind. I'm back to wearing my chocolate-colored gardening clogs again. The threatening hotspot on the ball of my foot erupted into a nickel-sized bubble of ooze. It is hard to believe there is any available real estate left on either foot to support another wound, and yet, here it is. I welcome the newcomer to *Blisterville* with a cushiony wad of Elke's magic fluff and a few strips of gauze tape.

As I wait for the kids at the bottom of the hill, I am shocked to see an old lady with a birdcage coming down behind them. It's her! This is my bird-lady I followed out of

Pamplona. I never expected to see her or her bird again. She is still wearing the pastel, plaid button-up shirt that clashes with her red stretch pants. Silver sneakers adorn her feet, and a pink bookbag slumps off her shoulders. Most remarkably, she still grips the handle of the gilded cage in her left hand. I can't believe she is also on pilgrimage. Back in Pamplona, I thought she was an odd little lady taking her bird for a stroll out of the city. Apparently, she plans to extend her stroll to Santiago in the company of her blue-green parakeet.

I take a long draw of water, swish it around, and spit it out in a patch of red poppies lining the trail. I can't get rid of the chorizo. After eating a hunk of bread, three slices of cheese, and four squares of dark chocolate, the putrefaction of dead hog lingers on my tongue.

When the kids catch up, Gretchen comes to my rescue with a stick of wintergreen gum. "So, what's your deal with pork," she asks. Jonny leans in and listens.

"It may be difficult to understand because you two do not farm." They admit to owning zero farm experience. "When I was in the fifth grade, I was lonely. I had only one friend in the world, and she was a pig." Jonny laughs, thinking I'm making a fat girl joke. "No, really. She was a *Yorkshire-Duroc* cross. An actual hog, weighing in at 700 pounds. We took long walks on the farm together, and I told her all my secrets. I raised her from a tiny baby. As a piglet, she fit in the palm of my hand." I stretch out my right hand for emphasis. "She was the color of lemons, and I called her Sunny." I pause because this should be the end of the story, but Jonny stares at me blankly. "Dude!" I feign exasperation, "Friends don't eat friends!"

Jonny was still enjoying an occasional chomp from his chorizo, so I didn't go into detail about how pigs smell exactly like their flesh tastes. But this is true. And I'm not talking about dirty pigs or pig poop. I'm talking about a freshly bathed hog sleeping on a bed of sweet straw at the Clackamas County Fair.

Sunny won more than her share of blue ribbons. Fairgoers complemented her wiry, yellow hair glistening like honey after a bath and rubdown with baby oil. She was quite the looker. If a pig could be pretty, Sunny was a beauty queen. Back then, neither she nor I could imagine the impact she would have on my life. She's the reason I grew up so fiercely independent. She is why I am who I am. And she's also the reason I cannot stomach pork.

It was 1979, and I was eleven and walking solo in rubber boots. I pulled open the barn door. Sunny heaved. Flat on her side, Sunny was unable to rise or grunt a salutation. Waves of purpled heat squiggled from her seven hundred pounds. Heat collided with November frost and disappeared in foggy puffs of steam. She let out a long sigh as if saying, "Thank God you're here, old friend." Her belly rocked in feverish knots as I stroked her golden hair.

A single piglet, shiny and blonde, emerged from a marbled sack of afterbirth. I wrapped sewing thread around a tube of bluish-white umbilical, slashed a length of cord with a razor, and positioned him to root at nipples dripping orange with milk, pus, and blood. I repeated these steps fourteen more times that night, but not before phoning for help.

"Yer hog's gonna die, little girl," said the Veeley boy who lived up the road. I hated calling for help, but I knew he would come. All five of the Veeley boys helped on my family's farm. The boys bucked hay, sheared sheep, rounded up stray cows, and offered extra hands in trying times. My parents were off on a hunting trip, and I was left home alone to deliver babies and save my best friend from dying of mastitis infection. I needed his help.

The barn air steeped damp and heavy, the odors familiar, like an opened wound and an Easter supper of pineapple-baked ham. I inhaled the salty sweetness and concealed a gag.

The first placenta cooled beneath a pulsating vulva the size of a coffee mug. I tried not to stare or show my curiosity and wonder, but I knew nothing of birthing babies. I wanted to be alone, alone with Sunny, alone with the stench, and

alone with the wonders of birth. But that boy stayed with me
all night. He coached me through each delivery and taught
me how to draw milky penicillin from an amber medicine
bottle. He kneaded thick skin on Sunny's neck and simulated
the injection. I nodded, held my breath, and slammed the
needle down. I repeated the process twice a day for two
weeks and prayed she would live.

Six years my senior, I hoped to make that Veeley boy my
proper boyfriend, once I was old enough to date. I dreamed
of marrying him one day. But that night in the barn, with the
birth and the stench and the threat of death, I aged. And the
crush of young love died.

After the last piglet found her place on a nipple and
Sunny was stable, the boy went home, and I walked back to
the house with my flannel nightgown tied in a bunch over
black rubber boots. The squalling little runt, now swaddled
warm and tight in my arms, drifted off to sleep. Brave and
powerful and alone. I knew I'd never want for that boy again.

That night in the barn, I became a midwife, veterinarian,
and piglet mama. I thought I could do anything and wasn't
half wrong, but I sorely misjudged future obstacles. I wish I
could go back in time, to be eleven once more, a self-
proclaimed feminist before I knew the definition of
feminism. I want that kind of self-assurance and grace, relying
wholly on myself – on my brains, on my sturdy little body, on
unwavering courage and intuition.

Jonny and Gretchen whisper about the bird-lady. She is in
front now, less than twenty-five meters. Her left arm is a
pendulum, and the swing of the gilded cage is hypnotic. I
listen to the rhythm of my hiking poles striking the packed
dirt, keeping time with the motion of the blue-green parakeet.

We walk along in a comfortable silence, and my mind
pays a visit to childhood and life on the farm. I think about
animals loved and lost and eaten. There was this bottle-fed
goat, named Periwinkle. He followed me to the bus stop
every day. One afternoon, when I hopped off the bus, he
wasn't there waiting for me. I screamed, "I hate you" to my

mother. She beat the hell out of me with a belt. My dad gave me a second whipping that night. A couple weeks later, my mother packed Periwinkle-pepperoni in my Wonder Woman lunchbox and expected me to eat him. I have always had a firm grasp on the food chain. But seriously. What in the fuck were my folks thinking?

At a makeshift rest stop alongside the dusty trail, Gretchen and I claim a plastic table beneath the shade. Jonny scrounges a couple of chairs. I slide off my pack and plop down so hard the legs of the chair threaten to buckle. Jonny puts a hand on my shoulder to steady me. "Easy does it, ole girl." I swipe at him with a half-hearted backhand, but he is too quick. Laughing, he joins Gretchen at the food truck.

"Need a brew?" Jonny calls to me in the deepest voice his fourteen years can muster. I shake my head and hold up the water bottle containing precious peregrino wine collected from the fountain in Irache. Jonny buys two Cokes, one for himself and the other for Gretchen.

Gretchen joins me back at the table, but Jonny mills around meeting new folk and greeting the dozens of pilgrims met earlier in his journey. The boy has such moxie. He is tall and well-built for his age, with caterpillar eyebrows that dance when he speaks. I marvel at his confidence and budding good looks. This kid is going to own the world.

Gretchen draws in a sharp breath. "There he is!" She tugs at my sleeve. By now, I know this look. I scan the trail leading to our rest spot, but I can't identify anyone of teenage-heartthrob caliber. "There," she insists. She's pointing at a dark man with a wild, black beard and pony-tailed hair.

"Him?" I shake my head. "But he's so old." The observation makes me laugh because he is much younger than me.

"Yes." She is breathless. "I'm so in love."

"You're a weird little girl. Dude is seriously old, at least thirty. And he is so hairy."

"I know," she sighs. "I just love em like that."

The hairy dude smiles and returns Gretchen's wave and makes his way to our table. He steps carefully through a maze of abandoned packs and carelessly strewn poles. As he draws near, I understand how she could find him attractive. He is South American, perhaps Colombian? His smile gleams and his dark chocolate eyes are ablaze with light. She jumps up to hug him and make introductions. "Pablo." She can barely utter his name without giggling. "This is my Camino mama. We met last night in Estella."

Pablo shakes my hand warmly and wraps his other arm around my shoulder in a half embrace. I absorb his electricity. When he releases, I'm left with a gushing dose of positive vibes. He makes me feel fuzzy and warm and a little speechless. Thankfully, Gretchen whisks him away. "Come on," she pulls him to the food truck. "I was about to fetch a beer for Mama." *Such a little liar*, but I nod and play along.

I shoot Gretchen double thumbs up while Pablo has his back turned to order his beer. She is blushing and bubbling over. How lovely and welcomed a crush would be right about now. That's what I miss. I miss the dreaming and scheming and flirting of a thrilling new romance. I miss the heartbreak Gretchen will undoubtedly feel in a few days when she sees her beloved Pablo holding hands with a beautiful, Swiss pilgrim born of his generation. She will cry, but she won't be sorry or jealous. Her crush isn't at all about permanent relationships, and it isn't at all about sex. She thrives in the mental ecstasy, in the raw and reckless heartfelt emotions. She still owns the ability to really feel. Yes. *To really feel* – this is what I miss.

I contemplate romantic disappointment and the doldrums of marriage, as Pablo and Gretchen sip their beers and slowly work back to the table. I glance down to pull out Gretchen's chair and notice what looks like one of *Rorschach's* ink blots. Hmm, *Starship Enterprise*, I muse. It takes me a moment to study the familiar shape. Yes. Stamped in a deep-maroon jelly and positioned in the middle of Gretchen's chair is the *USS Enterprise*. And then it hits me. I open the lid of my wine and feign a clumsy spill. The Starship is now safely concealed beneath a puddle of deliciousness.

"Damn it! My wine!" I grab Gretchen's arm. "Come. I need help cleaning this up." She struggles to free herself, but I tighten my grip and shoot her my meanest Mom-look. "Pleased to meet you, Pablo," I call to him over my shoulder while dragging Gretchen behind the food truck. By the time we round the truck, she is genuinely irritated.

"What are you doing? You're ruining everything!"

"Shh!" I command. "Turn around." She is angry but compliant, and I scan her from head to toe, quickly moving down her black tank top to her flowing, gauze pants of blue butterflies and wildflowers printed on a backdrop of white. It doesn't take long to spot another Rorschach masterpiece. *Murder on the Meadow.* "Honey," I speak gently now. "Your period. It's everywhere."

Except for the lone tree providing shade for our abandoned table, there is nothing to hide behind. I lead Gretchen into a field of tall grass. We both sit, and I dig through my shoulder bag for supplies. I know I don't have tampons or pads. I gave those up during my Camino training phase after successful experimentation with a cervical silicon cup. And one does not lend another her cup, no matter how dire. But I do have a few individually packaged feminine hygiene wipes. The wipes aren't enough to fix the pants, but it's a start. I hand them over. Gretchen thanks me and asks, "Can you fetch Jonny?"

"Jonny?"

"Tell him Aunt Flo is walking the Camino."

I interrupt Jonny in what I assume is a flirty conversation with two shapely Dutch girls. I whisper my message in his ear. I expect him to protest or at least shrug me off, but he doesn't. He offers a gentlemanly, "Excuse me, ladies," and rushes toward our pile of gear. He grabs a water bottle and Gretchen's pack. Remembering the brick of wet wipes in the bottom of Agnus, I snatch her up and take off toward our grassy hideaway.

When we reach Gretchen, she is flat on her back wearing only a tank top and tiny, black bikini bottoms. Jonny swoops down, plucks up the bloody pants, and soaks the stain with water. Theoretically, this is a promising idea, but the flood of water releases the stain from its tidy borders and sends a wave of reddish-orange down each leg. Undaunted, Jonny grabs my water and the wet wipes and starts scrubbing.

Gretchen roots around in her pack, pulling out a clean pair of pink briefs, plaid shorts, and a paisley pencil case filled with magic markers and maxi pads. Jonny keeps his back to us, busy with his work. Once Gretchen is dressed, Jonny helps her to her feet and tousles her hair. I loan a couple safety pins and attach her good-as-new gauze pants to her backpack to dry. We set off up the trail toward Los Arcos with Gretchen's pants flapping in the breeze.

At Gretchen's age, I would have sooner died than tell my siblings about Aunt Flo, and I can't imagine my brother or my sister coming to my rescue as Jonny rescued Gretchen. I can't pinpoint how or who reinforced the shame I once owned for my developing body or the horror I felt about my period. A menstrual cycle was something to hide. Leakage was devastating and humiliating. But no one here is devastated or humiliated or ashamed. There is something magical happening, a kind of familial love and care so foreign to me, and I am in awe.

The afternoon sun is unrelenting, and I tug at the floppy bill of my hat for shade. Jonny walks a few yards ahead, scuffing his feet and kicking up little trails of dust. I want to fuss at him, to tell him to pick up his feet, but I let it go. I stop for a water break but remember we donated our precious resources to save Gretchen's pants. I don't want to call attention to our lack of resources, so I pretend to be engrossed in a rolling blanket of yellow flowers. The flowers are an agricultural crop known by an unfortunate name, *Rapeseed*. The Spanish pronunciation sounds better, *rah-pe*. I introduce the field to Jonny and Gretchen as *Canola*, a common strain of the Rape family. We stand and absorb the yellowness and listen to the hum. The field is alive with honeybees. Buttoning my hiking blouse to my neck and fastening the sleeves around each wrist, I raise my arms and wade a few feet into the waist-high flowers. The cacophony of buzzing is deafening and much louder than it was standing a few feet outside of the field. The buzz seeps into my skin, and I can feel it in my heart. It's dizzying and delicious, and I sway with the windblown flowers. Bees ricochet off my arms and my torso and my hat. I'm allergic to bees, but not deathly allergic. This is probably why I find the experience exhilarating. It's risky but not deadly.

Jonny adjusts his khaki boonie-hat and gears up to enter the field. I realize how irresponsible I am behaving. He is in a tank top and long shorts. What if he gets stung? What if he is allergic? I shake my head in disapproval and work my way out of the field. He doesn't hide his relief.

On the outskirts of Los Arcos, our stopping place for the night, we pass a small bar. I check in with Gretchen about making a pit stop to visit the bathroom.

"Nope. I'm good. In fact, I am beautiful."

"And how is everything with Aunt Flo?"

"Oh, Flo is fine. And by the way, my vagina is so fresh and clean."

"You don't say?"

"What were those blue packets you gave me?"

"Do you mean the feminine hygiene wipes?"

"Yes! They are the bomb. I've never felt this clean."

"Good for you and good for your vagina."

"Can you use them every day?"

"Sure. But, why?"

"I like the fresh feeling."

"What do you normally use?"

"Use for what?"

"What do you normally use to wash your lady parts? You know, soap. What kind of soap do you use?"

"Soap?" She acts confused. "Wait. What? You can put soap on it?"

"Are you kidding me, Gretchen? I'm laughing now, "Do you or do you not wash your vagina with soap?"

She shakes her head. "No. No, I don't. And sometimes it smells. Nobody told me to use soap."

"Your mom…," I trail off, finding it hard to believe I'm having this conversation. "Didn't your mother teach you to wash your private parts?"

Gretchen shakes her head. "No. I thought you just hit it with the shower hose."

"Maybe you are allergic to soap down there. It's not uncommon. That is probably why your mom never taught you to use soap."

"Maybe." Gretchen is genuinely mystified as she mulls over her newly found knowledge vaginas can be washed.

"Why don't you purchase a feminine hygiene wash at the pharmacy? It's supposed to be gentle on lady parts."

I have never been thrilled to purchase anything specifically for my vagina, but Gretchen is elated as she skips up the street to find a pharmacy. I guess I was sort of excited about the menstrual cup. Using it makes environmental sense and its perfect for hiking. No more carting around tampons in preparation for my period and no carrying out used tampons in my pack. My personal Camino rule is if I pack it in, I pack it out. This rule also explains the bundle of red doggy poo bags in the front pocket of my rucksack. So far, I haven't had to use them. The possibility of needing to do a *big job* outdoors freaks me out. However, I can go potty like a total rock star, thanks to the little device enabling me to stand and pee like a man. Such freedom! The apparatus is an elongated, oval funnel with detaching tube. I don't understand why something like this wasn't a standard issue item during my twenty-four years of military service. The funnel, pink of course, is a great equalizer.

Jonny walks ahead to find his uncle and grandfather, while Gretchen and I duck into a small pharmacy. Unlike pharmacies in the United States, Spanish farmacias are usually small with most of the merchandise behind the counter. This isn't a problem unless you don't speak Spanish. Fortunately, Spanish shopkeepers along the Camino de Santiago are excellent at playing charades. Again, this fine, except if what you need is for *down there.*

Unabashed, Gretchen initiates conversation. She is pointing to her private parts while pantomiming a shower. She scrubs her armpits, washes her hair, and makes a swirling motion with both hands between her legs. I am dying! To make matters funnier, she requests "femenina hygiene sopa." The pharmacist, male, of course, is utterly confounded.

I love how many English speakers, including me, take to adding an A or an O to English words when trying to speak Spanish or *Spanglish.* As a soap maker in a former life, I know the Spanish word for soap is *jabón.* And being a foodie in this life, I know the Spanish word for soup is *sopa.* But the situation is too funny for me to interfere. I adore Gretchen, but no amount of adoration can make me stop laughing.

Eventually, I interject. "Ella necessita jabón para damas," I tell the pharmacist she needs soap for ladies, and I make a slight gesture toward the zipper of her plaid shorts.

We tumble out of the pharmacy and on the street in a burst of laughter. Gretchen holds a bottle of lady-wash high in the air like a trophy. It is such a release to laugh so hard about something so silly. We hug and cling to each other as we walk into town. Is this what it's like to have a daughter? Or is this something different, like being the cool auntie? Whatever it is, it is new and fresh, and I'm light as a feather fliting up the street to find our place to sleep for the night.

We catch up to Jonny, who is waiting outside for us, at the albergue *Casa Abuela* or Grandma's house. He motions upstairs where Uncle Drew and Grandpa are stretched out on their bunks. Jonny shows us to an adjoining room he calls *the kids' room,* and I'm thrilled to be welcomed to their youthful sanctuary.

Abuela, a real Spanish grandmother, offers to launder our clothes for a small fee. We dump our packs and sort our soiled garments into two collective piles, lights, and darks. I'm excited about a real washing machine experience. Handwashing is okay, but my socks don't feel as fresh when I pull them on in the morning. And Jonny's socks, even the so-called clean pairs, stink like hell.

I sort through the piles of clothes, rejecting anything that might discolor the crisp whiteness of my camping blouse. The blouse is UV-ray and insect shielding. It was a gift from my husband, and it is dear to me, like a peace offering of sorts. He gave it to me for Christmas, five months after I started training for the Camino. To me, it is more than a shirt. The blouse is a symbol of his support, or at least his acceptance that I would walk the Camino.

Gretchen carries the laundry downstairs to Abuela. Uncle Drew sneaks over and sits beside my bunk. In a whisper, he explains tomorrow is Gretchen's seventeenth birthday, but he's thrown together a surprise dinner party tonight in the plaza. Drew has invited a group of pilgrims she and Jonny met earlier along the trail. He also borrowed a guitar and purchased balloons. "I need you to distract her. Keep her out of the plaza until a quarter after seven," he says.

Distracting Gretchen is perhaps the easiest job of all. We sit on my bunk, eat chocolate, and talk about Pablo. When seven o'clock rolls around, I suggest we grab a sangría in the plaza. I slide into my green silk dress, the same one she admired last night in Estella. "Damn, I want that dress," she says.

I lift the lid of my pack and pull out the purple doppelganger. I toss the dress into Gretchen's arms. "It's all yours. For keeps."

"No way! Shut up!" She squeals, hugs me, and strips down to her pink briefs. I help pull the dress over her head and down to her hips. She is taller and thinner than me, but the sheered bodice conforms to her bust and waistline. I reach out and puff the silk of each capped sleeve. She is perfect, like a little doll with a messy bob of ash blonde hair. With matching dresses, we link arms and walk to the plaza. Now, this must be what it's like to have a daughter.

Fortunately, *Casa Abuela* does not enforce a curfew. Our group stumbles in much later than expected, tipsy on sangría and high on good cheer. "Hey, aren't you supposed to tuck us in?" Jonny calls to me from the top bunk. I like this setup, this home away from home I've found with my two Camino kids. I step on Gretchen's lower bedrail so I can reach Jonny. Looping one arm through the railing for balance, I use the other arm to tug his sleeping bag up to his chin. I lean as far as I can toward him, but I'm not close enough to deliver a goodnight kiss.

"There you go." I blow two kisses in the air and step down. "Now go to sleep."

"Hey, I want a real goodnight kiss," whines Jonny.

"Seriously, kid?" I step back up, and this time Jonny scooches closer to the rail, and I plant one on his salty forehead. "Happy now?" He signals thumbs up, and my feet return to the cool floor.

Gretchen is tucked in bed, but I go to her anyway. I pull her sleeping bag up to her chin, rest my hands on her shoulders, and then I do what my grandma did to me every time she tucked me in. Jostling Gretchen up and down in her bunk, I chant, "Night-night, sleep tight, don't let the bedbugs bite!" Gretchen giggles, just as I once giggled. As a child, I pictured friendly-faced, cartoon ladybugs and opalescent-green beetles hiding under my bed. Up until the Camino, Grandma's little ritual was my only exposure to bedbugs. Honestly, I had no idea there was such a thing. I kiss Gretchen on her forehead. "Sweet dreams, Birthday Girl."

"You know it. I'm going to have a romantic night with Pablo."

Pablo made Gretchen's birthday one to remember. The night was a blast and by far the most fun I've had in a long time. Drew orchestrated something from nothing. More than twenty pilgrims gathered at a long table in the plaza to eat, drink, and celebrate the birth of this adorable, young woman.

With a borrowed guitar, talented peregrinos took turns serenading Gretchen. When Gretchen took up the guitar and sang, I nearly cried my eyes out. A hauntingly defiant voice, I had no idea existed within her, came out in heart-wrenching belts. She completed three original songs, and not one of us took our eyes from her or spoke a word until she passed the guitar down the line. "Where did that come from?" I whispered to Drew.

There were peregrina-appropriate gifts. Thoughtful pilgrims dug through backpacks and hit the shops. There was a chocolate bar, a blue rubber massage ball with nubby spikes, and a tube of ibuprofen gel. She received a scallop shell, a small chunk of rose-quartz, a rainbow-colored rosary, and a pair of striped socks. But the gift she loved the most was a kiss on the lips from Pablo. I caught it on my camera, but as my gift to her, I pretended to miss the shot. "Dang it! I missed that one! Pablo, please. Please do it again." And he did. Pablo gave her the first kiss, and I gave her an encore. She floated upstairs to bed.

I toss in my bunk, unable to fall asleep. I listen to gentle shifts in Jonny's breathing as he falls into deep slumber. My boys are like him, wide awake and talking one moment and fast asleep the next. I joke with my husband about this phenomenon, claiming it's was a sure sign of a clear conscience and proof we are raising good children. If this is true, then Jonny, foul-mouthed and all, is a very good boy.

I fight with my sleeping bag. My restless legs hate to be confined. It's frustrating to be so awake with sleeping conditions this perfect. The room is well-ventilated, and no one is snoring. Yet.

Part of my sleeping problem is that I am so stinking happy right now. I'm inspired and energized by the collective love witnessed tonight. It was magic, pure magic. Drew counted eleven different nationalities gathered around the table. The sangría poured freely, as we all shared a common and unselfish goal of making Gretchen's day special. The world came together tonight beneath a blanket of stars to celebrate a sixteen-year-old peregrina on her way to Santiago de Compostela. It was beautiful. Totally beautiful.

This happens to me sometimes, these euphoric fits of wellbeing. But it's not unexplained or delusional like I'm happy for no reason. I am euphoric because tonight gave me such a high, a renewed faith and hope for humanity. This is rationalized euphoria. I don't know who I'm trying to convince, but let's say I've received criticism in the past for my great highs and deep lows. Nothing is on middle-ground for me. It's all beautiful, or it's all shit. At least that's what it was like before my illness. A touch of mania is my healthy normal, and it is good to feel normal again. To *feel* – to really feel is a beautiful gift.

My gift, self-diagnosed *hypomania,* is usually an asset. I find beauty in the darkest places. Sorrow and happiness and love and rage bloom or fester deep in my gut. But as smoothly as shifting a manual transmission into a new gear, I shift emotions. I howl with laughter one moment and bust out great sobs the next. The hypomania went on strike while I was stuck on the sofa. It was all down and no up. I love feeling it again, like an old friend who has been away too long. My hubby has the antithesis of mania. Jim serves as the yin to my yang. He rides the golden-mean, that impossible thread of emotional neutrality. He enjoys no great highs but suffers no great lows. I once witnessed him sink a hole-in-one while playing golf. I would have been ecstatic, but he nodded his head and gave the slightest of fist pumps. He didn't shout or raise his arms in the air. He didn't brag about it or relive the moment in the car ride home. Nothing. It was done. Just like that.

Jim and I are opposites, but together we strike a balance – an emotional equilibrium. I wonder how life will be without him if we don't survive? Who will keep me grounded? And can I find stability on my own? The imminent death of our marriage sends my heart plummeting into my gut, but so does the thought of returning home to the cognac leather sofa. I have walked myself into an emotional no-man's land, and now I'm caught between two electric fences. No matter which way I move, forward or backward, it's going to hurt. And standing still is no longer an option.

When I was a kid, I played this game with my little brother. It was our electric fence version of *chicken*. Each of us took turns moving an index finger closer to the fence without touching it. The thrilling fear of probable electrocution was addicting, and so were the bragging rights and laughter when the current arced and zapped the tip of the loser's finger. If I relaxed and stilled my breathing, I would sometimes hear the beat of electricity surging through the barbed wire. That's when I made my move, between the pulses. My brother never listened to the beat, even though I tried to teach him. I held my finger over the wire, and with my free hand, I held his hand. I'd call out the cadence in a whisper, "zip – zip – zip – zip." He never caught on. Neither did any of the Veeley boys. I loved playing the game with the middle boy, Marvin. He would only play if we held hands. This way, no matter who lost, both received the jolt. And he always lost. Marvin's rough, hay-hook mitts were no match for my nimble fingers. I wonder if I heard the current or if it was something felt. Perhaps, it was instinct – a knowing of when it was safe to make my move between the pulses.

Los Arcos to Logroño

I wake to Jonny's coughing. It starts as a dry tickle, and I'm able to doze on through. His cough gains momentum, and by the time he reaches a full hack, I'm sitting upright in bed. Gretchen is sitting up too. "Let's smother him with a pillow," she snarls.

"Let's try a little water first." I grab his water bottle from a side pocket of his pack. He is hacking, but he is still very much asleep. "Jonny," I give him a shake. "Jonny, wake up. Drink some water."

He sits up and scratches his head. "Aww. Time for school, already?" Gretchen and I stifle our giggles. If I had the energy to be cruel, I'd get him out of bed to catch the bus. That would be an excellent payback for last night's zucchini-in-the-bed stunt. Sadly, I don't have it in me. He takes a few gulps of water and flops back down on the mattress. Within seconds, I hear the shifts in his breathing. He is fast asleep again. Jonny's conscience is as clean as a whistle.

Mine, on the other hand, must be polluted. It's 0330, and there is no way I'm getting back to sleep. I fidget with my phone for an hour, flipping through the pictures of the last few days, before I give up and get out of bed. I dress quietly and pack up Agnus. Before leaving the room, I kneel and whisper to Gretchen, "See you in Viana." She mumbles back, confirming our plans created last night.

The plan was to get a head start on my little family, walk my own pace, and allow them to catch up to me somewhere on the trail; however, I hadn't planned on starting this early. Thankfully, Gretchen and I have secured our relationship via social media. If separated, we can stay in contact. Whoever finds Viana and WIFI first is supposed to send the other a message and then wait in front of the main cathedral. While neither of us has been to Viana, we are sure to find a cathedral because there is always a cathedral in villages and towns along the Camino de Santiago.

Agnus sits in a perfect beam of light provided by a scarce but strategically placed streetlamp. She welcomes the journey with a wide-open lid, and I satisfy her wanderlust by stuffing her full of my belongings. To avoid waking the others, her top remains open until I leave the quiet dorm.

Downstairs, Abuela has set out our breakfast. A lovely feast adorns the humble, wooden tables. I snatch two boiled eggs and a beautiful peach and make my way out the door.

I balance Agnus on a table in the plaza where we celebrated Gretchen's birthday last night. Rummaging through the hood compartment, I find my orange headlamp. I almost didn't buy one of these things, thinking there would be no way I would walk after dark. But I hadn't thought about walking before sunrise. This is twice now, two out of four mornings, I'm up before the sun.

The moonlight illuminates the genre-bending *Iglesia de Santa Maria de los Arcos,* a 12th-century Romanesque structure renovated in the 16th, 17th, and 18th centuries. I stood in the upstairs balcony last night identifying elements of Gothic, Renaissance, Baroque and Rocco. There's no way to take it all in. The blend is dizzying, but it works. I loved the fat flying babies, gilded roses, and explosions of Virgin Mary in every nook and cranny.

It wasn't until this morning while fiddling with my phone that I noticed a peculiar and creepy detail about the spectacular, 18th-century masterpiece of an organ. Each of the outer three principle pipes on both sides of the organ display a grimacing human mask painted over each pipe mouth. I hadn't noticed the odd detail when observing the organ. It wasn't until I magnified the photo on my phone that I saw six faces contorted in haunted agony. I'm not sure what this is supposed to mean, or if it means anything at all. At first, I thought the male faces represent the pain of sin. But their mouths deliver the sound, and the music is beautiful, so maybe it's not all about sin-shaming. Perhaps a parishioner had an odd sense of humor. I wish the church were open so I could investigate further.

I strap my headlamp on and adjust it to center on my forehead. The moon provides a fair amount of light, but I click it on anyway. I need to see and to be seen. In the dark, I'm nervous about missing a yellow arrow and losing my way, but I'm also worried about being hit by a car.

I am scared, but not as much as I would have imagined, had I imagined walking the Camino in the dark. I find my way through town and beyond the last albergue. The arrows lead me out of the village and to a graveled road. I pass a house with a tall chain-link fence and take note of the *Beware of Dog* sign. The sign isn't enough. Nothing could have prepared me as two German Shepherds slam against the fence, growling and gnashing their teeth. Their vicious barks shatter my nerves and almost knock me out of my shoes. Once my heart returns to the natural pace and place in my chest, a striped cat zips out from the bushes in front of me. I leap and let out a gasp. It's hard enough to keep my cool walking alone in the dark. I don't need this onslaught of domestic animals playing boogeymen.

I time each step into the darkness. Surging forward, I take advantage of the safe space between the pulses. The potential danger of walking alone in the dark thrills me more than it should. My senses kick into overdrive. I smell damp clay and wood smoke and something deliciously floral. I am vigilant and afraid and energized, and it is stimulating. I would never do this at home. Never.

After twenty minutes of startle free walking, I click off my headlamp and put my hands over my eyes and press gently. This is how I adjust to the dark and activate my *night eyes*. When I was a little girl, probably as early as five years old, my dad taught me how to turn on and use my night eyes. After a family gettogether at my grandma's house, he made me walk home through the woods and to the other side of the family farm. Sometimes he came with me. Sometimes it was only my siblings and me. And sometimes I walked alone. I never enjoyed walking alone in the dark, but I always felt accomplished after making it home alive. Alive – not lost, or frozen to death, or eaten by coyote or bear or cougar. Arriving alive was something to be proud of.

My night eyes don't work as well as I remember. Perhaps this is attributed to age-related decline. I stumble along, trying hard to avoid potholes. I take a break in the middle of the path to gaze up and admire the night sky. I've always been a stargazer, but I can't identify many of the constellations. The *Milky Way* is prominent. As a kid, I slept beneath its blanket of stars in backyard campouts. It shines above me now, like an old friend.

Humans followed the Milky Way across the Iberian Peninsula long before the Camino became a Christian pilgrimage. More than a thousand years before the birth of Christ, Celtic *Druids* used the route under this celestial body to lead them to Finisterre, or the end of the earth. On the rocky shore of Finisterre, they worshipped the sun at the altar of *Ara Solis*, and they called upon the crone goddess, *Orcabella*, for an invitation to the afterworld of eternal light. It is speculated the *Phoenicians* built the altar long before the Celtic peregrinations to the ends of the earth.

According to legend, it was none other than the Apostle James who ordered the destruction of the Phoenician altar to advance his evangelical attempts at converting pagans and spreading Christianity. But now, even without an altar, modern peregrinos of all faiths trek beyond Santiago to venerate the spot. They soak up the warmth of boulders smoothed by the sea and baked in the sun, and they admire the sun setting in the evenings. Following an ancient ritual, some burn their clothes and wash their bodies in the sea to clear away the dirt and grit of an old life and make way for the new.

Over three thousand years following the Celtic druids, here I am up before the sun and tracing their footsteps beneath a blanket of stars. Unfortunately, the trek out to Finisterre isn't in my plans, because I don't have enough time. However, something tells me I will be here again. It is early in my journey, but I sense the magnetic pull of the Milky Way.

The Camino and I have a connection – a relationship, something primal like I've been here before and will return soon.

The soft indigo of night slowly washes away to mottled dawn. The sky is the color of a nearly ripened prune. In the dim light, I can make out with certainty what I had expected since leaving Los Arcos. I've been walking vineyard side on a tractor road. Early on, I could smell the red clay and the smoldering brush piles of old vines. The grapes are far from ripe, but their floral sweetness, the promise of what's to come, dances in the wind.

The vineyard is alive in birdsong. Somewhere in the distance, a cuckoo bird sounds the morning wakeup call. *Coo-coo, Coo-coo, Coo-coo.* I almost take the call for granted, but then I realize this is the first time I've heard a real-life coo-coo from a real-life cuckoo bird. The little, blue, wooden bird emerging from my grandmother's clock every hour on the hour has a real-life doppelganger. The revelation stuns me. I stand frozen in place, so my clacking poles do not compete with the birdsong. And I listen. I can't believe in my forty-seven years this is my first cuckoo.

The tractor trail ends where the blacktop begins, and I hang a left and start up the main road, feeling the gradual incline in my thighs. There is plenty of light to see the path, but I click on my headlamp so I can be seen by oncoming traffic. While unlikely to meet a car this early in the morning, it's better to err on the side of safety.

The sky grows light, and ahead of me, the village of Sansol is a dark shadow set on a canvas of watercolor rose, lavender, and tangerine. Behind me, I hear the clacking of poles annoyingly offbeat with my own. The old Army me wants to yell, "For fuck's sake, get in step!" But, of course, I don't. That's no way to begin a morning as a pilgrim. I lift my poles a little, trying to get a read on the pilgrim behind me. Male? Female? Old? Young? Friendly…? I can't tell. A small jolt of fright leaps into my throat, but I push it down and chastise my foolishness. *This is a pilgrimage, dumbass.* Behind me is a fellow pilgrim. The clacking is the dead giveaway. How many murdering rapists stalk their victims with titanium walking sticks? Or at least I think the rods are titanium. They have a different sound than mine, softer and less metallic – more tap and less clack.

It doesn't matter how much I reason with my hypervigilant self. I still want to turn around. Pondering hiking stick composition isn't enough of a distraction. Not knowing who is walking behind me makes me feel edgy and out of control. I don't want to feel like this all the way into the village. In fact, I don't want this ever. I slow my pace and allow the clack to grow louder. When I turn to see with whom I share the road, a blonde young lady waves a pole in the air. I stop and wait. It's Anja, the beautiful Swiss girl who sat next to Pablo last night.

"Hey! Buen Camino, Anja. Lovely morning, don't you think?"

"It's so wonderful to listen to the birds without people noise," she says. I nod in agreement, and we walk without talking, eventually falling into step, tapping our poles in a natural cadence. I had hoped to make Sansol before seeing any fellow peregrinos. I had no real reason to make such a goal, and I'm pleased to have Anja's company. She has a warm smile and a gentleness that is so attractive. Her hair is the color of buttercream frosting, and she wears it in two classically Swiss braids that rope down each shoulder. She is tall and willowy and, of course, her eyes are an ice blue. She is perfect. She is the Disney princess of peregrinas. She is also articulate, athletic, and independent. As I said, she is perfect.

"How far are you going today?" I ask.

"Just to Logroño."

"Just Logroño? Logroño is thirty kilometers."

"Yes, but that isn't hard for me. Pablo and I often walk thirty-five to forty."

"Where is Pablo?"

"Still sleeping, snoring like an old bear."

"Did you stay at the municipal albergue?"

"Oh, no. Pablo and I usually stay in a tent together. Last night, we slept in the vineyard. I heard you pass by."

I want to pry. I want to know if Anya and Pablo are a Camino couple. But I don't ask because it is none of my business. Poor Gretchen and her mad crush, but Pablo is too old for her. She must realize this. Anja is probably twenty-five and much closer to his age.

Anja and I walk into Sansol together. The tiny village is still fast asleep. We enter and exit without waking two Spanish herding dogs chained to their small houses at each end of the village. We drop down into a ravine, cross a little stone bridge, and start a steep climb into Torres del Río. It did not look this steep in my guidebook, but my aching legs and thumping heart tell a different story.

The warm sunrise prickles the back of my neck and warms my bare legs. We stop outside the 12th century, octagonal *Iglesia de Santo Sepulcro*, the sister of the *Santa Maria Eunate* before Puente La Reina. Unfortunately, the church, like the café, is locked. I am grateful to have accidentally found my way to Eunate because Torres del Río is still asleep.

We rest at a table outside the closed café. Anya releases the locks on her telescoping poles and folds each one down into a tidy little club. "Titanium?" I ask. She nods. "Sweet," I say.

My feet are okay, but I need to take off my boots and change socks. Anja is hesitant to continue without me, but I bid her a *buen Camino* and make plans to see her this evening, in Logroño. She is an excellent companion, but I am slowing her down. Walking 30K will be a stretch for me today. If I'm going to succeed, I'll need to do it at my own pace.

I exit the village on a dirt track leading past a cemetery. There is nothing creepy about this graveyard, but I quicken my pace all the same. I climb 3K to a hermitage with an elevation gain of about 150 meters since Los Arcos. So far, the morning's ten-kilometer hike has gradually inclined with a couple of steep hills and a quick dip down between the villages of Sansol and Torres del Río.

I brace myself and lengthen my hiking poles to descend from the hermitage. Rocky switchbacks will drop me 170 meters in less than 3K. In the dim morning light, the trail is dicey. I rely heavily on my poles for balance and weight distribution. Despite my efforts, pain shoots from beneath both kneecaps, and my thighs turn to mush. I step on a loose rock and roll my left ankle. Falling forward, I try to catch myself with outstretched hands but fail and bash my knee on a jagged rock.

Flat on my stomach in the middle of the trail I roll to my side. An intense heat radiates from my right kneecap and the left ankle throbs. The fall knocked the wind out of me, and I'm too stunned to swear or cry. Afraid to move, I force myself to inventory body parts. Every digit wiggles. Each muscle contracts and relaxes. And all joints, although stiff, respond accordingly. I ease myself into a seated position and inspect the damage. My beautiful white shirt is streaked with dirt and covered in dust, but it doesn't look torn. My knee is bloody, but the damage is superficial. Bits of grit fill the gash, and I already dread the chore of scrubbing out the wound.

I contemplate removing the boot to inspect my ankle but think better of it. It's not horribly painful, possibly a slight sprain. I've sprained this damn ankle nearly every year of my life since initially injuring it in the Army in 1985. And just like in 1985, my ankle never fails to let me down at the least convenient of times. One time, I severely sprained it right before boarding a flight. I needed pain meds and crutches but survived without either. Instead, I downed four in-flight shots of vodka and slept through the throbs. I was stronger and harder back then. Sans vodka, I channel my old self. She's exactly what I need. When the former me finally makes her appearance, she tightly laces up my boots to control the swelling and then delivers a swift kick to my ass for not letting Anja stay with me. Safety in numbers.

It's about 6K before the next stop. I'm pissed off at myself for not letting Anja stay with me. Why did I refuse her company? She is lovely, and perhaps she could have used my presence. I assume nobody wants to walk with slowpoke me. I don't even want to walk with me right now, but I'm stuck. Besides, what could Anja have done? She can't prevent me from falling, and she surely can't carry me down this hill. I have a solid forty pounds on the girl. Sometimes, we are on our own even in the company of others.

I sit for a little while longer, examine the gash, and count the heartbeats in my knee. I squeeze the bite tube of my water bladder and soak the wound. I expect the water to sting, but I can't feel anything over the hot throbs pushing out spider-web trickles of blood.

I want my dog. Jasper would know what to do. He may have prevented the fall. Jasper senses when I am off balance. He knows when to pause and provide a brace, and he knows the right amount of tension to apply to the lead to keep me steady. Hiking poles, titanium or otherwise, are no substitution for him. If he couldn't prevent a fall, he would drop his heavy head in my lap and gaze up at me with his hot chocolate eyes, and I wouldn't feel so sorry for myself. There's not a piece of gear in the world that can do that for me.

The photo album on my phone contains at least a dozen candid shots of Jasper, but I avoid the temptation to look. The last thing I need is a homesick meltdown over my dog in the middle of this trail. While I do need a good cry, now isn't the time and this isn't the place. I must be strong, and I must be brave.

Steadying myself with the hiking poles, I ease into a stand and start the slow limp down the trail. True to my old self, I fight pain with an impromptu cadence of swear words, "Shit-shit-damn, shit-shit-damn..." Both legs are screwed, but the ankle is not as bad as I thought. The purple sock on my right foot is sticky with the blood trickling from my knee. I'm a wreck, but there's nothing to do but embrace the rhythm of my wounded gait and indulge in crafting perfectly horrid runs of expletives. Swearing is medicine. The creative potency of words releases endorphins. Like flipping a switch, I transition from a sorry-ass mush to feeling oddly thankful. It's weird, especially after so much swearing, but I'm compelled to pray. I start with the Lord's Prayer, my part in Grandpa's morning ritual. I send up thanks and ask for protection. I'm grateful to be walking, not only after this fall but after a lifetime of falling.

The Camino is a sacred gift I gave to myself after spending the past five years mourning my loss of health and identity. The gift didn't present during my darkest days, those days immediately following my military retirement. That's probably a good thing because I needed time to decide to recover. So, when my ankle gave way, I feared my Camino was over, that I had failed and would have to go back home to the sofa. It was a close call. I took a decent tumble, but I'm okay.

In non-pilgrim life, I don't pray often. I don't have the daily urge to do so, and I don't have the special occasion urge around Thanksgiving, Christmas, and Easter. Holidays are tough on me. Like many women, I end up working my ass off to please others. And I fret. What if the turkey is dry? What if I give the gift of *salmonella*? What if my sister acts like a total bitch again, spooning out insults disguised as cranberry relish? My mother will defend her. She will claim my sister is drunk and too stupid to know better. In my family, alcohol and ignorance go together like pumpkin pie with whipped cream. But it gets worse. One year, my father pulled a gun on my first husband. Now there is a Thanksgiving memory that never fades. My siblings will ditch the homemade gift baskets of my blackberry jam in the coat closet for me to find in spring while I hide the fucking Easter eggs. If ever there was a time to pray, it would be during the holidays with my family. We seriously need a little Jesus.

Ugh! What is with my ranting today? Thoughts of my dysfunctional family have hijacked my Camino. Even though I don't want to think about home, I can't seem to stop myself. I am a victim of sibling and parental bullying. I spend holidays wounded and fighting back, all while busting my ass to feed people and make merry. Every year, no matter how hard I try, it's another kick to the uterus. It's partially my own fault because I cannot find my grace, my God-given light when I am in their company. How sad is that? Now cushioned by thousands of miles of separation, it's hard to believe I'm the grown-ass woman whose feelings get hurt when they call me *Beeker*. You know, Beeker, the big nosed, frizzy-haired Muppet that bumbles around in a science lab screwing everything up. It's a stupid nickname, but try shouldering that when you are thirteen, late to enter puberty, and awkward as hell. And if it's not *Beeker*, it's *Pissy-Chrissy*, or *Bubble Butt* or *Feme-Nazi*, or something equally charming. When I revert to that wounded kid, I feel petty. I can't present *Pissy-Chrissy* or any of my cast of characters to God. Nobody, not even God, can endure so much whining.

I need to get over this crap. I didn't fly to Spain to feel sorry for myself by wallowing in childhood woes. I want to praise more and complain less – to focus on the beauty of now and forget about the pain of the past. I want to send out juicy rays of rainbow-flavored sunlight and catch the rebounds on my tongue. The *law of attraction* theorizes like attracts like. I receive light when I am light. This makes sense, but it is challenging to put into motion.

Melancholy accompanies me to the outskirts of Viana. The slog into town is draining. I'm roasting in the midday sun. My knee, which I've decided to let bleed, radiates an intense heat. My ankle is tender, but most of all, I'm dying of boredom from skirting the roadway through industrial sprawl.

Gretchen and Jonny catch up with me before entering the old part of the village. They greet me with pure enthusiasm, and we hug, and I kiss their sweaty cheeks. And like magic, I am happy again. It's a funny thing, how this mutual and familial affection bloomed between total strangers.

The kids walked out of Los Arcos this morning with an hour lead on Grandpa and Drew. They've adopted my idea to leave early, walk their own pace, and let the old jackrabbits overtake them later. We rest in a small park with a drinking

fountain and a lush splotch of green grass. I take off my
boots and inspect my ankle. A blackish-purple tint forms a
horizontal fringe from my Achilles tendon to my pinky toe.
Gretchen whips out her birthday tube of ibuprofen gel and
douches my whole foot in the stuff. The alcohol base of the
gel evaporates, leaving my foot pleasantly cooled. I rest on
my back in the grass, elevating my ankle on her lap.

Gretchen is hard at work writing in a spiral notebook. She
has her paisley pencil case, filled with felt markers and maxi
pads, spread out on the grass before her. I can't see what she
is writing, but she switches pen colors every few seconds.

"Gretchen, you know I'm done for the day, don't you?"

"I know," she nods. "But maybe Grandpa will let us stay
here tonight so that we can take care of you." She sounds
doubtful. I'm doubtful too. Grandpa is a man on a mission.
He is reliving his Caminos of yesteryear, and he likes to stay
in the same villages and at the same albergues.

Jonny is starving because it is lunchtime, and because
Jonny is always starving. I throw him a bag of walnuts to stop
his bitching, but he throws them back. Evidently, he's not
that hungry. On his prompting, Gretchen packs up her pens,
and I try to get my boot back on. Despite the liberal
application of ibuprofen gel, my ankle has doubled in size. It
will not go back into the boot.

"Damn!" Jonny glances down at my ankle. "You're so
hosed." We all nod in agreement. It does look that way. I slip
on my trusty gardening clogs, and Jonny carries my pack into
the old village. We find a café in the plaza in full view of the
portico of *Santa Maria,* the entryway into the 13th century,
Gothic beauty.

Gretchen returns to her spiral notebook, switching pen
colors every few seconds. Jonny devours an ice cream bar,
and I hobble over to the fountain to soak my ankle and knee.
The chilly water provides much-needed relief.

I wave to Grandpa and Drew when they come into sight.
They take a seat, and I can see Gretchen's hard sell to stay in
Viana for the night. I'm out of earshot, but I don't need to

hear to know the results. Grandpa heads off to afternoon mass, and Gretchen drops her head into her arms before writing a little more in her notebook. When she comes over to the fountain, I realize she has been writing her goodbye. She hands me a note folded into fourths, and she walks away. I open it and read the rainbow lettering.

Mama, thank you so much for being such a MILF queen. You are an incredible woman with so much strength and light for all to see. You have changed our lives with your grace and kindness. Grandpa is making us go on to Logroño, but you will be our Camino-Mama forever. I hope we find each other again!!! Love, Peace, and Sexy Sirs along your way, Gretchen & Jonny

I try not to cry, but these are truly the sweetest few sentences ever written to or about me. *MILF Queen* aside, I couldn't ask for anything more if this was my eulogy. Grace and kindness – to be a loving human being. This has been my prayer since leaving home, and evidently, I am succeeding.

My ankle is better after a long soak in the fountain, and I'm pleased with the gash in my knee. A red cross, with a striking likeness to the symbol of The Order of Santiago, oozes on my kneecap. Jonny comes over to inspect the damage, and he sees it too. Centered on my patella, is a dagger capped with an upside-down heart and flanked by two *fleurs-de-lis*. The fleur-de-lis may be somewhat of a leap, but with a little imagination, it's easy to see. I've never wanted a wound to scar as much as I hope this one does.

Jonny takes my place at the fountain. He peels off a layer of worn-out, white tube sock. I'm shocked at the carnage. His feet are much worse than mine, and I didn't know that was possible. "How are you walking? And why are you wearing tube socks? Don't you have hiking socks?" He shrugs his shoulders, dunks his feet, and pulls off his shirt to soak in the sun.

I leave Jonny at the fountain and hobble back out of the old village. I had noticed a hiking store before we entered. I plan to get the kid decent socks, but when I arrive, there are none to be had. Men's socks are sold-out. I eavesdrop on a conversation between a peregrina and the sales clerk. They are discussing the merits of the *Keen* hiking sandal. I admire an orange pair in the doorway. It's an impulse buy. But the clerk offers a decent discount and tosses in an ankle-support sleeve for my sprain. I wrestle on the sleeve, slide my feet into my new sandals, and I'm so thrilled to discover they do not rub in any of the spots already rubbed raw by my boots.

New shoe euphoria trumps body logic. I am not staying in Viana tonight. My feet are fine, never better. I'm not leaving my kids, not yet. Confident in my resolve and my new *Keens,* I grab Gretchen's arm and set off for Logroño.

We exit the old town of Viana and dally a moment for a photo-op at the 13th century, Gothic ruins of the *Church of San Pedro.* "Yes! This is the place. This is where I will marry my Pablo." Gretchen stretches her arms out like a windmill and turns circles in the nave. She jumps on a stone pedestal and pretends to flair out the long train of her imaginary wedding dress. I snap photos, pretending to be her wedding photographer, and frame her in a heavenly arch. This would indeed be a beautiful wedding venue.

We pass through the *Portal San Felices*, commemorating the Rioja saint who placed the cornerstone of the city in 1219. We trot downhill along a narrow path and run into the cutest gaggle of little schoolgirls. They are wearing crisp, white short-sleeve shirts, navy sweater vests, matching plaid skirts, and white knee-high socks. They flock around us and pump their dimpled fists in the air and chant, "Oui! Oui! Bon Camino! Oui! Oui! Bon Camino!" Gretchen speaks to them in French, and they circle around giving high-fives and hugs like we are celebrities. We wade through little girls and pass by their teacher. I mouth a *merci*, and she bids us a "Bon Camino." I have no idea how or why we crossed paths with French schoolgirls on a field trip in Viana, Spain, but I am thankful. It is the lift I need on this hot afternoon and sight and sound I shall not soon forget.

The joy of the little girls stays with me through the suburban sprawl and industrial wasteland leading toward

Logroño. Gretchen drops back to wait for the others who are scouring the village for a pair of men's hiking socks. I offered to loan the boy socks until Logroño, but Drew glared at me like I was crazy and said, "You see? This is exactly what I'm talking about. This is Jonny being manipulative. This is Jonny getting everyone else to solve his problems. And you're falling right into his trap."

"Dude, chill out. It's just socks, and he's only fourteen. Why can't you give him a pair?"

"Why? Because that's what Jonny wants us to do. That's what Jonny wanted all along. If he had planned better…"

I held up my hands in surrender. Apparently, this was *Camp Counselor Drew*, the guy who reprograms wayward youth with heaping doses of tough love. This was not the loving and caring Uncle Drew I've come to know. How such a sweetheart can also be a total dickhead is beyond me.

I walk at least two kilometers on my own before the heat gets the best of me. A park bench beneath the shade of a gnarled tree materializes just as I run out of steam. I flop down and watch a farmer on his tractor raking a field of mowed hay. He works his way around until he is perpendicular to me and my bench. He shuts off the motor and steps down from the cab. He is speaking and pointing up the road, but I can't hear him. He comes over, and even though my Spanish has improved beyond the survival mode, he is difficult to understand. He wants me to go up the road for food and drink. "A café?" I ask. He shakes his head, reaches out and tweaks my cheek and motions for me to move on. I thank him, but I'm not exactly sure why.

The farmer's tweak is fresh on my right cheek as I reach the *Ermita de la Trinidad de Cuevas*. A handful of locals gather in the grassy yard of the old hermitage to care for peregrinos passing by in the hot sun.

Platters of sausages and cheese and baskets of bread line cloth-covered picnic tables. When I enter the park, an old lady wearing a flowered housedress and a blue headscarf embraces me. A much younger man hands me a paper cup of water and motions to sit. I am not hungry, but I am force-fed. I've used all the Spanish I know to explain I ate lunch in Viana less than two hours ago, but when a bottle of wine is passed my way, I don't argue. I fill my paper cup and settle in.

Thanks to the wine, a velvety-soft *Rioja*, I'm fully relaxed and reclining against a tree when my Camino family arrives. Everyone except Jonny is in high spirits. Jonny is in visible pain. I see it in his limp and in the furl of his caterpillar eyebrows. His mood rapidly improves as lady volunteers force him to sit behind a tray of sliced chorizo and a cold Coca-Cola.

There is an air of tension between Drew and me. I expect him to come over and apologize or to continue arguing with me, but he does neither. He takes a few sips of wine and leaves, telling Gretchen he will wait up ahead. It's an awkward moment. Fortunately, Grandpa is oblivious. He drinks his cup of wine and engages with the locals.

Now that Drew is gone, I'm going to fix Jonny's feet. I tell him to take off his boots, and I rummage through Agnus for my first-aid kit and a spare pair of socks. Jonny is just a boy, and sometimes a boy needs a little mothering.

I tend to Jonny's feet with the help of three ladies. First, his feet are washed and dried with loving care by another woman wearing a blue headscarf. I don't know if these ladies are part of a religious order, but they each wear a matching light blue headscarf. Apart from the scarves, they wear ordinary clothes ranging from slacks to skirts to housedresses.

Peregrinos, past and present, differ in opinion when it comes to popping or not popping blisters. Typically, I'm on the fence. But today, I argue for not popping. We have another 7K to go, and I don't have anything to disinfect a needle or Jonny's wounds. My sole intent is to make him more comfortable.

I hate to share it, but I pull apart the last bit of Elke's magical blister-fluff to create four puffy clouds. I pad and tape the puffs to each of Jonny's raw heels and build soft pillows around the bubbles perched atop of his big toes. My purple wool socks are too small for his feet, but we stretch them as much as we can. They are not perfect but will provide a thick layer of cushion, and anything is an improvement over white tube socks with holes.

The final jaunt into Logroño is grueling. Drew went ahead to secure beds, and Grandpa is leading us on a *Peregrino Death March* toward the city. For an old man, he can step it out.

The three of us hang back out of earshot and craft our runs of hiking expletives. I know it's not responsible or pilgrim-esque of me. I should chastise their potty-mouths and encourage them to meditate and pray for strength. But I love words, all words. I love the graceful and heartfelt lines of prose poets, and I love the cadence and inflection of well-spoken sailors. We hold contests in categories of most creative, most elegant, and most disturbing. Jonny wins almost every time, but Gretchen runs a close second for most-disturbing. The kids award me a trophy for cursing elegance, but it's more like a participation award. I'm skilled, but I can't hold a candle to these kids. It's an odd and sophomoric way to pass the miles, but it makes us laugh and provides the comic relief we desperately need.

Part 3
La Rioja

Logroño to Navarrete

Walking out of Logroño before dawn, there is plenty of
light pollution to illuminate the yellow arrows painted on
sidewalks, curbs, and light posts. Today is supposed to be
another 30-kilometer trek to Nájera, but I don't know if I can
do it. I didn't sleep much, and while my knee and ankle have
improved, the swelling in my feet has returned in full force.
Gretchen and I agreed to meet in Navarrete, 12K up the trail,
for lunch and to reassess the situation.

Drew acted butt-hurt over our squabble back in Viana.
He hasn't spoken more than five words to me since. It's
awkward as hell, and I am surprised he saved a bunk for me
last night. I half expected I'd be on my own. After all, he is a
real-life family member, and I'm honorary. He refused to go
out to supper with us last night. Instead, he bought a *jamón
bocadillo*, a glorified ham sandwich built on a baguette, and
brooded in his bunk.

The rest of us hit the tapas bars – or were they *pintxo*
bars? Somewhere along the Camino, the name changes. The
style changes too, or at least that is what I've come to
understand. Pintxo is the Basque spelling of *pincho*. These are
smaller bites, just a pinch, like a skewer of olives and anchovy
fillets or a tiny piece of cocktail bread stacked with meat and
pickle and secured with a toothpick. My favorite pintxo thus
far is deviled egg filled with a dollop of crab salad and
adorned with a dilled cornichon, all held in place with a frilly
toothpick. Tapas are more substantial, like little plates not
held together with toothpicks or skewers. Logroño might be a
place of culinary fusion, a coming together of styles.

The tapas and pintxos were tasty, but I did not love
Logroño. I did enjoy plenty of local *Rioja* wine in the old
quarter last night. After all, we are in a region of renowned
bodegas. We bar-hopped with a captivating cast of characters.
Our entourage included a Jesuit priest named, *Happy*; a
California Barbie named, *Mimi*; a massive German with

permanent-resting-bitch-face named, *Bernard*; and a sad woman from Cincinnati named, *Denise*. Denise is walking the Camino to get over a breakup with her longtime girlfriend who is a mime. Y*es – an actual mime*, with Ringling Brothers Circus. She and her girlfriend traveled together, making their home on the circus train. Fascinated, I couldn't get enough of her story. I had to catch myself and reel in the enthusiasm because it was bordering on cruelty. Her story was incredible. Real life is stranger than fiction. Nobody makes this kind of shit up.

I pause at a small pond in a park on the outskirts of Logroño to admire a pair of graceful, white swans. My grandma had a thing for swans, or so I thought. Every Mother's Day, birthday, and Christmas, I'd scour the five and dime for the perfect collectible. And then one year, she announced she was sick of dusting her burgeoning bevy of swans. We all need a change sometimes, and we all get tired of dust.

I follow a paved track lined with young trees and stone benches. The path is hard underfoot, and the benches are harder under my backside. This newly developed stretch is aesthetically pleasing, but I'm thrilled to leave it behind after breaking into a pine forest.

Only 5K in, and I'm already out of gas. I don't see how I can make it to Nájera today. I rest at a closed café and enjoy a gorgeous view of the *Pantano de la Grajera* reservoir. Birdsong and the morning wakeup call of the cuckoo accompany my breakfast of two tangerines and a handful of walnuts. The sun inches higher in the sky. It's going to be a hot one today.

I lift Agnus from a plastic chair, sling her on my back, and cinch her down. Grandpa and Drew are coming up the trail. Drew bids a polite "good morning" but doesn't stop to chitchat. Grandpa and I doddle along, talking about swans and the pines and the beautiful reservoir. "Where are the kids?" I finally ask.

"Drew put them on a bus. We'll meet up in Nájera and walk on to Azofra."

Panic flutters in my chest. *My kids are gone? Gone on the bus to Nájera?* Yesterday was a total ass-kicker. Gretchen is still dealing with cramps, and Jonny's feet are a mess. Giving them a day off is wise, but I can't make it that far. Azofra is another 6K beyond Nájera.

We planned to stay in Nájera, at one of Grandpa's favorite haunts. Drew was to call ahead and save beds. Grandpa, the unwavering peregrino, has changed his mind. What if I never see the kids again? I didn't get to hug them goodbye.

"Would you like to recite the Rosary with me?" Grandpa asks as he fingers his beads.

"Sure." I try to sound chipper. "I'll do my usual part."

"Do you mean the only part you know?"

"Well, yeah."

"You aren't Catholic, are you?" He raises his eyebrows quizzically.

"Nope. Did you think I was?"

"Yes – A rather lapsed Catholic, but still a Catholic."

"Are you disappointed?"

"Disappointed? No. Not at all. I'm delighted with your daily participation in my morning ritual. The fact you are not Catholic is of little importance, at least to me."

Grandpa and I part ways after summiting *Alto Grajera*. I hug him tightly and instruct him to pass the hug on to the kids. I know, without a doubt, this is the last time I will see him or my Camino family again. Drew, strategically or not, performed a reset. I have been ousted. And it stings. Even though I often walk by myself during the days, it is odd to be alone again. There was comfort in knowing my little family was near.

I'm so busy clacking my poles up the hill into Navarrete; I fail to notice a fellow peregrina overtaking me until we are shoulder to shoulder. "Hot day," she sighs. I'm so startled at her unexpected but sweet voice, I lose my balance and stumble forward. She reaches out and steadies my arm. "I'm sorry. I didn't mean to sneak up on you."

"Oh, no, no. You didn't." I try to lie and act cool, but my attempts are ridiculous. I nearly did a faceplant into hot asphalt. She laughs at me, but her laugh is genuine and full of goodness. I like her instantly. We exchange names and home states and where we slept last night. Jana is from Tennessee, and she too walked from Logroño this morning.

"I'm ready for lunch," she says. I accept this as an invitation. Moments later, Jana introduces me to the Camino beverage of my dreams. *Tinto-Verano*, or red summer, is a fizzy lemonade and cheap red wine cocktail over ice and garnished with lime. It's love at first sip. The drink is simple and not overly sweet like sangría.

After a bunch of green olives, cubed cheese in herbed oil, and Tinto-Verano, we soak up the sun on the café's patio, stretching out our legs and elevating our bare feet in empty chairs. I nod off for a bit, and when I wake, Jana is smiling. "You look done for." I nod in agreement but argue it is too early to quit walking. "What's your rush? I'm staying here for the night." I see no reason not to join her. Although I only walked twelve easy kilometers, it is enough.

Angel, a sweet-faced hospitalero with a neatly-groomed dark beard, greets us at the entry of his albergue. He hasn't opened for the day, but he lets us in any way. He stamps and dates our credentials, our proof we have visited *La Casa Del Peregrino* in Navarrete, La Rioja. I examine the blue-inked sello bearing the cross of the Order of Santiago and glance down at my knee. The cross-shaped gash is yellow and weepy on a backdrop of feverish-red. Soaking in the Viana fountain was a regrettable error in judgment. The water wasn't potable water, but I assumed it would be okay for knees and feet. Now I wonder how many nasty feet, blisters, cuts, and scrapes came before me. I am disgusted. It would be my luck to pick up something.

Our early entry into Angel's albergue gives us a head start and first choice of beds. We select single beds furthest from the bathroom and beneath open skylights. It didn't take long to learn location and ventilation are keys to a restful night.

We drop our packs and move on to laundry duties and hot showers.

The bathroom is tiny but well-appointed. There are two stalls, one for the shower and one for the toilet. There are two sinks, one for handwashing and a deep basin for laundry. Jana showers while I soak our clothes. We switch places, and she scrubs our socks. After my shower, Jana retires, and I go about the task of pinning our clothes to a cleverly designed line on a pulley system running just outside the bathroom window.

I'm halfway out the window when a short, British man with graying temples and whiskers enters the bathroom. He chuckles and makes some comment, comparing the scene to a Princess Diana photograph. He's laughing, but I don't catch his inference. I look nothing like Lady Di. Regardless, I have made a fan. His name is Bruce, and he is clearly smitten with me and comes right out and says so.

A younger man enters the cramped bathroom and awkward conversation. Bruce introduces me to his son. "Thomas, meet your new step-mother." Thomas blushes and stammers a bit, embarrassed by his dad's flirting. He ducks into the empty shower stall and disappears. I finish the laundry while a very amused Bruce shaves off his gray stubble.

The albergue slowly fills up with road-weary peregrinos. Most keep to themselves, going about the business of laundry and hygiene. Bruce breaks out a small palette of watercolors, the kind little kids use in grammar school. He has come on the Camino to bond with his son and to paint. Meanwhile, Thomas rubs Jana's feet. Thomas is smitten with my beautiful, young friend. This is a coincidence both, father and son, find most convenient. I argue the coincidence isn't as convenient as they might like to think. "Give it time, my darling," Bruce assures. Jana, who is really enjoying her foot-massage, breaks into a peal of laughter. The ring of her laugh, so pure and honest, is a church bell calling our new devotees to worship.

I'm not a prude, and I can't claim to hate the attention. It's good for the ego and reassuring that no matter how wrecked I feel, someone finds me attractive. But, I'm not shopping for trouble and not in the market for a pretend trail-husband.

It is said a love affair awaits beneath a blanket of stars along the Camino de Santiago. Love will come to peregrinos with open hearts. Mine is not open. I have witnessed Camino love, predominately with the younger peregrinos. But last night, in a crowded dormitory in Logroño, I regrettably heard the hushed giggles and squeaky bed springs of new lovers.

I smile at young couples in the daylight and marvel at their endurance after dark. I wonder how, after walking all day in the sun and the wind and carrying a heavy pack, sweating, limping, tending blisters and bug bites and sunburns and chaffing thighs and chapped lips, can anyone have the energy to maintain standards of personal hygiene necessary to attract a mate. And how, how in the hell after walking thirty kilometers can anyone be horny enough to have sex in a dormitory filled with sixty-five or more exhausted strangers?

Camino romance isn't just for the youthful. It happens with older pilgrims too. There is a want of comfort, a need for security, a habit of falling into familiar roles, and a desire to share or shirk domestic chores. Most of the time, I find Camino love lovely. But there are other times when I find it confusing and a little gross. Consider the case of Greg and Juni. The kids and I walked a short leg into Los Arcos with Greg from Australia. He checked into the same albergue, *Casa Abuela*. When we entered, he was greeted warmly by a young Asian woman. After the couple shared a kiss and a long embrace, Greg introduced Juni. "She's my trail wife."

Juni suffered a knee injury the day before and hopped a taxi forward to keep pace with Greg. She gathered up his sweaty clothes as quickly as he stripped them away. Greg's introduction confused us because he told us about his real wife and kids. His non-trail wife is Megan. Megan is stuck at home, in Australia, too busy shuttling children to swim lessons and cricket practice to walk the Camino. Greg never mentioned Juni. Pretend-wife-Juni is South Korean. She and Greg met on the train from Paris to St. Jean Pied de Port. They don't share a common language, but she has been washing his laundry and fussing over him ever since. Greg is a married man on a spiritual pilgrimage, but he takes a temp-wife to handle the mundane domestics. The whole thing is skeezy. And what is in it for Juni? I'll never know.

For the most part, my wobbly marriage and romantic woes help me dismiss public displays of affection from fellow peregrinos. For the young couples, I write it off as hormonal-laden distractions to ease the daily grind of walking. But it isn't easy to dismiss the married, Spanish couples. My heart pings and aches when I bear witness to their wide-open love.

Yesterday, I watched an old Spanish couple walk out of Viana together. They held hands and made their way down the narrow path. They wore matching backpacks, small and light, and possessed ease of gate. They spoke intimately, just above a whisper. Keeping in step, they shared one set of poles. Clack-step-clack-step-clack-step. It was hypnotic and charming and annoying, all at the same time.

Romance, real and fiction is mine for the taking, but I'm still very married and not at all interested in coupling for convenience. I have no desire to cook for anyone, and I certainly do not wish to wash a man's stinky socks or skivvies. Besides, I didn't pack a razor.

Life and love with Jim are on my mind. With every church I enter, I light a candle for marital endurance. I'm hoping the ritual strengthens my resolve to see it through, regardless if I accept my dream job in Germany and regardless if he agrees to come along. However, there is no way to ignore the bitter irony of all my candle lighting while Jim is at home, on the sofa watching television, and very much in the dark.

Angel calls up from downstairs, announcing dinner is ready. It is a donativo meal. Peregrinos slip a donation into the donativo-box and find a seat around the humble, wooden table. The menu is simple: a crisp garden salad, pasta with pesto, bread, prepackaged flan cups, and an endless glass of wine.

An American woman and her teenage daughter come down the stairs. I scoot my chair over and motion for them to join us. "You can't be serious?" The mother speaks with a Jersey accent. "Pasta?" She rolls her eyes. "We own a vacation home in Tuscany."

"What a cow," mutters Bruce, as the pair exit the albergue. We poke fun at their expense before Jana hems us in, gently shaming our anti-peregrino behavior. In the few short hours of our friendship, I see I have much to learn from my graceful, new friend.

The dinner topic shifts to the beautiful scenery and Bruce tells an Irish couple about the bathroom scenery and Princess Diana photo. Everyone gets the joke except for me. The Irish lady sweetly explains a delicious scandal over a photograph in which Diana was not wearing a slip under her skirt. What I had failed to realize, while bending out the window to hang my laundry, is now transparent. My silk dress is see-through when hit by a beam of sunlight. Not only was I sans slip, but I was sans underpants.

Navarrete to Azofra

Jana and I leave the Albergue sometime after 0800.
Compared to my usual predawn departures, the morning feels
lazy. We pass the 16th century *Church of the Assumption* where I
attended mass last night and received my first pilgrim
blessing. The celebration was in Spanish, of course, and
delivered at a clip too fast for me to follow, but that didn't
matter. Sitting in the sanctuary of the church, listening to the
organ and choir, and breathing wafts of frankincense and
rosewood incense created an experience divine enough for
me.

The richly gold gilded interior was unexpected. Navarrete
is an unassuming place to possess such an imposing church.
The church is without a doubt, the hub of this humble
village. With the icon-studded altar, jewel-colored robes,
incense burners, and gold-gilding overload, the scene held a
Wizard of Oz vibe. Mass attendance was high, but not so
much by peregrinos. I counted nine of us. Parishioners
welcomed us warmly into the fold with handshakes and hugs
and kisses for our cheeks.

After the mass was complete, the priest invited us to his
chamber. He had to speak four different languages to
communicate with the multicultural gathering of peregrinos.
Mesmerized, I listened as he shifted from German to Spanish
to English and to Korean. He wanted to know where we call
home and what we hope to learn on our pilgrimage to
Santiago de Compostela. He then contemplated responses
before selecting a prayer card for each peregrino.

I couldn't give him the whole list of things I hoped to
learn, so I told him I needed to conquer my fears and learn to
be brave. I was surprised when he chuckled. He pressed his
right hand so firmly on my shoulder I had to shift my balance
to bear the weight. "But you are here, Peregrina, in a foreign
land, surrounded by strangers. You face hardship, pain, and

the unknown – every day. Your faith makes you master of your fear. You are already brave. Very brave."

The weight of his words and his touch brought tears to my eyes. I dug around in my shoulder bag and found Jim's brown hanky. I blew my nose, while the priest shuffled through his cards and pulled out the *Virgin of the Rosary.* "Yes." He said. "Perhaps the bravest of them all."

I try to show Jana the church this morning, but the door is locked. She took a pass on mass last night, opting for the charming company of Thomas and a bottle of *Rioja.*

We duck into a café across the street for coffee and a wedge of *tortilla,* a dense potato omelet. I'm not wild about tortilla, but it is filling and stays with me longer than a chocolate croissant or baguette smeared with butter and marmalade. The tortilla is bland and wants for jalapenos or a topping of diced green chili. Or salt and pepper. I'm not picky, but the taste is so underwhelming.

I slept well last night, which is crucial because we are headed to Azofra today. It's only 23K and not all that steep, but my knee is infected. It's not painful, but it is feverish and uncomfortable. Bruce gave me a dab of antibacterial ointment, but what it probably needs is a scrub and soak in Epsom salts. I foresee a hotel bathtub and fluffy white towels in my future.

Our British admirers left early this morning, but they are waiting for us trailside and drinking beer when we walk into Ventosa. I need a break and a brew, but Jana wants to keep moving. We agree to meet for lunch in Nájera. Thomas trips over his chair trying to gather his gear and catch up with Jana. "Young love," says Bruce.

I enjoy a beer, while Bruce paints on a postcard-sized canvas. I'm halfway through my beer when I finally realize what has transpired. Jana and Thomas are now walking together, leaving Bruce to walk with me. We've been coupled, and I can't help but wonder if the trio cooked up this little scheme while I was piously attending mass last night. So sneaky.

When Bruce isn't acting like a horny adolescent, he is a decent companion. He tells me all about his work as an electrical engineer in the Queen's army and about his divorce and the strained relationship he has with Thomas. He talks about finding watercolor as a means of therapy after his abrupt departure from the military. "I thought I'd always be a soldier, and now I don't know who I am anymore." I don't ask questions, and I don't offer my military history, but I listen with empathy. It seems Bruce and I have more in common than I thought. Like attracts like.

Bruce's pace is faster than mine, and eventually, I become frustrated with his attempts to hurry me along. I can't afford to rush, not with these feet. We come up with an excellent solution. He powers on up the road and then stops to paint. When I catch up, he closes his pallete and moves out ahead. We complete about five of these rotations under the hot sun before entering Nájera.

At first, Nájera is a disappointment. The long slog from the eastern quarter, amongst cracked sidewalks and graffitied buildings, leaves me unhopeful for a quaint reunion-lunch with Jana and Thomas. However, once Bruce and I hit the old quarter and cross over the río Najerilla, the scenery makes a dramatic shift for the better. From the bridge, I spy the perfect spot of lush grass to enjoy an afternoon nap.

Thomas and Jana wave to us from their place on a patio bar skirting the river. A cold Tinto-Verano and a bottle of water are waiting for me. It's a beautiful setting, and I couldn't be more thankful.

I haven't had a sip of water since meeting two thirsty Boy Scouts in a park about an hour ago. Bruce was in the park too, painting and waiting for me. I was walking toward him when I saw an overweight, red-faced man sitting on a bench in the shade with his teenage son. Both, father and son, sported *Boy Scouts of America* uniforms. The son, an Eagle Scout, rushed over to me.

"Hola," he said. "Habla English?"

"Yup, most of the time."

"Oh, Thank God. I hate to ask, but do you have any water to spare?"

"Yeah, of course." I strangled the urge to make a wise-ass comment about the Boy Scout motto – BE PREPARED.

"Is your dad okay? He looks awfully red."

"We haven't had water since Navarrete."

"That's more than 15K. Why didn't you take a pitstop in Ventosa?

"We must have missed an arrow or something. We never found the village or a fountain." He was embarrassed, and I wanted to kick myself for starting up an inquisition.

"It's okay. I have plenty."

"You're a Camino angel," he said with tears in his eyes. "We've been sitting here for about an hour. Nobody has had water to spare. My dad is on the verge of heat stroke."

"Does your dad need an ambulance?"

"Maybe. Do you have a phone?"

"Not one that works without WIFI."

"Yeah, same here."

"Well, let's get your pops cooled down and see how things go."

Fortunately, the kid was only half right. Dad wasn't on the verge of heat stroke, but he was on the brink of heat exhaustion. I knew this the moment we were introduced. Heat stroke victims are hot and red, but their skin is dry. Dad's handshake was junior high dance sweaty. I have a huge phobia sharing sweat with strangers, but this wasn't the time for my bullshit.

The boy was dehydrated and on the verge of heat exhaustion too. Untreated, heat exhaustion leads to heat stroke, but this wasn't anything water and a few preventative measures couldn't fix. I waved Bruce over to help. After all, two military veterans should possess enough collective first-aid skill to treat exhaustion and prevent stroke. But he kept on painting. It was obvious these guys were in trouble, but Bruce didn't seem to care.

I pulled the water bladder from Agnus. It held exactly two liters. This is more than I need between potable fountains and villages, and I shouldn't carry so much. The surplus adds an extra two to three pounds to my load, but I was glad to have it to share. I filled up both dry canteens and soaked their neckerchiefs to cool down their heads.

"Drink up," I ordered. "Both of you." They emptied their canteens while I knelt and unlaced Dad's boots. His socks were drenched, and his boots made a sucking sound when I pulled them away from his heels. Dad's feet were swimming in pools of sweat. *Oh, holy hell.* I tried my best to keep a poker face as I peeled off his socks and dumped his boots out on the dry grass.

"Unbutton your shirts," I commanded. And both complied. "Now unbuckle your belts." The kid balked, but Dad obeyed. Obviously, Dad is also a husband who is comfortable taking orders from a lady.

"And now you," I nodded to the boy. "Unbuckle and get your boots off." He reluctantly submitted. By the time I left the park, both scouts were flat on their backs beneath a shady tree, shirtless, legs elevated, shorts gaping open, and doing much better. I walked away rather proud of myself, but not necessarily for the deeds of sharing water and performing basic first aid. These tasks were more instinctual than anything else. My most impressive accomplishments include the touching of profusely sweaty hands and feet without making a scene and prohibiting the wisecracks about preparedness and boy scouts from leaving the tip of my tongue. I was a scout's angel today, and I earned a merit badge for kindness. To me, this is a significant Camino success.

Lunch with Jana and the Brits is amusing, but Bruce is wearing on my nerves. He retells the scout incident from his perspective, making me out to be a lusty Florence Nightingale saving two bumbling idiots from the grasp of Darwin's

Theory of Natural Selection. He criticizes me for giving them my water. "You risked your own life for those wankers."

"Hardly!" I roll my eyes. "We were less than an hour out."

Bruce pulls at the front of his shirt to form two peaks, apparently imitating my boobs, and then shifts into a falsetto. "Oh, me. Oh, my. Allow me to pop out my titties and save you stupid cunts."

Bruce acts out around his son, spewing sexual innuendos and lewd comments. Blue vocabulary doesn't typically bother because I swear more than most; however, I don't put certain words together in the same vulgar pattern, and I don't use the c-word. Apart from *dickhead*, I generally refrain from swear words involving body parts. And when I use the f-word, it doesn't have anything to do with sex. It's a multipurpose interjection.

Our waterfront table is perfect to people-watch. A miserable procession of peregrinos crosses over the river to the albergue. The schlep through the ugly side of town has wiped many of us out, and we can see it on their faces as they pass overhead.

Thomas and Jana discuss tonight's plans in Azofra, and I dive into a skillet of seafood paella. Bruce provides a stream of sophomoric commentary, pointing out peregrinos on the bridge and awarding them titles: *most-likely to succeed to Santiago, most-likely to have a heart-attack, most-likely to eat his fellow peregrinos, most-likely to get laid...* It's meanspirited, but the laughter is a welcomed distraction from the heat.

My paella looks fancy, but looks can be deceiving. I should have known by the glossy picture menu featuring six varieties and the phrase, "substitutions not possible," the dish would not be made in-house. It is the frozen pizza of paella. A prepackaged, *heat-n-eat* product, sealed in individual servings to placate the indiscriminate peregrino palate. This is the first of many paella picture menus I will see en route to Santiago.

"My God!" says Bruce. He bumps my shoulder and points to the other side of the bridge. "Look at those fat cows." We gawk across the water to see two women exiting a taxi. It's the mother and daughter team from Jersey, who refused to eat Angel's pasta in Navarrete last night. "They took a bloody cab?" Bruce is incredulous. "Lazy fucking Americans." Jana and I deliver a set of simultaneous elbow-blows to his ribs.

The fresh-faced mother and daughter duo cross the bridge and join the long queue of pilgrims waiting for the only donativo albergue in town to open. "Seriously?" Bruce continues, "And now these fat cows will claim free beds and leave the poor bastards who actually walk here without a bed."

While not a written rule, it seems polite to leave bed-by-donation albergues free for peregrinos negotiating financial hardship. If a peregrina can afford a taxi, she can afford to pay for a bed. A standard albergue bed ranges in price from five to twenty euros. Finding a donativo or donation albergue, where one pays what one can or nothing at all, is a unique bonus for pilgrims strapped for cash.

Bruce is all in a huff and anxious to complete the final 6K of our day's journey. He is convinced cab-riding peregrina whores will claim all sixty beds in the municipal albergue of Azofra. Everyone is ready to hit the trail, but I have my heart set on a nap. Jana, now our collective conscience and source of reason, offers a compromise. I will nap, and the three of them will go ahead and get our beds for the night. Bruce grumbles, but the plan is perfect. I need some time alone and a break from Bruce.

I'm not the kind to sleep in public, especially stretched out in the open along the river. If Nájera were not a historical pilgrim haunt, someone would mistake me for a bag lady. Agnus has exploded on the grass, spewing my meager belongings in a circle around me. My hair is a bird's nest, and I am dirty and sweaty. To complete the ensemble, I take a swig from a partial bottle of wine left over from lunch.

The canister of pepper spray is neatly concealed in the palm of my right hand, just in case. I'm out of my comfort zone, but I'm not afraid. Several peregrinos flopped in similar squalor line the river bank and tuck beneath the bridge. This provides would-be robbers, rapists, and murderers plenty of other targets to choose.

The wine relaxes my body, and the rushing white noise of the river rapids lulls me to sleep. I am either barely asleep or in a state of deep relaxation – mindful, but unable to lift my arms or wiggle my toes. My right leg twitches every so often at the kneecap, and I regrip the pepper spray in the softening clutch of my right hand. The rest of me surrenders, and like a dense clump of wet sod, I fuse with the riverbank. For the first time today, nothing hurts.

Water laps against rocks, and I hear distant laughter and squeals from a pod of school girls wading through the rapids. Conversation fragments drift from café tables and wiggle in and out of my ears. While I can't decode the words, the calm shifts in register indicate friendly conversations. A gentle breeze tickles my exposed limbs and ruffles the thin fabric of my sun shirt. This is peregrina heaven.

I enjoy snippets of a romantic dream or a meditative visualization. I'm not sure I know the difference. We are on the Camino, Jim and I, walking together. We are hand in hand, crossing the Pyrenees. And it is so stinking easy. I am wearing a polka dot sundress and flip-flops. My knee and ankle are healed, and my feet are blister free. Agnus is cinched high on my shoulders, but she is light as a feather. The sun is shining, and we hear cow bells tinkling, and the rolling green pastures are dotted with cotton balls of sheep. It's a lovely dream, splashed with watercolor poppies and blue violets. I want to stay here forever, but every time I turn to speak with Jim my restless leg twitches and jolts me from the dream state. I reenter with surprising ease, and I'm right where we left off, hovering beneath the cloud cover and gazing down the grassy valleys of the Basque region.

My restless leg takes me off and back on the mountain several times. How many rotations I make between the Pyrenees and Nájera, I haven't a clue. I try to slow my breathing and sink deeper into the grass. I isolate a small cramp in a quadricep, the source of the spasm responsible for jolting my knee up off the grass. I try to override the contraction by tightening and releasing the muscle in time with my breath. In and out, tighten and release, until I'm back on the mountain. To be on the safe side, I don't look at Jim or talk. Instead, I am content holding the warmth of his hand in mine.

We climb into the clouds. Wispy puffs of spun sugar conceal bucolic landscapes below. We can no longer hear the cows. Everything is blanketed in white, but somehow our feet find the trail. Step after unwavering step, we continue to climb. Hand in hand. Surefooted and confident.

Our idyllic hike into the heavens is rudely interrupted as a putrefied wave of cologne crashes down on me – too sweet for a man and too musky for a woman. The wave pushes me off the trail, down the mountain, and into the Army recruiting office of Sergeant Kenny Walker.

It's December 1985, and I'm home on holiday leave. At my sergeant's request, I drop by his office because he wants me to meet with a recruit and her reluctant parents. He wants her folks to see how positive the Army is for young ladies. He needs me because I'm the perfect example of *being all you can be*.

Before our meeting with the parents, I show off my new *Sharpshooter* marksmanship badge. "Well, I'll be Goddamned," says Sergeant Walker. "Our Private Betty Boop is a killer." I nod, thrilled with the recognition. "Hold on. Let me fetch the boss. He's got to see this."

Staff Sergeant Price runs the office. He is older than other recruiters, probably as old as my parents. A gelled brick of reddish hair strategically covers a balding and freckled dome. His speech tangles in my ear. He calls it hillbilly dialect. It sounds super creepy, like in the movie *Deliverance*.

Sergeant Walker leaves me standing at his desk. I hear them both laughing in the back room, but I'm sure it's not about me. I examine a photo on his desk of his wife and him at some formal event. He wears a dress blues uniform with gold buttons. He is handsome, but his wife steals my eye in her red velvet gown. His copper complexion mellows against her cocoa-cream, and the whole scene softens under the warmth of their skin. The photo glows. Smiles gleam. And a walnut frame captures a picture-perfect couple.

The sergeants rejoin me in the lounge. Price, the boss, holds two red cups and Walker holds one. "Orange juice, Private?" says Price as he hands me a cup.

"To Private Betty Boop," says Walker.

"Here. Here. To Boop," says Price.

I take a swig and pull a face. The orange juice tastes nasty, almost rotten. I sip it to be polite. Price notices and laughs. "Drink! Drink the whole damn thing," he orders. I obey, and the room starts to tilt.

"Sergeant Walker," I whisper. "I feel sick."

"Relax. It's just a screwdriver. Have another."

My head spins. I struggle to decipher what the sergeants are saying to me, but it is obvious they are angry. "Look at yourself," says Walker. "You can't meet parents like this. You're a sloppy drunk."

"Well. Well," sneers Price. "Thought you was a soldier and could handle yer liquor."

"Let's take her to your place to sober her up," Walker says to Price.

"I hope yer proud, private," says Price. Now git yer ass in the car."

I sit in the back seat. The car starts. My legs and arms turn to lead, and my head is a cannonball. My vision narrows, like peering through the peep-sight of an M-16 assault rifle. When the car stops, I release the door latch, and my gut squeezes like a trigger and shoots projectiles of rotten orange across the parking lot. I collapse in a river of my own vomit.

My body moves, but I don't. The sergeants struggle to heft my dead weight. I apologize, but my voice slurs and distorts like an old vinyl record played at the wrong speed.

The drink numbed all but smell and sound. Without seeing, I know Staff Sergeant Price owns a cat. The pungent ammonia of spent kitty litter comingles with cigarettes and stale beer. The odors permeate sofa pillows. I hear my first porn movie and slip deeper into the dark.

Semiconscious, I know I need to go home. I force my eyes open and release a moan I don't recognize. Sergeant Walker strokes my forehead. "Private, I'm going to put you to bed. Don't worry. I won't let anything happen to you." He scoops my dead body from the sofa.

He carries me into a bedroom and lays me face down on a blue synthetic bedspread, the kind that snags hangnails and calloused feet. I hear the door close. The cool darkness surrounds me. I relax and invite sleep.

I hear a rustle of keys, the metallic click of a belt buckle, the pull of a zipper, and the soft thud of pants holding a wallet hit the floor. "Sergeant Walker?" My voice sounds far away.

"Shut up, Private. Shut the fuck up."

Sergeant Walker wrestles my clothes and dead limbs. His breath of soured oranges and stale cigarettes gags me. Hand-to-hand combat diagrams scroll black and white. I hear drill sergeants calling out movements by the numbers. My mind repeats in ghostlike cadence, and I'm ready to fight, but my muscles fail to respond. I only manage to whisper, "No. Please."

He pushes the back of my head down into the bedspread. I gasp for air. I breathe through his pattern of suffocate, release, suffocate, release. My lungs burn, and eyes bulge red. I anticipate the pain of dry penetration. I cringe as beads of his sweat splat and pool in the small of my back. The pool overflows. Rivers trickle across my torso. I feel the rivers. I hear skin slap skin. His weight forces air from my body like a deflated balloon. But I don't feel him inside me. This part refuses to feel. This part is dead.

He collapses on top of me and whispers proclamations of love and admiration of my "sweet ass." A wave of cologne crashes down on me – too sweet for a man and too musky for a woman. I try to vomit. He shoves my head back down into the blue bedspread and resumes slamming and suffocating. He does not let up. I gulp air as the mattress gives way between thrusts. I fight for life with one defense tactic, stolen breath.

I hear a doorbell ring. I hear the excited voice of Staff Sergeant Price, "Kenny! Kenny! Your fucking wife is outside my door!" Skin stops slapping skin. Air rushes in. Lungs inflate. I hear a rustle of keys, the pull of a zipper, the metallic click of a belt buckle, and the opening and closing of the bedroom door. I exhale, alone and alive. I've been saved by his wife, the smiling lady wearing a red velvet ballgown and protected behind the glass of a walnut frame.

I roll to my side, pull knees to chest, and breathe – In and out, in and out. Fire rages in my gut. Salt burns my eyes. I know I've been had. Drugged. Raped. It was a setup. All lies. There weren't any parents to meet. Nobody needed my help. I am not an excellent example. I am Private Betty Boop, a cartoon soldier, and a whore.

I wake from my nap choking on angry sobs. Rage throbs in my temples. I scan the park and riverbank for the source, searching for someone douched in cheap cologne that's too sweet for a man and too musky for a woman. I'm hunting for an American, probably a fellow peregrino, between the ages of fifty and sixty-five years old. Maybe he received the cologne, *Jovan Musk for Men*, as a Christmas gift from his high school sweetheart back in 1975, and he's been bathing in the crap ever since.

The odor fades. It's just an olfactory flash – the boogieman's calling card. I crisscross my legs in a half-ass lotus and shut my eyes. I regain composure in deep, slow breaths. Adrenalin vacates my nerve endings and collects in a venomous pool in my stomach. I am queasy like I need to puke, but I can't.

There is nothing to do but walk it off, so I gather my gear and leave the park. On my way out of town, I pause to gape at the monastery of *Santa Maria la Real*. The site dates to the 11th century, but the current Gothic structure was built in the 15th century. I had intended to explore, but my two-hour nap and nightmare ruined my tourist plans and mood. It's just as well. *Santa Maria la Real*, with its high walls and few windows, looks more like a defensive fortress than a house of prayer. It is a magnificent pilgrimage halt, but I find it dark and uninviting. And right now, I need to stay in the light.

The climb out of Nájera is short but steep. A packed clay road through a natural preserve flanked by red cliffs artfully sculpted by rain, wind, and time takes my mind off the boogieman. The distant call of a cuckoo bird makes me smile. My shoulders relax as I fall into a comfortable stride. Walking in the sunshine and surrounded by nature is the boogieman antidote.

Before catching the Camino bug, I'd sit on my sofa and drown the boogieman in vodka, but he wouldn't stay down. He flashes more when I am still. This explains why the flashbacks coincided with illness. A little over five years ago, before Meniere's disease and chronic migraines attacked, I never sat still. The memory of Sergeant Kenny Walker couldn't catch up with me.

Unfortunately, boogiemen like Walker never die. He smoldered silently, compounding strength, and blazed on a trigger's squeeze. He rides a flash of electric currents back into my life, exposing scenes blackened by time, therapy, and substance abuse. He spares not touch, taste, smell, sight, nor sound. He is everyone, everywhere, at any time. He is perfume in the wind.

Military sexual trauma is not gendered specific; however, one in three women who serve in America's armed forces report military sexual trauma. I know the number is higher. My assault never made it beyond Staff Sergeant Price.

According to Price, I had it coming, and no one would believe a lowly private over two decorated Sergeants.

The rape flashback is a dirty cliché. I've heard similar versions dozens of times, and not only from lady warriors. It happens to men too. And it happens on college campuses, in high schools, and at places of work. It's the professor or the supervisor or the mentor or the sergeant. It's the abuse of power and misguided trust. That's the part I can't get over – the trust. It was never about my body. After all these years, what disgusts me most is those bastards took advantage of a kid, a dumb farm girl who swore allegiance and promised to defend the United States Constitution against all enemies. When my leaders became my enemies, it was a total mind-fuck, one I've subconsciously grappled with nearly every day of my adult life. And I'm not alone. Sixty percent of military sexual trauma victims develop post-traumatic stress disorder or PTSD. This is partly because many of us are held responsible, ashamed, and too embarrassed to seek treatment. Bullying, fear of reprisal, lack of support, and humiliation seals lips, and the cycle rages on.

The sun slips behind the clouds, and I'm treated to a soft rain. I take off my straw hat and allow the gentle drops to soak my hair and run down my cheeks. I pull the waterproof cover over Agnus but forego the rain jacket. The raindrops grow and gain momentum and slowly wash away the day's grit and shame.

I cross a paved road, leaving the *Zona Natural* and entering an agricultural area. The red dirt track, now marred with tractor ruts, is sticky beneath my feet. Each step is heavier than the last. I search for jagged rocks along the ditch to scrape the clay from my boots. The going is slow, but there is not much I can do about it. I'm not worried because Jana and the Brits have secured me a bed. And from what I've read about Azofra, it should not be a challenge to find them around town because town consists of two bars and a small tienda.

The red dirt road merges with asphalt and leads me into Azofra. Up ahead, a small gathering of people, probably peregrinos, are cheering and waving. I stop and turn and glance around to see what all the fuss is about. Perhaps there is a festival in the village or a parade. And here I thought Azofra was going to be dull.

As I get closer, it seems like they are waving to me. And then I hear the chanting, "Cody – Cody – Cody…" *Cody* is Jana's funny nickname for me. They *are* waving at me! I am their *Cody*, the *Codster*, the *Codemeister*. I have no idea why Jana calls me Cody, but I'm thrilled with my newfound celebrity status. I try to speed up to a jog but only manage a pathetic shuffle.

I was right about Azofra. There are only two bars, and Jana and the Brits and a handful of new friends I haven't met have gathered at the first bar in town to welcome me in. It's been a long day, 24K, roughly fifteen miles. My feet hurt like hell, but it's not the physical pain that got the best of me today.

The reception is warm and tipsy, just how I like it. Apparently, my friends have drained a few bottles of wine waiting for my arrival. Bruce raves on about how worried he has been and how he tried to muster a search party to go back and find me. "These lazy wankers," he slurs. "Yeah, these tossers wouldn't have it. They sat on their arses getting bloody-well trolleyed." I hug Bruce, and he is so *trolleyed* he loses his balance and knocks me to the floor.

I'm surprised we don't get kicked out of the bar, but we don't. Instead, the host helps us right ourselves again, and the waitress sweeps up a broken wine glass. We eat our peregrino meal, a chicken hindquarter stewed in *cerveza* and served with fried potatoes. I inhale the chicken and sop up the grease with my fries. My plate is clean, but I hardly tasted my food. But I tasted the wine, several times. Despite our display of drunkenness, we keep right on drinking the delicious and local *Rioja*.

Jana gently rocks in her chair, wearing a Mona Lisa smile and shifting into her redneck accent. "Out there on the road, Cody," she says. "The going gets hard – so hard. But you're never alone. Never. Alone. I'm your buddy, Codester. I got your back." Wrapped in her wine-soaked proclamation, I am safe and warm.

Azofra to Viloria de la Rioja

Despite waking with a mild hangover, my stay in Azofra was fantastic. We followed our supper last night with more wine and a soak in a peregrino foot fountain. There were about twenty of us around the pool, laughing and telling stories, and tending abused feet. This is what I love about pilgrimage, the communal effort to survive and still have fun. I meet folks from all around the world, and we always find common ground when it comes to feet.

Feet, specifically blisters, are exhaustive topics of debate no matter where pilgrims gather. Everyone has an opinion. There are poppers versus the non-poppers. There are those who cover with *Compeed* patches and those who let-it-breath. Some peregrinos drain the ampule fluid and flood the skin beneath the flap with iodine. Others insist on rubbing alcohol or hydrogen peroxide. For me, I'm starting to prefer the eccentricities of the needle and thread tribe. The idea is to thread a bit of string diagonally through the center of the blister and double back to form a tidy cross-stitch. The trick is to leave a short length of string flapping in the breeze to serve as a wick for draining fluid.

The intricate needle and thread operation draws a crowd, and last night Bruce and I were center-stage. My latest edition, a bean-shaped bubble on the inside of my big toe had a personality and a pulse of its own. There was no way to let it be. Bruce was beyond tipsy, and I was gaining on him. He convinced me he was sober enough to perform the cross-stitch surgery. Surprisingly, he was as steady as a surgeon. It was me who was shaking and flinching with each poke of the needle. The scene was a train wreck. No one wanted to watch, but everyone gathered around. Some gawkers were more useful than others by shining headlamps into the operating space. Others let out great gasps and squeals and were far less helpful.

After the surgery, Bruce claimed to be an army medic. His occupational story is shifty. When I first met him in Navarrete, he was an electrical engineer. The next day, he waxed on about his prosperous career as an architect. One thing is clear; his shifting stories coincide with his reason for walking the Camino. "I've forgotten who I am."

"Haven't we all, Bruce. Haven't we all…" I hate that we must be a specific something, a job, or a title. And I'm growing bored and frustrated with cue card inquiries: Where are you from? What do you do? Why are you walking the Camino? The origin and occupational questions are simple. I rattle off the facts. However, the why-question catches me off guard, and this doesn't make a bit of sense because I hear it more than a few times per day. I should have a canned answer, but I can't condense my motivations into an orderly thesis statement. Part of the problem is motivations evolve and dissolve the further I move down the trail. Sometimes, I don't want to talk about it. To avoid a deep conversation last night with a very persistent peregrino, I claimed to have run away from my sofa to improve fitness. It's not a lie, but it's not exactly the truth either.

Jana and I are slow to leave Azofra this morning. We loiter in the albergue and hit the last bar in town as it opens for breakfast. We slept well, but we need coffee and chocolate croissants to get us moving. So far, the Azofra Municipal Albergue is my favorite. The 60-bed facility is partitioned into thirty particleboard rooms, making it a welcomed surprise and a bargain at seven euros. The albergue is described in guidebooks as *purpose-built*, meaning it wasn't once an old gymnasium, monastery, or schoolhouse repurposed to serve pilgrims. Purpose makes all the difference. Except for the communal bathrooms, the place was built for me.

I can handle showering next to the dude in the adjacent cube, so long as my cube is equipped with a locking door. Toilet stalls are another thing altogether. I can't perform certain biological duties when I see a man's feet aligned with mine. Sure, I can focus enough to potty, but I can't do the big job. It's not just the feet. There are sounds and smells that make it impossible to relax. I waste too much energy contemplating bathroom issues. As a temporary solution, I've become *The Midnight-Pooper.* Yes. I set my alarm.

Agnus is ridiculously light today because the beautiful Jana, with her calming wisdom and persuasive charm, encouraged me to empty out all nonessentials to send forward to Grañón in her bag. Besides water, I carry a change of socks, my medical kit, sunscreen, and a red apple. In my shoulder bag, I carry my phone, pepper spray, a Swiss Army knife, and gum. Jana uses a bag-forwarding network. For a small fee, a company transports backpacks and luggage from one albergue, pension, or hotel to the next. She tried to get me to do it in Navarrete, but I turned up my nose. I have this silly idea that to be an authentic pilgrim I must kill myself in the process.

I lobbied for a short day to Santo Domingo de la Calzada, but before I staggered into Azofra last night, the new tribe had already planned a full 25K day. I don't want to be left out. Jana offered a compromise, a long break in Santo Domingo to enjoy lunch and visit the chicken church. Bruce and Thomas agreed to go ahead and secure our beds in Grañón.

I'm excited about the chicken church and ask Jana if she knows the legend. She shrugs. We are walking at a fast clip and uphill, but I have enough breath to tell the story anyway.

"A long time ago, a German couple and their son were on a pilgrimage and stopped in Santo Domingo for the night. They were put up by a farmer. And like every old story or joke that includes a farmer, there was a farmer's daughter. Well, the farmer's daughter fell madly in love with the German boy. His name was Hugo, and he was not feeling the connection. This pissed off the farmer's daughter. To seek revenge, she took a silver cup from her parent's collection and hid it in Hugo's rucksack. In the morning, as Hugo and his folks were ready to set out, she accused him of stealing the cup. Hugo was hanged in the village gallows, and the only thing his grief-stricken parents could do was continue to Santiago and pray for Hugo's soul." Medieval pilgrims not only walked to Santiago, but they had to walk back home. "When Hugo's parents passed through Santo Domingo on their return, they went to the gallows to see their dead son. To their shock, Hugo, still dangling by a rope, was alive and kicking. Hugo credited his miraculous survival to the divine intervention of Santo Domingo. The parents rushed to the village priest, who was sitting down to a roasted chicken dinner. They told him of the miracle and begged him to cut the boy down and absolve him of his crime. The priest laughed and said, 'Your son is no more alive than this cock on my plate.' And just like that, the roasted chicken jumped up, belted out a cock-a-doodle-doo, and ran away. Of course, the boy was released and proclaimed innocent. And to this day, a rooster and a hen are kept in the church as a reminder of miracles."

"Hmm," says Jana. "I thought it was the mayor."

"What?"

"The mayor. The parents visited the town mayor, not the priest."

"Wait a minute. You already knew the story?"

"Yeah. I read it somewhere. And I don't think it was a farmer's daughter either."

"Well, why didn't you stop me?"

"Oh, Cody. You sounded so excited, and I didn't want to ruin the fun."

"Well, thanks a lot. I about had a cardiac arrest trying to talk and walk uphill."

The climb is kicking my ass. In my guidebook, the stage from Nájera to Santo Domingo de la Calzada is described as expansive country tracks through farmland. This part is true, but it's a gross understatement when Brierly describes the path as *gently undulating*. There is nothing *gently undulating* about the climb into Ciruena.

Jana and I are quiet, walking side by side, for two hours. She breaks the silence as we enter the village. "How are your feet," she asks.

"I'm afraid to look." I glance down at my hiking sandals and notice a bit of blood oozing through my toe-socks and staining the orange suede leather. It serves me right. I should have known better than to let a drunk man operate on my blister. However, I'm less concerned about my feet than I am about my right knee. Angry red streaks spread from the wound to my thigh. My leg is hot and itchy. Hopefully, it is nothing a bit more antibiotic ointment cannot fix.

The long slog into Santo Domingo is disheartening, but it's not the same brand of urban decay as in Nájera. I'd call this an agricultural-industrial wasteland. Rusty farm implements and dilapidated buildings dot the landscape. I'm comfortable with farm smells, but this is different. I catch a whiff of a nasty but familiar stench – like tons of rotting compost. We pass a metal building with expansive bays, and I ponder the playpen-size wooden crates. And then it hits me. Potatoes – or more precisely, moldy potatoes decaying in the hot sun. Jana covers her mouth with a scarf, and we both pick up the pace.

We enter the village of Santo Domingo and dive into the inviting stone shelter of an albergue run by Cistercian nuns. I'd love to stay here and spend the rest of the afternoon stretched out in the lush grass of the shady courtyard, but our stuff was fast-forwarded to Grañón this morning. This is the huge disadvantage of using a backpack-express system. You can't stop whenever you need, and I feel the need.

A couple of Canadian college girls comment on my knee, and one runs off to get help. The girl returns with a peach-faced nun armed with a medical kit. Refusing care is out of the question. The young nun won't have it. I grit my teeth and squeeze Jana's hand as the sister dumps hydrogen peroxide into the gash on my knee. The wound and peroxide cocktail is a spewing volcano of orange foam.

The nun lectures on wound care and the importance of treating my body gently. Her English is near perfect, but her adorable accent and deeply dimpled cheeks make it hard to take her seriously. Regardless of charm, the nun is adamant and refuses to us leave the convent on foot. I have too much respect and gratitude to argue. She calls a cab and stands on the corner with us to ensure we get in.

I'm sobbing as we climb into the back seat. The cab driver watches us in bewilderment through his review mirror. Jana links her arm into mine and speaks softly, "What is this all about, Cody?"

"I failed! I'm a loser – like those cows in Nájera."

She looks surprised, "Codester, this is *your* Camino." She drapes her arm over my shoulder. "You must take better care of yourself. Who are you competing with anyway?"

"Nobody, but I don't want to be a taxi-cab-riding-whore!" And with that, we both start laughing. The driver shakes his head.

Jana is right. I risk my health to sooth ego and feed competitive nature. I create false pressure. I'm not even Catholic! And if I were Catholic, the cab ride still wouldn't matter as long I walk the last 100k on my own two feet. Many peregrinos start in Sarria and walk the five-day trek into Santiago. There is no need to kill myself earning a Compostela to cut purgatory time when I don't even know if I believe in purgatory.

We arrive in Grañón to learn our British boys failed to secure our beds for the night. To make matters worse, the albergue is completo. Jana collects her bag from an apologetic hospitalero, who thoughtfully locates two beds at an albergue 8K ahead. Luckily, our cab driver is enjoying café con leche at the bar adjacent to the albergue. He is reluctant to let two crazy women back into his cab, but we convince him to take us to Viloria de la Rioja, the birthplace of Santo Domingo. He pulls right up to the albergue door to drop us. As he pulls away, I sense the disapproving stares of *real peregrinos* who would never take a cab. The scene is familiar, but this time Jana and I are the ones facing judgment.

My pride is in the toilet as the host greets us with disapproval. He has two beds but doesn't want to shelter us. His albergue is for real peregrinos, not "tourists in taxis." I'm humiliated and want to walk on. I can do it. My feet and knee are better already, and it is less than 4K to the next village. Jana shakes her head. She knows what I am thinking.

She gently nudges me aside and takes over the negotiation. She smooths her long, blond hair over one shoulder before she begins. With a slight tilt of her head, she softly explains our day's walk, the ongoing troubles with my feet, and the suspected infection on my knee. Jana is graceful in word and manner. How could anyone refuse? Our host is a tough customer, but Jana reels him in with her persuasive charm.

We are led into a cozy dormitory. The converted space once served as an old milking shed, but we are the only cows now, taxi-riding cows. It is rustic but well-appointed and impeccably clean. The hostess meets us to go over house rules, and there are many. Before she begins, she condemns, "You arrived by taxi." Jana and I nod our heads and offer no further explanation. The story is getting old. We know. We suck. We are shitty peregrinas...

Jana and I forget all about the hostile welcome after learning about laundry service. The cost is five euros per load for washing and drying. We team up and create two piles, one for lights and one for darks. I scrutinize the light pile, making sure there is nothing that will dull the whiteness of my hiking blouse. Jana delivers our two stacks and ten euros to the laundry room. So easy.

Noting numerous *Do not waste water* signs, I zip in and out of the shower and dry off with my *towel of disappointment*. The towel of disappointment is a piece of purple-shammy-bullshit I found at an outdoor recreation store during my planning phase. Unfortunately, I did not test it out before packing.

When unfolded, the thing is just large enough to wrap one thigh. However, it is lightweight and dries quickly.

There is nothing to do in the village, and I shouldn't be walking anyway. So, I tend to my knee and put up my feet in the common room to read and wait for supper. Jana joins me carrying a yellow bucket of warm salt water for my feet. The host sizes up the amount of water and shakes his head at her lack of frugality. He holds his thumb and forefinger about an inch and a half apart. "That is all," he scolds. "That is all she needs."

These people are incredible. The albergue is beautiful, and the soup on the stove smells delicious. Authenticity and charm ooze from walls. This should be a peregrino paradise, but these must be the grumpiest hosts along the Camino. Jana is unfazed. She rises above, and I stew in a pail of salt water. I am held hostage by my feet. Peregrinos are supposed to be grateful for the hospitality received. I get that, and I'm trying. I'm not collecting handouts here. I paid for a bed and dropped a twenty-euro note into the donativo box to cover supper. I'm not expecting quality customer service, but I want to be treated kindly or at least ignored. Ignored would be satisfactory.

Dinner is heavily orchestrated. We take our assigned seats. Jana and I are separated, but I'm looking forward to the shared conversation of a communal meal. The host sits at the head of the table with the hostess at his right. Instead of an evening blessing, the host proselytizes on the writings of *Paulo Coelho* and the true meaning of pilgrimage. He urges us to throw away guidebooks and stop following arrows. "Just walk," he assures. "You'll find your way."

I get the concept, and it's a lovely idea to wander in self-discovery. Maps and guides and schedules may not lead to enlightenment, but they are not the antitheses either. I can't help but wonder if I'm the only one at the table noting the irony of what the man preaches and how he runs his albergue. Everything, even conversation, is scripted, rule-based, and controlled. These are not hippy-dippy, live and let live kind of hosts.

We are instructed to pass our bowls clockwise and one by one to the hostess for a ladle of soup. The soup is potato and leek, and it is perfect. She rations the servings, but the wine flows freely. Thank God. After the second course, a tasty rice dish, the host announces how we must earn dessert. Sticking to the clockwise order, each peregrino confesses the reason for walking the Camino de Santiago. The good news is I am last and have plenty of time to think. The bad news is I am last and have plenty of time to fret.

Consumed with crafting my defense, I cannot focus on confessions of my fellows. If I could, I'd find a spinoff to piggyback. A hundred reasons enter and exit my head, but nothing is shareworthy tonight. I'm grappling with life-changing questions, but I don't want their input. I'm facing down fear, but I don't want to disclose this to hosts who don't deserve this brand of intimacy. They visibly dislike me, but it's not just that. Despite ongoing problems with my feet, I am emotionally and spiritually well. I don't want to rip off the scab. Not for them.

When my turn rolls around, I accentuate the positive and share what is right in my world. I settle for the most recent event. "I'm walking in a state of thanksgiving because my youngest of five sons graduated from high school last week. All five earned diplomas, and I'm relieved and grateful." The mature pilgrims around the table nod as if they understand the angst of pushing teenagers toward success. I don't know why I do it, but I look to the hostess for approval. Family photos on the wall indicate she knows a thing or two about raising a son. She shakes her head and in a matter-of-fact tone says, "No. Not believable."

The table falls awkwardly quiet. The hostess gets up and goes to the refrigerator and grabs two stacks of chocolate pudding cups. By the time she gets to me, she runs out and goes back into the kitchen. When she returns, she drops a plastic cup of plain yogurt in front of me. This is what I get for being an approval-whore.

I hate plain yogurt. Yogurt isn't a dessert. Yogurt is for breakfast. I pull back the foil lid, lick it clean, grab my spoon, and take a bite. I openly declare my love of yogurt – of plain yogurt. I rave about the superior quality of Spanish dairy products and beg to know where she purchased it so I might enjoy it tomorrow. Jana shoots me a look across the table.

The hosts push us off to bed like we are schoolchildren with a geography test in the morning. We are locked inside our dormitory from 2100 to 0700. This is out of the norm. I understand a curfew, but I want to retain my freedom to leave. What if there is a fire or an earthquake or a suicide bomber?

I'm almost asleep when the hostess reenters the dorm with our bundle of clean laundry. She sets the stack down on Jana's bed, selects my hiking blouse from the pile and holds it up with outstretched arms. "Your shirt." She gives it a snap. I clap my hands in anticipation.

"*Gracias!*" I reach for it, but Jana grabs it before I can. The hostess turns sharply on a heel, exits, and relocks the door. Jana holds my shirt to her chest.

"What is it? What's the matter?'

"Oh, Codester. Your beautiful shirt. She ruined it."

In the dim light and without my glasses, I can't see what she is talking about. She walks into the bathroom, and I follow, and together we inspect my blouse. It was laundered with jeans. The shirt is light gray and streaked with indigo. My rage flashes but quickly melts into sorrow. "She did this on purpose. Why? Why would she?"

"Because she is a little bitch," hisses Jana.

I'm shocked at her sudden lack of grace and bust out laughing. My laughter is met with annoyed hushes from the dorm. "Sorry. Super sorry," I whisper out the bathroom door.

I wiggle my shirt free from Jana's clenched fist and lead her back to bed. She is rigid and steaming with anger. "Shake it off," I whisper. "It's just a shirt."

I try not to dwell all night and ruin my sleep, but I don't understand. If it was an accident, why not tell me. I would have shrugged it off. It is just a shirt, and it will still protect me from the sun and insects. But it's not about the shirt. It's about the passive-aggressive act. Why did she bother? And why snap the shirt so proudly in my face. Was she asking for a fight?

This can't be all about taxi crimes. It was my first ride and less than fifteen kilometers. It's not a designer shirt or anything to envy. It's a hiking shirt, a gift from my hubby. While white is impractical, it looked lovely in the sun against my tanned face.

Because one of my goals is to be kind, I try a little self-reflection. Maybe I took too long in the shower. Was it presumptuous to expect lights and darks washed separately? I stretched the yogurt thing a bit far, but my shirt was already through the wash cycle. It must be tough running an albergue. Peregrinos can be very rude. I want to rise above, but even Jana struggles. It's all about balance. How do I be a kind and forgiving human without turning into a doormat? The old me would have walked to the next village, but maybe this has nothing to do with me. That's the challenging part of being so vulnerable out here. I'm juggling expectations to be humble and grateful. Most days, I succeed but not without the struggle for equilibrium.

Part 4

Castilla y León

Viloria de la Rioja to Villafranca Montes de Oca

At 0700, the hostess unlocks the dorm and flips on the light. The wake up is harsh but not surprising. Jana and I hurry to get the hell out and avoid further conflict. I pretend not to notice my ruined shirt. I drape it over a peach tank top and roll up the sleeves. Graciously, I thank the hosts and exit to the patio. Under a judgmental scowl, Jana arranges bag-transport to Villafranca Montes de Oca, about 20k away, and I don't argue.

As I'm lacing my last boot, I sense the hostess standing over me. When I glance up, she says in a snotty tone, "Shall I call you a cab?"

"Oh, no. I'm well today. But thank you for your kindness." I stand and wrap her in a tight embrace. She gasps and stiffens like a board, but I don't let go. I'm going to hug her until I mean it.

Jana and I wait until we are safely out of sight to burst into mad laughter. We shush each other because we are probably still in earshot, but the more we shush, the harder we laugh. We stop at a patch of grass beneath an old tree to collect ourselves.

"Oh, my God, Codester. Did you see her face?"

"Her face? No. But you should have felt her body. It was like hugging a steel girder."

"Not only did you hug her, but you rocked her back and forth. What were you thinking?"

"I thought if I held her long enough, I could love her."

"And?"

"Love is a rather generous term. But at least I'm not angry about my shirt."

Jana adopts her exaggerated version of a redneck accent. "Dang, Cody. That's some Zen shit right there."

"Well, I'm learning from the best."

"It's tough out there on the road, Codes. It'll learn you. Yup. It'll learn you."

I'm glad we've stopped for a bit to soak in the village. Viloria de la Rioja is the birthplace of Santo Domingo, the illiterate saint who worked tirelessly for peregrinos. This isn't just the place where my shirt was ruined, and that's not how I'm going to remember it.

Born *Domingo Garcia* in 1019, Santo Domingo devoted his life to God but was rejected by monasteries because he lacked intelligence. Instead, he became a hermit in a forest which is now the village of Santo Domingo. The saint dedicated his life to serving pilgrims. He built roads, a bridge crossing río Oja, and a pilgrim hospital, which is now a swanky *Parador* hotel. Late in life, he built a little peregrino church where the much grander *Cathedral of Santo Domingo de la Calzada* now stands. Sadly, the original church and his birth house were demolished. His birthplace is marked by a fenced pile of rubble. His baptismal church is next to the park, but it is locked. No matter. It's surreal to stand where he lived and breathed.

I'm no saint, but I do have a soft spot for illiteracy. My first teaching job was with a nonprofit, family literacy organization in Washington state. After marrying Jim, I left the Army, completed my masters and got my first break. It wasn't glamorous, but I was thrilled. I taught basic literacy and English as a second language. The grassroots organization partnered with the local community college, and it wasn't long before I was teaching at the college too. Literacy was my gateway drug into the intoxicating world of adult education. I held night classes at a community center and lectured in the county jail. I knew I had found my life's work. I belonged in the classroom helping adult students of the *hard-to-serve* populations.

Despite my vocational epiphany, my military hubby requested orders to North Carolina to further his career. I wasn't included in the decision-making process that uprooted my family and interrupted aspirations. My oldest boy, Nicholas, was entering high school. He didn't want to move again. By the 8th grade, he had attended six different elementary and junior high schools. He was done. He moved in with my parents. He needed stability I could not deliver.

Nicholas fills a house, and his presence was sorely missed. I laughed much less after the move. I don't know why I didn't stay put. My life would be different had I stayed with the college and lived with my sons in the fixer-upper house I made into a home. Life would be different, but maybe not better. I find it hard to fathom I never considered the option.

Jana and I walk on. Tension moves into my shoulders, and my poles strike harder against the blacktopped road. Why am I angry about something from so long ago? Jana notices my mood and stretches out her stride to leave me alone with my thoughts.

Jim and I met in the Army. Back then, it took little convincing to choose him over my career. I transferred to reserve status and moved with him to Washington. I understood the sacrifices of an Army wife but was happy to give up my enlistment. I had been all I could be.

Despite the sacrifices, it was my partnership with Jim that made it possible to return to school, obtain a master's, begin a doctorate, and land my first job in adult education. Life with Jim was easier. The ongoing struggles to pay bills, find daycare and feed the boys vanished. Marriage elevated me from survival mode to crafting a meaningful life. This is probably why I tried to make the best of North Carolina. After the move, I found another teaching gig but at half the salary. Eventually, I landed a director position in a family literacy project. I also completed a doctorate and earned a commission in the United States Coast Guard Reserve. I owe much of this success to Jim. While I was busy rebuilding a career, and caring for the boys, Jim was drifting. And while he drifted, his conduct as a married man was somewhat questionable.

Somehow, we survived North Carolina and found our way back to Washington state. Things felt more normal, but I was lonely. Jim rarely spoke to me. To fill the void, I sought camaraderie with military brothers and sisters again by accepting an active-duty tour with the Coast Guard. My love for adult education took a back burner to simmer. For the most part, I was content. Jim and I lived together, more like roommates, but it was okay.

My little boys, who were no longer little, kept me busy and entertained. I never relied on Jim for friendship, and he never offered. Instead, he was a dutiful partner with comfort and preference toward matters of logistical support. He kept the woodstove stoked, set up retirement accounts, and performed automotive maintenance. Emotional components of love, marriage, and parenting held little interest for him.

And then I got sick. First, it was vertigo and then migraines. It spiraled downhill with anxiety, depression, and agoraphobia. Forced to retire from the Coast Guard, I lost my comrades, my confidence, and my identity. I tried to hold it together, keeping busy with the boys and the garden. But I was slipping, and Jim didn't know how to help.

My middle son, Garret, graduated from high school and joined the Air Force. He left a mess in his room and a mess in my heart. Jaden, the baby, was next in line. He too would graduate and move on. The thought of an empty nest made me sick. What would I do without my kids? Where would I place my energy, and who would talk to me? But most of all, who would make me laugh? No one. That is who.

Jaden just graduated on the 14th of June. He packed his car and moved across the water, near Seattle, to live with his dad. I flew to Madrid, to walk the Camino, the very next day. And now, I am here – trying to come to terms with what just happened. Up until now, I hadn't laid out all the facts. I refused to stay home in my empty nest long enough to celebrate my wedding anniversary on the 17th of June. Admittedly, I could have endured a few days of empty nest to honor fifteen years of marriage. Did I run away? Is this what my pilgrimage is about – an empty nest? Maybe I am nothing more than a runaway mama-bird.

We enter Belorado, but I'm so consumed with thought I hardly notice. Jana is ahead of me but stops to wait. I almost walk on by. "Wait! Cody, check this out." She is standing in front of a triple bell tower that provides the framework to four stork nests. The bell tower, attached to the church of *Santa Maria y San Pedro*, is nestled in the backdrop of limestone cliffs complete with ancient cave dwellings and castle ruins. The scene is beyond postcard perfect.

Two of the nests are occupied by single storks, and two nests are vacant. One of the vacant nests is constructed, in part, by long strands of toilet paper. I assume the toilet paper is a byproduct of peregrination. I pop in the church and light a candle for my boys. I can't help but think the storks, and the empty nests vacated by runaway mama birds, and the strands of toilet paper are somehow symbolic. Maybe it's a bit of light humor, compliments of Saint James.

Before exiting Belorado, Jana and I happen upon an outdoor market. There are textiles and handicrafts, antiques and used clothing, produce and artisan cheeses. The market stalls are a pleasure to behold after a mind-numbing walk shouldering a blacktopped roadway. I stock up on walnuts, dried prunes, figs, and green olives scooped from a wooden barrel of brine. If I didn't have to carry my pack another 12K to Villafranca, I would purchase more.

I pop olives and spit the pits as I walk. Jana works her way through a bar of dark chocolate with almonds. We are quiet, placated in culinary satisfaction, but I can't stop thinking about runaway mama-bird syndrome. Up until today, I've tried to ignore the empty nest issue. It was not one of the reasons I was walking the Camino. My motivations, multifaceted and convoluted, evolve as bits of everyday life demand my attention.

Jana offers a penny for my thoughts, but I don't sell out. She is in her late thirties, never married, doesn't have kids, and isn't eager to share details. I haven't asked her why she is walking the Camino because I overheard Thomas inquire, and she told him it was none of his business. It's probably best to keep the mama-bird thing to myself. Nobody likes an oversharing-peregrina.

We continue in silence to Villafranca Montes De Oca, where we will hopefully meet back up with the Brits. The entire route, all twenty kilometers, is uphill but scenic. The beauty and tranquility of the trek compensate for the burn in my lungs and the ache in my thighs.

Our arrival into Villafranca is an esthetic buzzkill. The village is basically one big truck stop. We endure an onslaught of rumbling trucks by pasting ourselves to the stone walls lining the narrow but busy road. We make our way to safety and duck into a small tienda to purchase supplies. I need fresh bandages, a cold soda, some fruit, and this magical foot treatment called *Peregrino Crème*. Basically, it's petroleum jelly infused with camphor and essential oils. Jana swears by it, and she remains blister-free. The label doesn't list which essential oils are used, but I detect peppermint, lavender, and a touch of rosemary. It smells lovely and keeps the feet fresh. It is also a blessing for chaffing thighs.

I impulse shop, grabbing what I need and what I do not necessarily need for tomorrow's ridiculously steep climb. We will ascend not one but three peaks before leveling off in San Juan de Ortega, and then we will descend slightly to our planned stop in Atapuerca. We hope to get an early start so we can check out the prehistoric caves of *Homo antecessor*. This location of our early ancestors, now a UNESCO World Heritage site, was uncovered in the 1980s during excavation for a railway. This site, a source of the earliest human remains found in Europe, dates back over 900,000 years. Even the earliest of us felt the gravitational pull of this magical trek tucked beneath the blanket of stars known as the Milky Way.

I unload my basket at the checkout counter. I have tape and gauze, magical foot cream and antibacterial ointment, almonds and dried apricots, a fresh apple and a container of yogurt, and an icy cold diet soda. I dig out a credit card, but the cashier shakes her head and smiles. Evidently, no credit cards are accepted. I dig out my cash, but I only have eleven euros, which is not enough. After cab fare and the donativo dinner last night and today's shopping in Belorado, I am broke.

I panic. But then remember the emergency fifty-euro bill stashed in the secret compartment in my pack. I rifle through the pocket, but it is empty. I ask the cashier, in stuttering Spanish, where to find a bank machine. She smiles again, seemingly amused by my situation. To my horror, there is no bank machine until Burgos.

Embarrassed, I restock my items and leave the store. I don't have enough money for supper and a bed tonight. How did I let this happen? I forgot to grab cash before leaving Belorado. What am I supposed to do? I'm two days away from Burgos.

Jana comes out carrying my soda pop. I'm freaking out, but I'm grateful for the cold drink and her thoughtfulness. "Don't worry, my broke-ass Cody. I got you." I thank her, but I'm horrified. Money has always been a big, fat deal for me because I went so long without. When the boys were young and before I met Jim, my checking account balance was often in the negative a full week before payday. I prayed nothing would break on the car and no surprise expenses, like school pictures or field trip fees, would demand attention before the end of the month. Familiar tick-tick-ticking blooms in my chest. *Panic* has come home to roost.

We locate the 60-bed, municipal albergue where Jana sent our bag. The Brits found a smaller place with more amenities up the road, and we've decided to join them. Jana pops in to get our stuff while I wait outside. I hear her arguing with the hospitalera. Apparently, the woman won't give Jana our bag unless Jana pays for a bed. I can't keep up with the whole conversation, but we are being swindled to stay or pay for the bag. Had I the money to burn, and I don't, I'd give the old bat the cash and forgo argument. But Jana isn't playing that game. The baggage tag clearly states delivery does not constitute a reservation. This was the case in Grañón when our bag arrived at a sold-out albergue. Why is Villafranca different?

And out of principle, Jana won't throw away money, and the lady won't budge. We are shown to bunks in a cramped dormitory overflowing with our fellow stinky peregrinos. Jana is visibly pissed off, which apart from last night's shirt incident, is out of character. I try to cheer her up, but she pulls her sleeping bag over her head. She's shutting down and needs privacy.

I hobble to the communal bathroom and find an empty shower stall. Despite the crowd, hot water is plentiful. Fully clothed, I stand under the shower and lather up my shirt and hiking skirt with a bar of homemade cedar soap. Next, I strip off the wet clothes and wash out the insides. Finally, I scrub down my body with an exfoliating puff thoughtfully clipped to my pack before leaving home. It's the little luxuries. For a moment, I forget I'm flat broke.

I exit the shower, hang my clothes outside, and return to brush my teeth. The albergue, a recently converted school, is modern with adequate amenities. The bathroom is designed for peregrinos. There are multiple shower and toilet stalls, and the trough-style sink of stainless steel is impressive. A dozen or more peregrinos could brush their teeth at the same time. Above the sink hangs a long mirror at the perfect height, at least for me.

I'm busy brushing away when three French bicyclists enter the bathroom. Without ducking into stalls, they strip away colorful riding shirts and padded shorts. I'm treated to nearly naked, paunchy, middle-aged men wearing sweat-stained undergarments that reveal everything the Lord gave to them. From my perspective, not one of them received much.

The men crowd beside me at the sink. The intrusion is perturbing because there is plenty of sink real-estate. I don't get why they slither up next to me. One of the bicyclists lets out a long and thunderous belch while scratching his balls. As a woman who raised boys, I'm not easily offended. I stifle a giggle and concentrate on my poker face in the mirror.

The shortest man stands on my left. In my peripheral vision, I see the top of his balding head. I also see he is digging around in his shorts. I avert my eyes until I catch a waft of acrid urine. *You've got to be kidding me.* I glance over to see his beans and frank resting on the edge of the sink as he takes a pee. *What the fuck?*

Jana buys dinner, and I repay her with a delightful tale of the peeing Frenchman. I try to make her laugh, but she is a terrible audience and has not rebounded from her argument. "I'm taking the bus to Burgos," she announces. "I've got to get out of this hellhole."

"Wait. When?" I'm shocked.

"Tomorrow morning. It leaves right outside the truck stop. You better come with me."

"But why? I don't understand."

"I'd get out tonight if I could. I need a break, a real bed, a bathtub, some privacy..."

"What about the Brits?"

"Forget the Brits. They didn't save us beds yesterday. Thomas is engaged but looking for a side-piece. It won't be me." I nod sympathetically. She really seemed to like the guy.

"Okay, but are you sure you want me tagging along?"

"Of course, Cody." Her face softens into a smile. "You need to soak your knee, and you're broke as a joke. Plus, won't it be terrific to have an extra day to explore Burgos?"

It doesn't take much to convince me. My knee and I need a hot bath, and I could also use a full day off my feet. Plus, my money problems can be resolved.

Instead of pulling a reset on a fellow peregrino, Jana and I will pull the reset lever on the entire village of Villafranca. I'm excited but a bit ashamed. Not only am I a taxicab-whore, but tomorrow I'll be a bus-riding-bitch. This isn't how I visualized my journey. Never had I questioned my naive assumption I would walk every step of the way.

Villafranca Montes de Oca to Burgos

Following the most miserable night of sleep since starting the trek, I board the bus-of-shame bound for Burgos. With only six euros to line my pockets, Jana pays my three-euro fare. I protest, but my words are drowned by the roar of traffic. Trucks rumble by like they did all last night. I felt them in my sleep, as the metal bunk beds shuddered with each passing.

Jana is without her warm smile and sparkle this morning. This truck stop village has taken its toll on her. She looks sad and vulnerable. To be a pilgrim is to be vulnerable, but I hadn't grasped the magnitude until last night. The vulnerability is hard to ignore when your busted flat in Villafranca with blistered feet and a bashed-up knee. Thankfully, I have a buddy. I don't know what I would have done without my Camino angel, Jana.

I have met mendicant peregrinos relying on handouts and the kindness of strangers. Some are genuinely indigent or vagrant. Others exploit temporary poverty as a challenge to embrace the journey as *true peregrinos*. These true peregrinos are hard to take seriously when they look as if they jumped from the cover of a sporting goods catalog. Like the false mendicants, my poverty and a sizable portion of my vulnerability are curable. All I need is a bank machine. Jana needs a hot bath and comfy bed, and I intend to see to her needs in Burgos.

Between episodic fits of restless sleep last night, I surfed the Internet for Burgos hotels and landed 4-star accommodations near the cathedral square. In the hotel's special-request block, I wrote: *Two broken peregrinas in desperate need of a bathtub, spa-quality toiletries, fluffy towels, cozy robes, good wine, and chocolate.* When we arrive, we are not disappointed. Every request is met.

We strip our hiking clothes and slip into thick, terrycloth robes. A housekeeper drops by to gather our laundry, and I open a beautiful bottle of complimentary wine. Decadent truffles and strawberries dipped in chocolate await on a silver tray lined with an intricate paper doily. In the bathroom, bottles of shampoo, conditioner, exfoliant scrub, shower gel, body lotion, foaming bath salts, toothpaste and toothbrushes, and disposable razors line the vanity like a ritual offering. We are children on Christmas morning, hugging and celebrating life's simple luxuries once taken for granted.

Jana hops in the tub first, while I sit on the balcony drinking red wine and eating chocolate strawberries. Villafranca is miles behind, and I cannot be more thankful. We've had a rough couple of days between the surly reception and peculiar treatment at the albergue in Viloria and last night's fiasco at the truck stop village of Villafranca. We were in desperate need of a karma-cleansing, a reset, and we pulled one off in grand style.

I pour a glass of wine for Jana, intending to deliver it to her in the bath. Instead, I find her tucked in bed with a towel wound around her wet hair. I peek closer to see the gentle rise and fall of her chest. She is fast asleep. I lower the blinds but leave the windows and balcony door open to invite the fresh air. Jana's glass waits on her nightstand as I tiptoe to the bathroom. Our room is dark and cool and relaxing, a stark contrast to the section of trail we abandoned when we boarded the bus.

Despite this beautiful room and the glorious wine and chocolates, guilt finds a way into the party. The invasion is subtle like I cheated or ripped myself off. I was looking forward to the climb out of Villafranca to the old pilgrim hospital of San Juan de Ortega. And I was excited about Atapuerca and the archeological dig site of *Homo antecessor*. Rationalizing the fast-forward is easy based on my need for cash, not to mention Jana's needs. What pisses me off is the need to justify. Why must I be Super-Peregrina? I need to shake this overachiever mentality and enjoy the journey, but I'm a slow learner.

I met a Spanish teenager back in Azofra. She was from a small village outside of Pamplona. As we sat together soaking our feet in the communal foot bath, she explained how European peregrinos often complete the route to Santiago de Compostela in chunks. She rides her bicycle and finishes a section every weekend. Her mother drops her at an albergue on Friday night, and she rides all day on Saturday and Sunday. When she concludes her ride on Sunday, her mother is waiting to take her and the bike back home. "Only crazy Americans must do the whole thing in one trip," she told me with a smile. My guess is there are plenty of crazy Australians, Koreans, and Canadians to keep us company.

People I meet always say, "The Camino is a once in a lifetime trip." I say this as well, but why should it be? Humans followed this path long before Christianity and will continue long after I've passed through this life. Why should it be a once in a lifetime gig? It's not going anywhere. I vow to return. San Juan and Atapuerca will wait.

Shaving my legs after two glasses of wine is an unnecessary risk, so I forgo the razor. A little stubble is the least of my worries. Cleanshaven legs will hardly compensate for the gash on my knee and the raw sores on my feet. Following a luxurious shampoo and a head to toe exfoliation, I drag from the tub. I'm tempted to tuck in for a nap, but I'm also anxious to explore the cathedral and the cobblestone streets of Burgos. I scribble Jana a quick note, suggesting we meet for supper, and then slip on my dress and slip out the door.

The 13th century, Gothic *Catedral de Santa Maria de Burgos*, another UNESCO World Heritage site, is more than expected. Brierly's descriptions in my guidebook didn't prepare me for the splendor and sheer magnitude of this place. Brierly mentions overcrowding, but this is not what I am experiencing. I'm swallowed up in the sanctity, mostly alone, moving at my own pace and enjoying an audio tour through a rented headset. I go about snapping photos and lighting candles before finding myself awestruck in front of Leónardo da Vinci's *La Magdalena*.

Da Vinci's rendering of Magdalena's full figure takes my breath away. Her radiant skin, nudity shielding locks of chocolate-cherry, and her innocent expression are more than I can process. The painting glows as warmly as the gilded encasement. I can't explain why, but I'm profoundly touched. Standing next to her makes me weep.

Something about *La Magdalena* makes me long for a do-over. At forty-seven, I'm only now experiencing this kind of intense emotional reaction to art. This is tragic as all hell and makes me cry harder. Where has this deep appreciation been hiding all my life? It comes down to choices, choices I made early on, like the choice to join the Army out of high school instead of pursuing a college degree. Or casual decisions I made daily, like taking the kids to the zoo instead of an art museum. It's about exposure too. I do not hail from an academic or artistically inclined family. As a child, I never visited an art museum or a theatre or the ballet.

When I take stock of my life, I am thankful. I have experienced romantic love, deep friendships, and motherhood. I've obtained academic goals and enjoyed career success. I can also field strip an M16 military assault rifle and reassemble it in record time. I'm witty, intelligent, attractive, and reasonably healthy. From the national perspective, I'm living the American dream. On the global perspective, I'm a freaking rock star. Honestly, I have nothing to complain about – and yet, here is *La Magdalena* breaking my heart.

Although romantically patriotic, I often question my choice to serve in the military. What if I had gone off to college instead? In 1980s rural Oregon, high school guidance counselors didn't waste time on girls like me, farm kids with uneducated parents or insufficient funds. I'm sure my last name drifted across desks. It was a well-known name. My parents and grandparents attended the same school in a town where family name seals fate.

Military recruiters feed on depressed towns like mine, places where money and dreams are tight. It's always like that, back then and now. The defense of a nation is proxied on the backs of the lesser of us. Kids of affluence go off to college and study beautiful things like the arts, and the broke kids hit the factories and mills or take up arms.

I remember when my high school offered the *Armed Forces Vocational Aptitude Battery* or ASVAB, proctored by servicemen. I didn't plan to take the test, but I was a bird attracted to shiny objects. I admired the uniforms and the recruiters wearing them. Sparkly insignias, badges, and awards lured me in. Hypnotized. To me, the men were exotic and refined, like nothing I'd seen before. With test booklet and *No. 2* pencils in hand, I stumbled into action, irreversible change, a wormhole out.

A month later, Sergeant Kenny Walker called wanting to talk about test scores. I agreed to meet for lunch in the school cafeteria. We sat across a small table in the corner. I tried appearing aloof, but my insides gushed, and my heart pounded from the personal attention and a lunch date with a real-life soldier. "So, what's all this crap mean?" I tried to sound cool.

"Young lady, this *crap* means you can be a military policewoman in the United States Army. You can be all you can be!"

He had me at, *"You can be."*

The memory of Sergeant Walker makes me sick. Recalling his name brings bile to the back of my throat. My head whirls and the painting rocks back and forth. I stumble away from my beautiful *La Magdalena* and find a pew. Sweat beads on my upper lip, but my body shivers. I bow my head to pray, but I can't close my eyes. I'm afraid of the dark. I'm afraid of having a flashback. And so, I stare down at my Mary Jane clogs and mumble my prayer.

I am supposed to pray for guidance in the art of forgiveness. *It is only through forgiveness, we find true peace* – or at least this is the mantra espoused by the hippy-dippy and my last therapist. But I don't buy it. Evil motherfuckers like Walker and Price don't deserve clemency, at least not from me, not yet. Besides, why I am I the one stuck with the impossible labor of forgiving? I know my part of the equation and where I went wrong. I blame an insatiable need for attention and approval, combined with blind trust for authority and a naïve belief in human kindness. But I was just a stupid kid. And now, I've held the pain and shame for thirty years. I've flashed in hot rage over smells, names, and drink orders. I can't forget Walker and Price, but I'll make a bet I never cross their minds.

I pray for freedom. I want to be free from the shame and free from the fear of boogiemen lurking in the shadows. What I want is to forget, to erase my past, or at least come to terms with it sans flashbacks, hot rage, and cold sweats. I walk for relief, and when I reach the *Cruz De Ferro,* I will dump Sergeant Walker and Sergeant Price as I leave my white rock in the pile of stones beneath the iron cross. I will drop them just as thousands of peregrinos before me have dropped their burdens in preparation for the clean slates they will receive in Santiago de Compostela. This is what I really want – *Tabula Rasa.* I walk to clean the slate.

I exit the cathedral three hours after entering. I planned to be only an hour, but I lost track of time. The art and architecture got the best of me. I scan the plaza for Jana. In my note, I suggested we meet in the plaza at 1900, but I don't see her. However, I do spy Bernard, the grumpy German I met in Logroño. His shock of white hair sticks up in tufts like baby bird feathers, and his overly tanned face draws down at the corners of his mouth. He appears angry and uninviting. This is probably why I always see him sitting alone.

I wave to him, but he doesn't return the salutation. Nor does he give me the head-nod. Undaunted, I cross the plaza and plop down at his table. "Buen Camino, Bernard." He's playing hard to get, pretending he doesn't remember me from five nights ago. I jog his memory. "Oh, come on, Bernard. We hung out in Logroño…"

"Where are your children?"

"Oh, those weren't my actual kids. They were Camino kids – siblings who adopted me."

"And they gave you back? Un-adopted you?"

"Yes, it seems so."

Bernard drinks his beer, and I enjoy a sangría. We watch zombie-like peregrinos stagger across the plaza in search of beds for the night. "Do you stay in the albergues, Bernard?"

"Never. Why would I?"

"It's part of the process. Besides, it can be fun."

"Fun? There is nothing fun about pretending to be poor."

"I suppose you're right." And I know he is right because there was nothing fun about last night. "But isn't it hard to meet people?" I press on.

"Unfortunately, not." He is referring to my intrusion, but as if on cue, Mimi-the-Barbie-girl spots us from the cathedral steps. She is waving and jumping and calling out to us like we are her long-lost pals. Her blond hair is pulled into a side ponytail that leaps and shimmies with a life of its own.

"You see what I mean?" says Bernard. I nod and brace myself for the onslaught that is Mimi. She is coming in hot and sweaty and ready for hugs. Denise-the-mime-lover and Happy-the-Jesuit trail behind, crossing the plaza without hoopla. I receive Mimi with open arms, and she all but knocks me to the pavement. Bernard puts up a passive resistance by staying in his seat and holding fast to his beer. She hugs him anyway, draping her arms around his shoulders, pressing her sweaty breasts into the back of his neck, and planting a kiss on his flaccid cheek. Bernard tries to remain stoic but fails as a blush spreads across his face and creeps down his neck. His eyes narrow and he grimaces a partial smile, like a baby negotiating a bubble of gas.

I wait for Jana with the old Logroño gang. Eventually, we give up and start another tapas crawl. The streets fill with hungry pilgrims, tourists, and locals. It's an eclectic crowd. Mimi strips down to a hot pink sports bra to pair with her pleated, black hiking skirt. Conveniently, her knee-high socks match her bra perfectly. She looks more like a cheerleader than a peregrina. Her blond locks, newly released from the ponytail, cascade across her bare shoulders. No matter what bar threshold we darken, Mimi is always offered a table. She is extremely popular with male bartenders and locals alike.

Mimi is bright and bubbly, but she is hard to engage in conversation. Her responses are scripted, and her body language contrived. When I speak, she widens her eyes, twirls a strand of hair, and nods appreciatively. She uses several key phrases: "Oh my God!" and "How magical!" and "So spiritual!" Pre-peregrination, I would find her annoying. But now, her behavior is so over the top. I can't take her seriously enough to become annoyed. Bernard tries to ignore Mimi, but he can't take his eyes off her. She leans forward to speak and dumps a set of perfectly sculpted breasts on the table between us.

Denise and Happy speak intimately together, while Bernard and I entertain Mimi or vice-versa. I catch snippets from Denise and Happy's conversation. Denise waxes on over the break up with her mime lover. Happy nods sympathetically. I want Mimi to shut up so I can hear the details. But that is not going to happen. Instead, I settle for bits and pieces. It's impolite to eavesdrop, but I cannot resist.

It is after midnight before I head back to the room. Jana is still asleep with the towel wrapped around her head. Her glass of wine is untouched on the bedside-table along with my unread note. I fill the tub and enjoy another hot bath before tucking in for the night.

In the morning, Jana and I part ways. She hops a bus, fast-forwarding a hundred kilometers to Terradillos de los Templarios, while I hang back for another day in Burgos. I am sad to see her go, but I need one more day to relax and enjoy the city. She wants to reconnect with friends she met on the first day in St. Jean Pied de Port. The reset is mutual. We need what we need. Jana hugs me and says, "Don't let the road get you down, Cody."

Unlike medieval pilgrims, goodbyes don't have to be forever. Jana and I secured our friendship via social media. She will post bits of her journey, and I will post mine. I'll keep up with her progress as I've kept up with Gretchen's.

Technology is a gamechanger in modern peregrination. Everything is more accessible, but I wonder at what cost? We are distracted and taken out of the pilgrim scene by the same device making it easier to get here – The *smartphone*.

On the cobblestone streets of Burgos, Mimi bobs up and down in front of me. She is wearing earbuds and dancing to a beat only she can hear. Oblivious to the sound of church bells in the square and oblivious to the fact she is being followed, Mimi ducks into a farmacia. Like a creeper, I trail in behind her. She is too busy testing tinted sunscreen and lip glosses to notice me.

The pharmacist examines my blisters and recommends *Compeed* patches. She instructs me to apply the plasters and leave them alone until they fall off. I've now moved from the *let-it-breath* mindset to the *cover-it-and-forget-it* approach. After I make my purchase and patch up my feet, I reach over and gently tug an earbud from Mimi's ear. "Hey, wanna do lunch?"

"Oh! My God! Like, you totally scared the crap out of me!" She applies another coat of gloss directly to her lips from the sample tube applicator. I cringe in utter germaphobia.

"Hey, girlfriend." She creates a duckbill with lips lacquered in the shade of Barbie's dream home. "What do you think of this color?"

"Wow!" I tease. "So magical!"

Mimi and I enjoy lunch at an outdoor café near the cathedral square. I'm plowing into a plate of buttery sea scallops when I hear the ding-ding of bicycle bells. I glance up to see the mother and daughter duo from Jersey straddling two mountain bikes. "How's the food," asks the Jersey mom.

"Excellent. You would love it." She sniffs and rolls her eyes. They stand in front of us for an awkward moment before I pose the obvious question, the question they want me to ask. "Hey, where did you guys get the awesome bikes?"

"We rented them," chimes Jersey daughter.

"Yes. We rented these," confirms the mother, "to ride through the boring *Meseta* and on to León." She is pleased with herself. "We'll cut our time in half!"

"Oh-My-God," squeals Mimi. "You girls are geniuses! That's such an amazing idea! You're such an inspiration!" The mother and daughter nod proudly.

After lunch, I follow Mimi through a maze of streets to the bike store. I explain my vertigo and the fact I haven't ridden a bicycle for at least ten years. "Let's just see," she urges. I admit I'm curious to experiment. My balance is terrible, and I assumed bicycling, horseback riding and skating were things of the past.

Once we find the bike store, Mimi turns on her charm. She bends all the way over in mock inspection of bike pedals to expose the booty-shorts beneath the pleats of her hiking skirt. It works. The store manager is a drooling mess of putty in her hands. He loans us the bikes, free of charge for an hour, so she can see "if her poor, old, girlfriend can still ride." Something about the power of *free* makes her description of me more palatable.

I make a few cautious circles around a shopping plaza and test out the brakes. There is a lot to remember. I follow Mimi as she expertly winds through narrow streets and uses all the correct hand signals. She's a natural, but I'm warming up and starting to enjoy myself. She limits our test ride to the old part of town and doesn't expose me to busy traffic. I'm not ready for that yet. We ride around for about twenty minutes before working our way back to the bike shop. I try a dismount but learn the hard way the bike is too tall for me and my short legs.

The manager promises me a lady's bike in the morning, a complimentary gel seat, and a sweet discount. Before I talk myself out of it, I sign a rental contract for 0900 tomorrow morning. This is so out of my comfort zone, but I'm thrilled to face a new adventure and overcome an old fear of what I thought was a nonnegotiable obstacle.

Peregrinos complete the Camino on foot, bicycle, or horseback. As a Camino virgin, I dismissed bikes and horses. I would walk, not ride or bike. I would be *a true peregrina* and carry my pack and suffer each mile. After all, a pilgrimage is not a vacation. It makes me smile to think about my pre-Camino self. That was when I suffered *Camino Purist Syndrome* or CPS.

Thankfully, my affliction with CPS was fleeting. I have Jana to thank for helping me examine the limitations and needless hardship of my narrow mind. I'm relieved she taught me to use the baggage transport services, and how she sided with the obstinate nun who stuffed us in a cab back in Santo Domingo. Once the taxi cab cherry was popped, I lightened up, and my emotional and physical pilgrimage has been all the better for it.

All this fuss about being an authentic peregrino is nonsense. Like it or not, I am a tourist as much as I am a peregrina. We are all posers in our hi-tech, ultralight, sweat wicking, quick drying, sun shielding, overpriced, made in China, synthetic shirts and hiking trousers. My fall from the Camino purist pedestal has been a humbling but welcome transformation. I've wasted too much energy judging myself and others, and I've operated in constant survival mode, doing whatever possible to keep myself physically in the game. After a night of peaceful sleep and two hot baths, I have no worries about the physical portion of the Camino. My next hurdle is to build up the mental clarity and stamina to tackle my inner journey.

I invite Mimi to crash the night with me so we can make our way over to the bike store together in the morning. She takes the spare bed once occupied by Jana. She doesn't mind the secondhand sheets, and I don't apologize. After all, she's the girl who smears on layers of tester lip-gloss directly from the applicator.

Burgos to Castrojeriz

Our ride out of the city goes as planned, except for the manager's promise to find me a lady's bike. I must make do with man's green and black Schwinn mountain bike at least four inches too tall. The seat is dropped as far as it goes, but the gel cushion adds another half-inch. There is absolutely no way to execute a graceful dismount, but I will survive.

Our backpacks are strapped to the back of our bikes by a cobweb of bungee cords. The extra weight makes maintaining balance a little more difficult, but I quickly adapt. We contemplated a backpack forwarding service, but we have no idea how far we will be able to ride today. As a novice, I'm thinking conservative, like thirty to forty kilometers. Mimi believes we can do sixty. We could go further and faster without these awkward bundles weighing us down, but I'm not willing to risk sending my Agnus further than my legs might take me today. Besides, I would miss her too much.

Regardless of the extra weight, I'm so excited to be whizzing down the smooth blacktop path meandering through a beautiful park and leading me out of the city. Mimi rides at a safe distance behind me, so she can watch how I'm doing and supply me with ongoing coaching and commentary. I learned something new about her last night. She is a *CrossFit* coach. This explains her constant encouragement and perky demeanor.

I soar like a cuckoo bird down the trail and speed past the walking peregrinos. I call out a chipper, "Buen Camino!" But I seldom hear replies. I can't believe how fast I am going. I'm flying, and it is so liberating!

Once I run out of smooth pavement, I realize I'm not prepared to comfortably negotiate rough terrain. Each rock, pothole, and bump hit me somewhere very deep in my bottom half. I can't precisely pinpoint the anatomical location of the pain. It is new and unexpected and takes my breath away.

Based on the seat shape and where I bear my weight, I assumed bike riding would hurt my lady parts, but that area isn't painful – or at least not yet. I was excited about the complimentary gel seat, but I'm not sure it's doing any good. This is probably why it was complimentary. What I should have purchased was padded riding pants designed to handle a bike seat. I considered buying a pair, but the shorts were too expensive for three or four days of wear. I would be reluctant to toss them once back on foot.

Mimi and I tackle the first 10K without taking a breather. My butt, or whatever this is, aches. However, the resting of my knees and feet feels brilliant. It should take about four days to reach León if we keep up the current pace. Initially, I calculated nine days on foot. The bikes will more than cut our time in half, all while giving my blisters friction-free days to heal. Perhaps this is one of the better decisions I've made, and I owe it to the Jersey duo and to Mimi's enthusiastic encouragement.

The sun is hot on my back, and there isn't any shade. Our bike helmets are ventilated, but wearing one is a buzz kill. I can only imagine how lovely it would feel to have the wind whipping through my hair. As a kid, I never wore a bike helmet. None of us did.

At least I'm on a bike and have some air circulating around my body. The walkers look miserable in the morning sun. It's expected to get hotter this afternoon. I've already veered around two groups of ladies slathering on sunscreen in the middle of the path.

It's funny how perspectives change. When I was on foot, the bicyclists annoyed the crap out of me as they whizzed by or rang bells, signaling me to get out of the way. Now that the shoe is on a different pedal, I realize how dicey dodging potholes and peregrinos can be. At times, it's downright death-defying. The bell helps, but it's not foolproof. I give plenty of warning, ringing my little bell two times at least twenty meters out and then again at ten. My goal is to avoid startling the walkers, but sometimes I can't help it. Earbuds pose a big problem. Peregrinos tune into music and tune out of their surroundings. I don't use earbuds because I like the sound of birds chirping and the trail crunching beneath my feet. Besides, I'm afraid of being crept up on or ran over. Hypervigilance won't allow me to sacrifice one my senses.

Some peregrinos walk shoulder to shoulder, three or four abreast, blocking the entire path. Typically, the group parts down the middle and moves to each side of the road to let me pass, but there is always one pilgrim consumed by indecision.

Despite the complications involved in responsible cycling, I'm satisfied with our pace. We will make it through the Meseta in no time. "Biking is so stinking easy!" I yell to Mimi as she rides up beside me.

"You're doing great! Super inspirational!" She feeds my ego and her need to coach. "Let's make a pitstop ahead. We need to rest up for the monstrous hill!"

Hill? There are no hills on the Meseta. Are there? I thought it was flat and dull. This is the reason many peregrinos hop a bus, bike through, or skip it entirely by starting in León. In last night's anticipation, I forgot to study my Brierly guide. Pouring over the guidebook and burning each village and elevation peak into memory is my nightly ritual.

Heeding Mimi's advice, I pull into Tardajos and find the perfect stopping place. I try a dismount but clumsily rack myself on the crossbar. This is supposed to be more painful for men, but I'm doing all I can to not cry out and clutch my wounded lady parts.

We park our bikes against the rock wall of an old flour mill. The mill is now an albergue and a bar. The inside is fresh and dark and inviting. We find seats in the back and lean against the cold stone. A homemade gazpacho served cold and without spoons hits the spot. I never think of soup as a refreshment, but it's the perfect pick-me-up.

It's tough to leave the shadows of the albergue and return to the open sunshine. The dusty red path leading to our first hill climb sends up wavy vapors of uninviting heat. I let out a long sigh, and Mimi fires up the CrossFit mantra. "You got this girl! No pain, no gain..." Ugh. She is such a cheerleader, but I do appreciate her optimism.

The incline into *Rabé de las Calzadas* is slight but steady. My quadriceps tighten and threaten to cramp. I try standing up to take the strain off my thighs, but I don't have that kind of balancing skills, at least not yet. I used to stand and pedal when I was a kid; perhaps, all I need is practice. I alternate from sitting to standing until I'm able to complete a few pedal rotations at a time. This is a useful way to relieve my thighs, but it exacerbates the ass pain. The pain in my ass, or wherever this is coming from, radiates up through my guts whenever I lift from the seat. It's a punch to the stomach or uterus or some mystery organ I didn't know I owned.

We leave the asphalt again for the rocky path up *Alto Meseta*. It's only a 100-meter gain in elevation, taking us from about 850 to 950 meters, but it happens in less than two kilometers. Mimi grinds slowly by. She is red-faced and out of breath. When I need it most, she offers no coaching tips or words of encouragement. I watch her strong legs push harder up the hill and lengthen the distance between us.

My pace is at a near standstill. Peregrinos I whizzed by this morning are now passing me on foot! It's embarrassing. The taste of crow makes me choke. I stand and shift all my weight from pedal to pedal, but it is no use. I'm moving so slow I can no longer maintain balance. I attempt a pain-free dismount, but it's not in the cards. The bike falls on top of me, and I bust open my right knee again.

Two ladies on foot help upright me and the stupid bike. One lady tends to my sagging backpack and cobweb of bungees. The other lady fusses over my knee. I overexplain the situation that I'm usually a walking peregrina. I blame Mimi for the dumb idea of renting bikes. But they aren't judging, and they're not even curious.

Mimi waits halfway up the hill. Together, we push our bikes to the plateau of *Alto* Meseta. We have officially entered the Meseta. Despite my grumpiness, I can't help but enjoy the windswept and wide-open landscape. The Meseta is hot and dry. Beyond the scrubby sagebrush and stubbles of mowed wheat, it lacks vegetation. But the Meseta is not without beauty. We ride the four-kilometer path across the rough, plateau table. The ride is not what I imagined while I pushed my bike uphill. I thought once we reached the top, it would be smooth and easy going, but the path is deeply rutted with tire tracks and pocked with jagged rocks. It demands all my attention. My view is limited to a few feet in front of my tire.

The ride down from the plateau is worse than our climb. Evidently, I've reached the age where I prefer the safety of uphill scrambles to the ease of downhill sashays. The loose rocks are treacherous and require cycling finesse. We lack the skills to survive and must get off and walk again. A cycling team of eleven Italians shoots passed, pumping fists in the air and hollering, Buen Camino!" We halfheartedly respond, keeping both hands firmly on our handlebars as we gingerly ease the bikes downhill.

Mimi's bike gets away from her and takes the skin off her shin along with it. The bike careens down the hill before toppling over and sliding another few meters. Fortunately, no pedestrians were in its path.

The grippy spikes of the left pedal acted like a cheese grater on Mimi's shin. The injury is only a surface wound, a long and jagged scratch down a perfectly tanned and cleanshaven leg. But it bleeds like crazy, and I'm sure it stings.

Tears stream down Mimi's cheeks. She is hopping up and down and waving the backs of her spread hands at chest level. This is what is referred to as *white-lady crying*, and she looks great doing it. It's as if she is trying to dry her tears and nails at the same time. I would be swearing and throwing rocks and kicking up dirt. But she quietly hops on her uninjured leg and shakes her hands and doesn't utter a blue word. How ladylike. I am impressed.

I tend to Mimi's scrape and to her bruised pride. I hug her until she stops hopping, and then I force her to sit down on a boulder. She winces as I dump water across her raw shin. And now it's me, coaching and encouraging my young friend. While neither of us is enthused about the ride, the scrape has humbled her to a dangerous level.

She rebounds after lunch, and we find ourselves in a déjà vu. We push our bikes up another steep hill, ride precariously across another rocky plateau, and then gingerly pick our way down loose gravel and tumbling stones. Pushing our bikes up and down and across two plateaus has eaten up the time we gained whizzing out of Burgos.

Before we left Burgos, I worried I'd be a burden to Mimi. She is two decades younger, much fitter, bikes all the time, and volunteers as a CrossFit coach. Her physical resume is daunting, to say the least, but the path through the Meseta is a great equalizer. The ride is more laborious than Mimi predicted, and her scraped leg is proving to be more than she can stand. The Camino is more of a mental journey than a physical one. I know we won't die out here. We will make it to an albergue tonight and shower and eat and drink an entire bottle of wine together. I know we will survive. I know, but Mimi does not.

She responds well to self-deprecating humor, and so I give it my best. I try to describe where exactly the bicycle seat hurts me. The pain is intense but impossible to pinpoint. Before long, she is laughing and joining in. "Is it a pain in the pancreas?" She suggests.

"No. No! It's more like an ovarian obstruction."

"How about a kick to the prostate?" Mimi raises her eyebrows.

"But Honey, we don't have prostates."

"Huh?" She is serious. "Of course, I do! That's where prostate cancer comes from!"

I spend the next hour convincing my silly girlfriend that in no way, shape or form does she own a prostate. She is adamant, and this makes us laugh hysterically. Despite the heat and our sore asses and my bleeding knee and Mimi's skinned shin, we are feeling lucky. Our newly found vigor is a blessing of epic proportion. We laugh and joke about our hard luck because it's better than crying. There is nothing we can do except keep riding. We can't quit or call a cab. We are stuck in the middle of the Meseta in the afternoon sun, and all we have is each other. It is perfect, and I wouldn't want it any other way. It's the kind of *suck* I haven't felt since my military days. There is something addicting and bonding about suffering together. Nothing builds comradery like a hardship.

To pass the time, I try to tell Mimi a story about my early days in Army boot camp, and how the extreme adversity bonded me with girls who remain in my memory forever. Mimi interjects comments, "Oh, wow! I totally know what you mean. One time at cheerleading camp…" Or she makes a cross fit reference. I know she's only trying to participate, but I fall quiet and revisit my sisters in arms.

We stop for the night in Castrojeriz. I am totally wrecked and cannot bear bunk beds or communal toilets or snoring peregrinos. I spring for a caravan cabin at a remote campground filled with pull-behind trailers, campers, and motorhomes. The campsite is not occupied by fellow peregrinos; instead, it is filled with tourists. It's odd to be so far removed from our kind.

Our cabin is adorable and provides more amenities than Mimi or I need. We have two bedrooms, a kitchen, sofa, television, and all the hot water we can use. Neither of us has the energy to ride back into town to gather dinner supplies. Instead, we abandon our cabin kitchen and make our way to the campground's snack bar. But once there, I cannot stomach any of the menu options. The pain in my seat radiates up through my guts. There is no way I can sit down and eat. I buy a bottle of pop and a bag of chips and head back to the cabin.

Castrojeriz to Villarmentero de Campos

In the morning, I have the same problem. I cannot eat. The sight of food makes me nauseous. I nurse another soda before getting back on the road. With nothing in my stomach, my energy lags. If I didn't know better, I would swear I was pregnant. This is how I remember morning sickness some nineteen years ago when I was pregnant with Jaden.

Unfortunately, we have another hill to climb. My legs are lead, and I find myself pushing the stupid bike up, only to ride less than a kilometer across the table, before easing the bike back down the hill. This is not the motivating start we need. Within the first hour of our day, we are both deflated. The good news is the rest of the way to León is relatively flat. We have completed our final Meseta plateau. The rest should be easy. Right?

Mimi and I don't speak to each other or anyone for the next 20K. Spirits are low, and heads are hung. I focus a couple meters ahead of my front tire. I watch rocks and ruts and potholes. Pedaling is easier, but the wind chaps my face, and the sun beats down on my throbbing head. There is no joy in today's pilgrimage. And I am not having fun.

Outside of *Frómista* and consumed in my own misery, I don't notice the sheep until I ride straight through the middle of a huge flock. I slam on my brakes and nearly fly over the handlebars. In a bailing dismount to protect my private parts, I leap from the bike and let it crash into a pile of sheep. Unharmed, the sheep circle around me. They are curious but cautious.

Mimi flies up the path behind me. Her head is down. Her earbuds are in, and she's listening to music. I holler out. She glances up just in time to scream and leap from her bike. She lands with a solid thud on a patch of grass formally occupied by sheep. Her runaway bike also crashes into the flock. The sheep shake off the second intrusion and continue grazing.

I rush over and help her to her feet, and then laugh at the sheep shit smeared all over her right hip. "Hey, Speed Racer! That was a seriously close call."

"What the fuck!" screams Mimi. "Where did they all come from?"

We scan the flock and nearby bridge until we spot a shepherd dressed in blue coveralls. He is perched on a bridge abutment, shaking his head and enjoying the scene. At his feet, two shaggy herding dogs sleep peacefully. The dogs are unfazed by our rude intrusion. I call out an apology. He waves his hand and laughs. Apparently, he is accustomed to crazy ladies on bikes trying to wipe out his herd.

We gather our bikes and what is left of our nerves and walk toward the bridge. I hold up my phone and ask permission to take a photo. The shepherd indulges me by reclining slightly and plastering a beautiful smile on his weathered face. His dark blue eyes sparkle for attention. I snap his picture and point out to Mimi how perfectly his eyes match to his coveralls.

We stop for lunch in *Frómista*, but I'm still unable to eat. We are only 25K in, and I am done for the day. I want to quit, but Mimi insists we go further. She is right. We didn't rent bikes to ride the same distance we could easily have walked. Biking was supposed to be so much fun, but it sucks. It totally sucks.

Except for the sheep incident, my day's view is tedious and narrow. I don't have the skill or self-confidence to look up and enjoy the experience. To make matters worse, I'm not making new friends or engaging in peregrino small-talk. The bike creates a bubble separating me from the world. It works just like my car does for me in real life.

I sip a can of *zitrone*-flavored *Aquarius*, Spain's answer to lemon Gatorade. Mimi engages in flirty chitchat with two American cyclists. Opting to eavesdrop instead, I don't join the conversation. The men boast of 100K days with a daily minimum of 75K. With only two weeks of vacation from their stressful jobs, the guys plan to knock out the ride in ten days and take another two days to ride out to Finisterre before flying home from Santiago. Mimi is overly impressed, but I'm on the fence. While I am envious of their vigor, I don't envy a stressful job with fourteen days of freedom per year. I don't want to *knock out* the Camino. Even so, I can't help feeling impressed. I haven't completely lost my competitive spirit, but I am learning to tone it down. And for the most part, I'm relieved.

About 10K post-pitstop, a migraine blooms. It's probably caused by the lack of food or too much time in the hot sun. The telltale spots in my vision, or migraine *aura*, indicate I'm in for a doozy. With or without Mimi, I must find a place to crash immediately.

I ride up to a small chapel in Revenga De Campos and perform another painful dismount. My private parts suffer the crossbar, and I want to swear. Two nuns dressed in baby blue and gray sit at a picnic table beneath the only shade. The sisters are within earshot, so I keep obscenities to myself and suffer in silence. I duck inside the empty church and find a pew. It is dark and refreshing and perfect for migraine recovery. I slip a *rizatriptan* tablet under my tongue. It's a minty-flavored meltaway that usually does the trick in fifteen minutes, but it comes at a price. I'll be too drowsy to safely continue. I'm most certainly done for the day.

Mimi plops beside me and searches her guidebook for a place to stay. She finds something two kilometers ahead. There is nothing closer. We wait in the sanctuary of the church for the tablet to take effect. The timing must be just right, so we can travel in that medicated sweet spot between relief and zonked out.

With sunglasses on and eyes half-shut, we make it to *Casona Dona Petra*. Mimi takes over, handles everything, and tucks me into bed. I'm thankful for her help. One of my significant anxieties before coming to Spain was figuring out how I would survive a migraine. I have a crash-kit packed for such emergencies. The kit includes meds, a black sleeping mask, a tincture of lavender oil, and a bug net. I am prepared to face a migraine alone and in the middle of a bug-infested forest, but I'm thankful to be here instead with Mimi taking care of me.

Mimi heads downstairs to lock our bikes in the pension's barn for safekeeping. I beg her to leave mine parked in the street with a sign saying, *Gratis* or free, but she doesn't take me seriously.

Villarmentero to Sahagun

We pedal out of Villarmentero feeling rested but apprehensive. The icepick stabbing in my forehead subsided, but I still have the aura. I need to take it easy today.

We spend another morning staring at the dirt path in front of us and deeply regretting the rentals of these damn bikes. The pain in my ass is excruciating, and I'm still too nauseous to eat. We stop several times to rest and drink *Aquarius*. I can't stomach food, but I try to keep up my electrolytes. At each stop, I leave the bike unlocked, hoping somebody will come along and steal it. But no such luck. Rural Spaniards are too honest for my liking.

Thankfully, the ride is relatively flat with the final stretch downhill. So, we make it to Sahagun, our intended stopping place, well before expected. I should be happy, but I'm crabby and ready to bite Mimi's head off at the littlest of things. I'm thankful for a migraine-free ride, but I am not having any fun, and I am not behaving like a proper peregrina. The love and light I promised to shine are all but lost. Something needs to change and fast. I need an emotional reset.

We walk our bikes through town, shopping for a place to stop for the night. Sahagun is in various stages of decay. Piles of rubble and crumbling facades dot the cityscape. We veer around a white van blocking the sidewalk, while the driver delivers backpacks to an albergue. I'm almost around the delivery-van before it registers. There is a bike rack on the back of the vehicle! It's as if the skies have parted, and God plopped the van in my path. I take it as a sign of divine intervention.

I'm far too excited and motivated to explain the plan to Mimi. When the lady driver emerges from the albergue, I nearly tackle her. I expect my request to sound absurd, but she nods her head and smiles at me knowingly. We negotiate a price. I almost weep with joy as she straps our bikes to the van and jots down the delivery address in León. To make the moment brighter, Mimi jumps in the passenger seat. She claims to be uncomfortable trusting the rental bike with the driver, but she is probably just sick of my shit. And I can't blame her because I'm totally sick of my own shit.

Mimi has ditched me. She has performed her own reset, and I am thrilled. Gone is Camino-Barbie along with my stupid mountain bike! I don't feel bad, although I probably should. I had only intended to get rid of my bike, but Mimi wasted no time unloading hers. She also stuck me with the entire transport bill, but I don't mind. I would have paid double to rid myself of that pain in the ass. And I do mean the bike, not Mimi.

The good news is my feet are healed. Only dried-out patches of skin and thick callous remain. The knee oozes a bit of blood but doesn't look infected. My feet fall softly on the sidewalk, and my pack and spirits are surprisingly light.

I walk almost out of town before seeking refuge in *Convento Madres Benedictinas.* An elderly woman collects ten euros for an evening meal and a bed and shows me to my dorm. It is a six-bunk dorm with a private bathroom, but I'm the only occupant. It feels odd to be all alone. I haven't spent a night by myself since meeting up with Krystal, the German girl, way back in Puente La Reina.

I take a long shower followed by a short nap. I planned to hang out in bed until dinner, but the austereness of my lonely room gets the best of me. I feel the familiar old prickle of anxiety, but I'm not going to let it win. I dress in my best, the same old green dress and rubber clogs, and head out to explore the town until it's time to take in mass.

Although I'm not in the mood to walk, I meander off the beaten path and find myself in a neighborhood plaza occupied with kids kicking soccer balls and riding skateboards and by old men playing dominoes. It's perfect. I claim a table beneath an umbrella and settle down to enjoy a refreshing Tinto-Verano and a taste of local culture.

Sahagun to Calzadilla de los Hermanillos

I walk out of Sahagun in the early morning. Last night was a peculiar night, one I'm sure will remain in my memory for some time. I fell apart during the church service. The strength and beauty carried in the voices of the nuns singing evening vespers were too much to handle. I sat in my lonely pew, in a poorly attended mass, and cried my eyes out. I wasn't necessarily sad, but something in their voices soaked into my skin and eventually broke my heart. I cried for everything. I cried for myself, my kids, my marriage, the world. And I cried about things I have not thought about in years.

When I was seven, my big brother died. It was so long ago, but a force stirred the memory last night. I closed my eyes and tried to imagine him hunched over his plastic airplane parts. He was always building models. I inhaled to catch a huff of model glue but came up empty. I can't recall much about my brother, but I do remember the day I learned he had died. There was no accident, no twisted metal of a car crash, or a fall from a tree. There had been no known illness, and no surgical scars to follow as a roadmap. There was an influenza misdiagnosis on one day and death, itself, ten days later. A few months passed, and I learned a new vocabulary word, *leukemia.*

I don't know why memories of my deceased brother are stirring, and I don't know what to do about this melancholic mood. It's cathartic to revisit old memories, but I can't let myself dwell in this state. It's not good for me to hang out here for too long. It's hard to pinpoint the exact emotion or mix of emotions I'm experiencing. It isn't sadness, but something close – maybe despair? I feel uneasy and a little out-of-body. I'm trying to make sense of an old puzzle, but time has stolen most of the pieces. I need a distraction, but I have overtaken two separate groups of pilgrims and tried to strike up conversations. I have no luck. I am the leperperegrina no one wants to befriend. It must be the gray cloud over my head.

After a short break in Calzada de Coto, where I continue to strike out meeting new companions, I resign to go it alone until I've sorted out the mess in my head. I take up the remote earth track cutting through scrub brush and barren fields toward Calzadilla de los Hermanillos. I don't know the significance of my intended stop for the night, but I do know the name translates to *Road of the Little Brothers*. The name is fitting, given my preoccupation with my own brother today. I like the visual the name conjures in my mind, a town gone wild with overall-clad little boys riding bicycles and scooters and playing ball in the courtyard. Despite the visual, I assume the little brothers in question have more to do with a religious order of monks and less to do with my own experiences with brothers.

I stop at a peregrino fountain to rest and replace my warm water with fresh. A young American woman sits on the bench. I safely assume she is American before I speak to her. She owns a style I've noticed in young, college girls from home – purposefully androgynous. Basically, she resembles a thirteen-year-old boy. Prepubescent and all.

"Hey," I say. "How's life?"

"Hot out here," she says.

"Yup," I nod and go about my business. I need a distraction, but I don't want to sound desperate.

"How far you going?"

"Probably the next town." I've walked only 10K, but I can still feel the ghost of that damn bike seat crammed up my ass. To make matters worse, I've developed some sort of chaff spreading from front to back and everywhere between. And it hurts like hell to pee. I noticed the rawness and itching before riding into Sahagun last night. While I haven't tried to take a gander with a hand mirror, the inflamed outline feels like a full-fledged diaper rash. I tried treating it with Jana's magic *Peregrino Crème*, a gift she tucked into my pack before parting ways in Burgos, but I still I feel it prickle and burn with every step.

"Walk with you?" the young woman asks.

"That'd be lovely." I offer a hand and pull her to her feet.

McKinley is from Vermont, which is cool because I don't know anyone from Vermont, and Vermont is one of a small handful of states I have yet to visit. I ask her questions about her home, partly to fill in the time but also because I'm curious. She isn't helpful.

"You know," she shrugs. "Maple syrup and autumn leaves."

"Right, but you've got Ben & Jerry's Ice cream."

She shrugs again. I quiz her for a while, but tire of her unwillingness toward rhetoric. McKinley isn't a huge distraction. In fact, if it were not for the scuffing of hiking boots and gentle breathing next to me, I'd swear I was walking alone. I want out of my own head today, but she isn't going to deliver me.

Fortunately, I don't have to be in my head for long because we stop at the first café we see. Mik and I belly up to hearty bowls of lamb stew and cold bottles of *cerveza*. The beer is refreshing. And the yummy stew, with huge chunks of lamb and carrots and potatoes, hits the spot. We sponge the bottoms and sides of our soup crocks with torn hunks of baguette, sopping up every drop of the rosemary-herbed stock.

The café is a pension and an albergue too. I'm interested in staying the night, but it is beyond Mik's nightly budget. She is a part-time bartender and full-time student. She saved up her tips for a year to scrape together enough cash for this trip. I understand, so we agree to investigate a donativo albergue on the other side of the village.

After lunch, McKinley lights up a cigarette. I lean back against the stone wall under the covered patio and absorb the earthy coolness. Usually, I throw a fit about secondhand smoke. I find this is true with other reformed smokers. Instead of becoming nonsmokers, we become anti-smokers.

But today, the smell is oddly relaxing. I nod off a little, hanging somewhere between light sleep and deep relaxation, and it feels lovely.

Sooner than I want to be, Mik and I are back on our feet and making our way through the village. I've never been one to nap, but the stew and the beer and the wall proved a perfect combination. I'm anxious to check out the donativo albergue, as this will be my first one. To be safe, I'm keeping my expectations low.

Hermanillos is a sleepy place, and it doesn't take Mik and me long to walk from one end to the next, exploring each little oddity and snapping photos. Yellow spray-painted arrows on the blacktop lead us to a part-time tienda, a grocery store about the size of my walk-in closet at home. Dusty stacks of canned goods and boxed pasta line the back wall. I examine a lone crate of mixed produce and admire the tomatoes and red peppers and five brown mushrooms. Fresh veggies would be tasty tonight.

Behind the register stands a peculiar man. Mik tugs my sleeve, but I don't make eye contact. I know exactly what she is thinking. While it is not kind to say out loud, I cannot help but think of it too. Our grocery store man is a doppelganger to one of Roald Dahl's *Oompa Loompas* from the film adaptation of *Willy Wonka and the Chocolate Factory*. He gives me a silent and slow nod, and I can hear the movie soundtrack in my head. Speaking Spanish, McKinley promises him we will return and shop after we've checked into our albergue. He offers another slow nod and remains silent. McKinley bobs down the street humming the familiar tune.

Our albergue is delightfully small. There are twenty-two bunks split up in cubicles. The hospitalero shows Mik and me to a cube containing four handmade, bunks. I'm thrilled with the setup. Since we are first to arrive, we claim bottom beds and spread out our stuff and plug in our phones. There is a laundry room, co-ed lavatory and shower, and a small kitchen with a few pots and pans. I stuff the donation box with six euro and feel like I have scored a bargain.

Mik calls dibs on the shower, and I head back down the street to the tienda. I've got my heart set on those five brown mushrooms and want to snag them before another hungry peregrino happens upon them. The little man behind the register greets me with another slow and silent nod. I point to the mushrooms, and he plucks them up and places them in a brown paper sack. We carry out the same routine with two tomatoes, two brown eggs, two red apples, a yellow bell pepper, a clove of garlic, and a single stalk of green onion. The whole while, he never utters a word. I help myself to a dusty sleeve of angel hair pasta and a modestly priced bottle of red wine. He pumps out a few draws of olive oil into a paper cup, scoops a handful of olives from a crock filled with brine, and wraps a baguette in brown paper.

This is by far the most fun I've ever had shopping for groceries. I love this guy. When he secures a massive cleaver to slice me a wedge of pearly white cheese, his eyes bulge, and he appears positively maniacal. I can't resist. I pull my phone from my shoulder bag and ask if I might take his photo. He smiles broadly and strikes a pose behind his beautiful wheel of cheese. I know before I snap the picture I'm about to capture one of my most treasured Camino memories.

I pay my bill of five euro including the wine, shake his tiny hand, and thank him from the bottom of my heart. This is one of my most intimate exchanges with a local. He never spoke a word to me, but I left his shop feeling understood and accepted. He is the cure I needed to shake away the blues.

To make my life even better, I stumble upon an overgrown rosemary bush and a leggy clump of oregano sprawling over a garden wall. I quickly secure a few pinches. I rub a branch of rosemary between my palms and huff its aromatic perfume. I am so happy and free right now. There is nothing but light and love – light and love and the promise of pasta for supper.

Calzadilla de los Hermanillos to Mansilla de las Mulas

In the morning, McKinley and I eat leftover spaghetti, and I dump the dregs of the olive oil on two stubs of stale baguette. I wrap a piece of the bread, a boiled egg, and an apple in a brown paper bag and give it to Mik. I put the same in my pack. Mik smiles and says, "Gee, thanks, Mom." I reach over and swat her on the butt. As it turns out, she is only a year younger than my oldest son. In fact, she will celebrate her 25th birthday in two days.

Together, Mik and I walk a picture-perfect stretch of surviving Roman road through fields of wildflowers and scrub. It is hot and dry, and the wind carries our voices away, making idle chitchat too costly on our energy reserves. I'm content with our silence and enjoy the side by side march toward our intended destination, Mansilla de las Mulas. Before we finish today, we will complete a long and lonely 24K along this deserted track.

McKinley is a full head shorter than me. To my left, I can see the top of her head in my peripheral. Her brown hair is matted into dark curls. She told me last night she gave up washing her hair six months ago. She claims it to be a "completely unnecessary task promoted by toxic detergent manufacturers and cosmetic companies pimping their poisonous chemicals." I use her proximity to nonchalantly search for lice, fleas, bed bugs, or clumps of dandruff. I find nothing. The kid looks and smells clean.

We manage to walk 15K before stopping for lunch. We rest at a riverside park, one of only two shady spots along today's path. The oiled bread and boiled egg go down easy, and the apple provides the dose of energy I desperately need to complete the final 10K.

My rash itches and burns. Jana's *Peregrino Crème* provides some relief. I keep the area well lubed, hoping to prevent further damage. I use my unfortunate situation to entertain McKinley. She is in stitches, listening to my dramatized account of riding bikes through the Meseta with Mimi, the Camino-Barbie. It's a little mean-spirited of me. Mimi is a fun girl, but not one I could or should spend an exorbitant amount of time hanging out with, on or off bikes. And Mimi with her beautiful blond hair and perky demeanor is the opposite of my new walking companion, a natty-headed little hipster.

After lunch, Mik smokes her cigarette and finally talks about her life in Vermont. She talks about her bartending job, college courses she loves to hate, her misfit band of roommates, and about the relationship struggles she has with her parents. "My dad is really disappointed in me right now. He hopes I learn something out here, maybe find Jesus." I stay quiet, inviting her to continue. "I'm gay," she blurts. "Did you know?" I give her an exaggerated nod. "Really? Is it that obvious?" She acts bemused like her *trail coming-out party* should surprise me.

"Yes, Mik." I smile. "It's obvious."

She pretends to be offended and punches me in the arm. Then she shoves Agnus off the rock I've propped her up on.

"Hey, now!" I scold her, "Leave your mitts off my Agnus." I jump out of the way to dodge another punch, and she gives chase. We play the shortest game of tag ever. Thoughtfully, she slows down to let me escape.

I'm stuffing the contents back into my upset bag when we hear a distant crack and a roll of thunder. Startled, we scramble from beneath the park trees and out to the open path. Another round of thunder rumbles, and then the sky opens. We are drenched before we can dig out raincoats, but we put them on anyway. I hate how the waterproof vinyl sticks to my wet skin. I pull Mik's hood up and over her brown curls and help with her pack cover. In a moment of clarity, she grabs my hiking poles, folds them down, and tucks them beneath my pack cover. I don't know if a peregrino has ever been struck by lightning, but I don't need to increase my chances by holding out two perfect lightning rods.

This is my first downpour, even though I've carried this rain jacket for three weeks. As it turns out, the jacket is useless. The water comes in sideways, running down our legs, and filling our boots. This is clearly poncho weather. I leave my hood off and allow the rain to soak into my scalp and run down my face and neck. It feels soft and lovely as it washes away the dust of the old Roman road.

Mik and I walk against the sideways rain, and the wind keeps blowing her hood from her curls. Despite our circumstance, we are not unhappy. Instead, the opposite is true. We are giddy schoolchildren linked arm in arm and splashing in every puddle in our path. We laugh and kid each other all the way into Mansilla de las Mulas.

We dive into the first albergue we come across *Jardín del Camino*, a modern place with thirty-two beds divided into two dormitories. The prime attraction of the albergue is the lovely outdoor bar with covered patio. We are some of the first pilgrims to arrive, but we didn't leave Hermanillos early, and we didn't walk all that fast. There is a municipal albergue with seventy-six beds deeper into town. At only five euro a bunk, perhaps that is where everyone else is sleeping tonight. Our albergue is a little expensive, ten euro, but the rate includes a breakfast of coffee and toast with butter and marmalade.

I suppose we didn't need to dive into the first place we found. It's not like we were going to get any wetter if we searched for the cheaper place. But here we are, in an open dorm with a vast, gender-specific bathroom all to ourselves. We claim two bottom bunks adjacent each other, plug in our phones, and hit the showers.

The rain lets up, and Mik and I tour the town. It's livelier than the last, but most of the action is at our albergue's bar. A huge screen shows tonight's game, the *FIFA World Cup* hosted by Brazil. I wonder about Krystal, the German girl I met my first night. Puente La Reina was so many miles and faces ago. I'm surprised I haven't bumped into her yet. I would enjoy seeing her tonight. Back in the Irish pub in

Puente La Reina, she proclaimed Germany would make it through to the final game, and she was right.

Tonight, it is Germany versus Argentina for the championship. Every German walking this section must be sitting at this patio bar. A handful of Brazilians and Spaniards pull for Argentina. The Germans sit stoically, while the grossly outnumbered Brazilians and the Spaniards provide all the drama and emotion the German peregrinos lack. I spot my old buddy, Bernard, and wave him over. He declines. Instead, he sits at a long table filled with his countrymen, drinking his beer, and swallowing bursts of outward emotion.

I never knew I liked the game of soccer until I watched this match. Free flowing beers and bottomless bowls of green olives and *Marcona* almonds help. Marcona is the caviar of the almond world. The nuts are sweeter, rounder, and softer than the California version. I'll never be satisfied with ordinary almonds ever again.

Mansilla de las Mulas to León

I wake with a pounding headache. It's not a migraine, just a plain ole hangover headache from last night's revelry. Excessive beer may be at fault, but I blame the losing team. Never have I heard such a small gathering of men make such a cacophony. It was fun watching their highs and lows, especially late in the game when the Brazilians and Spaniards were joined by the Italians. After Argentina fell, the German peregrinos slipped off to bed. The losers lamented and sang and drank all night long. Mik and I left the party before midnight, but we were privileged enough to hear it until the wee hours of the morning.

McKinley celebrates her twenty-fifth birthday today. As a delightful surprise, her parents booked her a room at the Parador hotel in León. The *Hostal San Marcos* is an impressive 16th-century monastery turned 5-star luxury accommodation. She asks me to join her and explains the hotel is featured in Emilio Estevez's, *The Way*. This is where the main character, *Tom*, treats his companions to a night of luxury. I remember the scenes in the film and cannot resist.

The state-owned Parador chain is exclusive to Spain. Founded by *Alfonso XIII* in 1928, the program promotes tourism in Spain and saves historically and culturally significant buildings, like the San Marcos Monastery, from ruin. The first Parador along El Camino Francés was back in Santo Domingo in the old pilgrim hospital built by its namesake. I eyed the hotel lobby wishing I could stay a while. I love the idea of staying in a Parador. It' a luxurious splurge for a worthy cause.

McKinley takes off toward León, while I rest a few more hours to shake this headache. Later, I'll jump a local bus into the city center and skip the long slog through the industrial wasteland and urban sprawl. Despite my late start, I should arrive at the Parador before Mik. I'll make myself comfy in the hotel bar and await her arrival. I don't feel sorry for hopping the bus. In fact, my guru, John Brierley, recommends doing so in my guidebook. According to Brierley, the route into León is busy and dangerous and unnecessarily wearisome. He doesn't need to tell me twice. The din of cities and busy traffic exasperates my Meniere's disease.

Vertigo is the worst symptom of Meniere's. Or at least it is the most embarrassing. The accompanied staggered gait runs a close second. Fortunately, the gait and the dizziness are intermittent. Sometimes, I hardly notice. Most symptoms come and go, except for tinnitus. I live with constant tinnitus, another classic symptom. Most sufferers describe tinnitus as a ringing sound in the ear. For me, it is a roar. It was the tinnitus that came first, my first symptom in the downward spiral that glued my ass to the sofa.

At first, I liked the sound of tinnitus, a dull roar of phantom waves crashing into nothing, my private ocean, like a seashell affixed to my left ear. I found the phantom charming and appropriate given my line of work in the U.S. Coast Guard. The sea lived in my ear – forever. But the roar took over. It moved me in and out of my job like the tide. It crushed concentration and pushed me beyond the thresholds of stress.

Tinnitus is not rare, affecting seventeen out of every hundred people. Tinnitus is not an illness or a disease; instead, it serves as a symptom of another problem. My tinnitus was like having a hydrophone positioned in the fluids of my inner ear, an underwater warning system that detected severe threats. Debilitating vertigo and migraine headaches lay on the horizon. The hydrophone whispered, "Meniere's disease." But it took two years of tests to rule out benign positional vertigo, vestibular tympanic dysfunction, diabetes, thyroid issues, multiple sclerosis, and an uncommon tumor called an *acoustic schwannoma*. I blamed the disease on stress and waited for symptoms to subside, to roll back out with the tide in the same way the sound first came to me. My inner ocean swelled in the semicircular canal of my left ear. It was only a matter of time before the disease swallowed my career with a roar. A private ocean, a souvenir of sound, leaving just the vibrations of an identity lost before fully found.

The hangover-headache lifts after breakfast, but a midmorning anxiety attack prevents me from crossing the threshold from the street into the bus station. I'm surprised. Typically, this is a transition problem I experience when trying to move from the safety of my car across the threshold of the gym or grocery store. Something similar did happen in Madrid when I was trying to cut across the airport terminal to get to the train station, but I wrote that off to stress from the harried travel day. My last bout was before Estella when I couldn't cross the threshold from the hot sun to a cool albergue. But that was miles ago. I've crossed into bars and restaurants and albergues multiple times per day ever since. This shouldn't happen today. I've been through forests and fields, in and out of villages, up and over mountains, and stranded in the vastness of the Meseta. Entering a bus station should be a cakewalk. But I can't do it! The place is full of old men playing dominos. How dangerous can it be?

I pace around outside of the bus station, visit both little churches in town, light a few candles and say my prayers. Finally, I give up and start walking. What else can I do? Unfortunately, there is no way to let Mik know I'm on my way, or that I'll be very late.

Today's walk into León is short, a bit more than 18K, with a gradual incline before dropping down into the outskirts of the city. Despite the reasonable terrain, I'm not enjoying myself. I'm jogging, trying to make up for lost time. To make matters worse, I need restroom facilities. Thanks to my stand-up-&-pee-device, this isn't typically a problem. I unzip, point, and shoot. But this isn't about potty. I desperately need to make a big job.

The pathway out of Mansilla hugs the major roadway into León. A scrubby skirting of trees and bushes provides an unsatisfactory privacy screen, so dropping my pants here is less than ideal. According to my guidebook, there are a few albergues and cafés ahead, but I'm not sure how far I've gone already. I've been traveling much faster than my usual pace, so perhaps relief is up around the next corner.

My stomach gurgles and churns. I'm paying the price for eating too many olives last night. Tummy pains are unusual for me. I don't often suffer gastro-drama, but one does not forget the feeling of diarrhea-related cramps – and that is precisely what I'm feeling now. I am prepared to poop in the woods. I have all the necessary equipment, but I don't want to use it.

I devised brilliant poop kits. I keep a kit stuffed in the bottom of my shoulder bag for an emergency. I prepared four kits before leaving home, making use of large doggie-poo bags I found in a park and free wet wipes from a fast food restaurant. For zero expense, I created the perfect poop-n-carry system. Each kit contains two red bags, one whole and one split open. Wrapped in the poop bags are three individually-packaged wet wipes. Three wipes may be excessive, but a peregrina never knows what she'll be up against. The idea is to take the red bag that is split open and lay it out flat on the ground. This forms the drop zone. Once the drop is successfully executed onto the zone, use the wet wipes and deposit them in the drop zone. Next, slip the uncut bag over the right hand like a glove. Now, simply draw the corners of the drop zone together and collect in the gloved hand. Gingerly turn the glove inside out and peel it off the hand. Finally, tie the top and walk it out. *Voila!*

Sweat beads across my forehead, but I know it is not from the physical exertion. I am out of time. I am now convinced I will indeed poop outside. It's only a matter of deciding if I will handle it in a purposeful fashion, as I've prepared, or will I be a victim of my own hesitation. I hike another five minutes, scanning for the perfect cubby hole in the shrubbery to shield me from both the road and the trail. I find my mark, drop my pack, duck into the bushes, and prepare the drop zone.

Everything goes according to plan. The system couldn't
be better. All evidence is carefully sealed in the outer red bag
and slipped carefully into an outside pocket of my pack. I'll
dump this dump in the first trash bin I find.

In less than fifteen meters, a break in the shrubbery
exposes a café and a bar. I was so close! I could have made it
to safety. How ridiculous! I make my way toward the café,
drop my baggie in a dumpster, and head in to wash my hands.
I'm disappointed I had to poop in the woods when I was so
close to a proper washroom. On the bright side, my invention
worked like a charm. Like it or not, this is another Camino
success.

Back on the trail, it is easy to see that John Brierley, my
guru, is not wrong. This section is best when bussed through.
There isn't much to gain from the confrontational slog into
the city. There is very little shade. Nothing but a sparse
barrier to protect the peregrina from the rumble of the
freeway. I follow North 601 from Mansilla de las Mulas
without enjoying a moment of quiet or a grand vista. I
sincerely regret my inability to cross the bus station threshold
and save myself from this bullshit. Peace and enlightenment
are not found on freeway overpasses.

Rattled and confused from the road and close to tears, I
finally make it to what should be the Parador. I stand outside
for a long while, thinking it is a museum instead. The façade
is stunning, and I examine the intricate details. I pace the
length of the building twice, trying to figure out where the
actual hotel entrance might be. A cab pulls up to the building,
and I ask the driver. He points to the door in front of me,
and I feel like a dumbass.

Once brave enough to push open the glass door and
move through the entryway, I find myself standing in a
museum that is also a hotel lobby. It's hard to wrap my head
around the fact I will be sleeping in a museum tonight. It is
overwhelming, but I make my way to the front desk. It is
more than evident how disheveled and inappropriately
dressed I am for such an establishment. I want to turn and

run, but a bellman gently reaches out and touches my elbow. "Come, Peregrina." I allow him to steer me to the front desk. He takes Agnus and waits while I check in. I must look utterly shell-shocked from the road.

Mik hasn't left a message for me at the desk, probably because she assumes I am not coming. I do not know her last name, so I play a game of charades with the front desk clerk, trying to describe my McKinley. Finally, I'm able to describe her in Spanish as a dirty, little American girl. Only then does he know exactly who I am talking about.

He calls McKinley's room, and she invites me to bunk with her, but I decline. I'm an emotional wreck. I need privacy and a long, hot bath. I'm given a room right next to her, and we settle for a visit instead of a sleepover.

After my bath, I slip into a bathrobe and out the door to visit Mik. She greets me wearing only her robe and holding a glass of champagne, compliments of her mother and father. We drink a toast to her birth while admiring the boxwood labyrinth in the courtyard below her window. I offer to take Mik out to a birthday dinner in the hotel's renowned dining room, but she has gorged herself on chocolate dipped strawberries, grapes, and fine cheese. She wants to lay low for the evening. We hang out for a little while, but I can tell Mik is needing some down time too. I slip back into my room and slide into another hot tub infused with lavender and grapefruit soaking salts.

The Parador was thoughtful enough to provide a complimentary razor, but I'm still not interested in shaving my legs. It's too much work. Besides, hairy legs beneath a hiking skirt is an unusual combination. It's my little experiment or rebellion or maybe both. I guess it is a bit like Mik's shampooing abstinence but with far less commitment.

I head down to the dining room alone. I'm wearing the only halfway decent thing I have, my green silk peasant dress, but I feel out of place and uncomfortable amongst the other diners. The Maître D is kind enough to tuck me in the far corner of the dining room, but only after I balk at a small table in the center of the room. I am panicky and uneasy tonight. Today's walk through the city has left me frazzled. My body feels fine, but my nerves are shot, and my stomach is in knots.

When my food is delivered, a beautifully roasted rack of lamb with fingerling potatoes, I can't look at it. I try eating a bread roll to soak up the acid in my stomach, but it's no use. My hands are shaking, and I feel as though I might throw up. I motion to the waiter. He responds immediately, making me think I must look as bad as I feel. "Lo siento. Estoy enferma." I apologize for feeling ill. He waves off my apology and offers me a hand. He steadies me to my feet and then does a most remarkable thing. He escorts me out of the dining hall to my room. I'm touched by his concern and the fact he left the dining room during the busy dinner service to see to my comfort.

Moments later, there is a knock at the door. When I answer, I'm surprised to see the Maître D. "Perhaps Madame's appetite will return?" He speaks gently and in perfect English. I step aside, and the Maître D pushes in a well-appointed dining cart complete with a vase of roses, a carafe of wine, a bottle of sparkling water, my rack of lamb, and a glass terrine of flan dolloped in whipped cream. The kindness and care extended to a ratty peregrina with hairy legs bring tears to my eyes. The Maître D makes a hasty exit to avoid the drama. After a few tears of gratitude and a half glass of wine, I relax. Suddenly, I am starving.

León to Villar de Mazarife

McKinley knocks on my door early in the morning, and I'm already awake, packed, and dressed, but I'm not ready to leave the Parador. Over breakfast, an international spread sure to please peregrinos and tourists from all corners of the world, I offer a proposition. "Let's hang back this morning to check this place out." I continue, "After, we can cab forward, beyond La Virgen del Camino. Then it's an easy 15k to Mazarife." This will be Mik's first fast-forward. She agrees without hesitation, but I feel like a bad influence.

Mik and I enjoy a leisurely breakfast, return to our rooms for a second-morning bath, and then we haunt the empty corridors checking out old tapestries and antique furnishings. We are schoolgirls playing hooky today. We visit the cloister and walk together through the boxwood labyrinth before finding our way into the consecrated chapel. The monastery has served many purposes, to include a military barracks and outpost, a horse breeding stable, and a Spanish Civil War prison complete with a torture chamber. The karma, both good and bad, is ripe. I wish I had another entire day to soak in the history. This may be my first Parador experience, but it will not be my last.

Mik and I contemplate another night, but neither has time nor money to spare. Reluctantly, we ask the bellman to call us a cab. We load our backpacks in the trunk and depart the beautiful Parador at much higher speeds than we arrived. McKinley squeezes my arm in the back of the cab as we pass by our fellow peregrinos making the miserable trek along a narrow and broken sidewalk moving out of town. Cars and trucks flank the walkers the entire route to La Virgen del Camino. Mik slouches in her seat. She tries to act ashamed, but I can see she is delighted with her choice to fast forward out of this crap. I sit straight up and smile. I own no guilt. For me, there is nothing to gain walking amongst car dealerships, gas stations, and industrial wasteland. I may not be a fount of spiritual or religious wisdom, but I know enough to recognize this is not where I seek or find enlightenment.

The driver takes us through the mess and drops us before a quiet little park in the sleepy hamlet of Ocina. Initially, I had requested he dump us behind the freeway overpass outside of La Virgen. He recommended otherwise, and I'm glad I listened. The grassy park, complete with picnic table and children's play yard is a welcome contrast to León. There is also a freshwater fountain. We dump our city water and refill with something more refreshing.

We follow the steep incline along a dirt track dotted with sheep poop. It is quiet, except for the light scuffing of McKinley's boots. She is like a child ruining her Sunday shoes. I want to scold her and make her pick up her feet, but I know that is not my job.

Neither of us speaks, and there isn't an urgency for conversation. We are content to soak up the morning sun and each other's silent presence. As it turns out, Mik is an excellent walking companion for me. She is decades younger, but she is much shorter. Her choppy stride is quick, but I'm able to keep up with her while maintaining a longer stride and more relaxed pace. We are a well-matched team.

The dirt track dumps us on a quiet road where we walk single file in the heat of the midday sun. The going is slow and uninspiring and without much visual distraction. A few cars pass us by, kindly swerving to the far lane to cut us a wider berth. My eyes follow a tractor with a round bale of straw skewered on a sharp spike that protrudes from the rear. The tractor is a giant bumblebee. I've never seen anything like it. I grew up hauling rectangular bales of hay with my beloved Veeley boys, and I've seen plenty of round bales too, often bundled in thick, white shrink-wrap and left on the field like humongous marshmallows. I've seen these round bales transported by forklift or in the bucket of an excavator, but I've never seen one stuck on the stinger of a small tractor. It's genius, really. I point out the novelty to Mik. Unimpressed, she shoots a glare that says, "And your point is…?" Perhaps the stinger-thingamajig is an invention only a farm kid can appreciate.

Like a couple of hungry cows, we follow the tractor and hay bale to the outskirts of Mazarife and stop at the first albergue. It is promising. I read a sign offering a communal supper of paella and a bed for twelve euros. Anxious to try real paella after my fast-food paella experience in Nájera, I raise my eyebrows in a suggestion. Mik declines because she has her heart set on a colorful albergue she read about in her travel guide.

Mik guides me into *Casa de Jesus*, where we are greeted and given a hilarious orientation to the layout by none other than *Jesus* himself. A five-euro bed is always an appreciated bargain, but if I'm to be completely honest, Casa de Jesus is too rustic for my style. This is grossly illuminated after spending last night in a Parador. However, if this is what it means to be flexible, I'll buck up and remain optimistic.

Jesus leads us to a four-person room crammed with two sets of wooden bunks. We both claim bottom beds and pray to remain roommate free. The bunks are old and rickety, and the top mattresses sag without any added weight. I cringe as McKinley flops across the tattered and badly stained mattress. My mother instincts get the best of me, and she gets an earful about bedbug prevention. She laughs at my hypervigilance and rolls on her side to take a nap.

I'm not taking chances, so I stretch out the tent foot I use as a bug barrier and secure the corners to the bedposts with elastic hair bands. It is a near perfect fit. I purchased the tent and barrier before researching the feasibility of camping. While I have met several peregrinos who do camp, it's not for me. I want a hot shower, a glass of wine, and a place to charge my phone. Basically, I prefer glamping over camping.

The tent foot, douched in permethrin, is odorless. The treatment is supposed to last six weeks and through six wash cycles. I haven't washed the shield since treating it three weeks ago. I'm banking on another two weeks of protection.

The nylon barrier is free from odor and residue, but I avoid sleeping directly on it. Instead, I use a silk sleeping sack. The system is lightweight but not perfect. The nylon shield and silk sack pose traction issues throughout the night. When restless, it's easy to slip right off the mattress.

McKinley naps and I wander back to the first albergue in hopes of joining the communal supper. For five euros each, I reserve two spots at the table. I'll give Mik paella as a belated birthday gift. I am honored to have shared in the birthday celebrations of two young women, and I can't help but wonder how different life would have been had I carved out the time in my teens or early twenties for pilgrimage.

I meander through the small village and pop into a tiny grocery store to purchase snacks and breakfast for tomorrow. I wonder how Jonny and Gretchen are getting along. I was hoping the fast forward to Burgos, and the bike ride through the Meseta would enable me to catch up with them. But so far, no luck.

While I haven't met back up with the kids, the same cannot be said about Luke the Australian. Luke walked into Los Arcos with us and stayed at the same albergue. He sits across from me now at the communal paella dinner and pretends we've never met. I don't bother jogging his memory or inquiring after his pretend-wife from South Korea.

Our host prepares the paella over a propane flame in a frypan the size of a backyard kiddie pool. The spectacle delights. Diners take turns capturing the idyllic image of the old man tending to the rice. We *ooh* and *ah* as he dumps kilos of fresh shrimp into the mixture before killing the heat. His timing is an art form. The rice is tender. The vegetables are slightly firm. And the shrimp are a touch beyond translucent. It is a masterful demonstration of paella perfection.

The communal table falls silent as we work our way through mounds of paella heaped on our plates. Once dessert is served, assorted yogurts in individual cups, the conversation picks up. McKinley and I are the only

Americans at a table of fifteen. We are also the only ones who claim yogurt is a breakfast food and not a dessert.

The conversation takes the usual peregrino detour. Each pilgrim explains why he or she feels compelled to walk. I'm still uncomfortable tackling the question, but I articulate something closer to the truth. I share the disappointment I felt in losing my military career and talk a little about my empty nest. Fellow diners nod. Apparently, I've touched some universal truths regarding parental and occupational displacement. I don't talk about illness, or my upcoming professorship or the conflict the job may cause in my marriage. I've used enough oxygen for one dinner party.

There are a few pilgrims recently separated from work. One had his job eliminated. One admits to getting the sack. And one woman, beaming with vitality, scoffs as she tells us how she was forced to retire because of her advanced age. We all laugh at the thought of it. She is too old to continue her work as a bus driver, but she is spry enough to walk 800 kilometers across Spain.

When the table works its way around to Luke, he raises his hand in a universal stop sign and says, "I'd rather not." There is an awkward lull in conversation before a couple of British math teachers fill the gap. They are a husband and wife duo, tackling the Camino and teaching the junior high world about quadratic equations.

"Before we departed for the summer," says the lady teacher, "we set up a collection box in the teachers' lounge." The pair nods at each other as if confirming the story. "We asked each of our coworkers to anonymously write their burdens on a slip of paper and insert it into the box."

"And now," the husband interjects. "We carry their burdens along the way." He beams, holding up his man-purse to show us where these secret burdens are stashed. "When we get to *Cruz de Ferro*, we will pray for our fellow teachers and deposit their burdens in the pile of rocks below the cross."

"Isn't that just beautiful?" exclaims the lady teacher. We all nod our heads in agreement. It is a lovely sentiment. And then, rather unexpectedly, the lady begins to weep. She buries her face in her hands and comes unglued. Her husband pats her back and explains one of the burdens is infertility. For the past five years, a colleague has tried every fertility method covered by their crappy medical plan in the hope of having a baby. "Can you believe the responsibility on our shoulders?" cries the woman. "We must succeed!" She gesticulates wildly. "We must lift the burden and give this woman a baby!"

It's hard to know how to respond to such an emotional outburst. Each of us shifts a little uncomfortably in our seat. Mik takes a stab at lightening the mood, "Oh, sure. You'll carry her paper burden to *Cruz de Ferro*, and then she'll be stuck carrying the real little-burden over the next eighteen years." It's all I can do to keep the yogurt from shooting out my nose, but oddly enough, no one else appreciates Mik's humor.

We head back to the albergue and tuck into bed. My imagination gets the best of me. I swear I feel the patter of tiny bedbug feet across my skin. I get up and down several times during the night and shine my headlamp on my mattress, but I never see anything. And then my scalp begins to itch, and I'm sure I have fleas. I give up the fight to sleep before the break of dawn. I dress in the dark and stuff my bedding into Agnus.

"Mik. Hey, Mik. I'm hitting the road." She mumbles something and pops upright into the sitting position and nearly bashes her head on the top bunk. Her eyes are saucers. She is frightened, and I do my best to soothe her back down onto the bed. I tousle her hair and whisper my goodbye. I do hope to run into her again, but we haven't exchanged emails or solidified our friendship via social media. I hadn't intended on doing a reset with McKinley because we are compatible traveling companions. However, I am convinced we are not alone, that we are sharing our room with all sorts of vermin. And I'm freaking the hell out. This is a reset to preserve my sanity.

Villar de Mazarife to Astorga

It's been a while since I've set out before the morning light. I use my headlamp to make sure I don't miss a yellow arrow. There are no tidy shell placards in Villar de Mazarife, only yellow spray-painted arrows fading into the blacktop or barely visible against the crumbling façade of an old barn or house. It's funny, how even in the dark, my eye is trained to find any spot of yellow. When I'm lost in thought and autopilot has taken hold, my eyes stay vigilant, jumping from one arrow sighting or shell to the next. It is an incredible phenomenon, how quickly I've adapted to finding my way.

Perhaps this is what makes El Camino Francés so alluring to lady pilgrims – the ease in which we turn away from our busy lives and shut down the clamor of competing demands and focus solely on the journey. Last night at dinner, I met an 84-year-old woman from Austria. Her name is Erika, and this is her fourteenth Camino. She walked her first one when she was seventy and has made it a yearly ritual. She shared one regret. She regretted not starting in her fifties when her life was particularly chaotic and demanding. She claims she would have been a much kinder human had she discovered the journey years ago.

"You would think kindness comes easy at my age. What do I have to get worked up about? The kids are raised. My husband is dead, and there's nothing left to do but tend to the garden." Everyone around the table listened intently, but I was captivated by her humility and charm. "I must practice," she continued. "It is simple to envy and keep a small-mind. It is harder to be kind. I pray and make time to reflect. It is what I do out here. I pray, and I think."

I'm glad I discovered the Camino when I did, in my late forties. Truthfully, I wouldn't have been ready for it any earlier. When everything was going well, I didn't make time to think or pray. If I stayed busy, there wasn't a problem I couldn't tackle on my own.

Illness is humbling. It slowed me down long enough for my past to catch up. Unfortunately, my boogiemen caught up too. I don't suppose I can have one without the other. When I was well, my subconscious goal was to live at breakneck speed, never slowing long enough to examine my mental history and address how this history impedes the present.

Erika is an inspiration. I hope I have the bravery and physical stamina to hike into my eighties. I also hope I have the courage and the mental perseverance to continue a reflective practice of self-improvement and kindness. She is right about making time to think. I've never enjoyed so much time to myself, and I now understand the value of the scarce commodity of silence. It is in the quietest moments where I slip into some sort of introspective trance. People and places and memories long forgotten, tucked away in some dusty compartment in my mind's storage closet, emerge. It's been three weeks since I've put anyone's needs over my own. Sure, I've compromised and tended to the needs of my fellow peregrinos, but not with the persistence or personal sacrifice required when a mother tends to the daily needs of her sons or when a wife takes care of her husband. I don't have to cook for anyone, or pick up dirty clothes, or replace the empty jug of milk, or swing by the post office... I have nothing to do but walk, sleep, think, pray, and find good chocolate and wine.

It is such a novelty and a delicious absence, this lack of responsibility. The freedom of stripping away life's mundane complexities is intoxicating. Many say the Camino is addicting, and I believe it. I hope it is addicting, especially for Levi, the heroin addict from Holland I met on my second day. I hope thru-hiking becomes his junk – the fix he cannot live without. I hope he walks the trail again one day in the company of his daughter, Eugenia.

I cross a major road and leave the quiet street from Villar de Mazarife for a dirt track cutting through what I assume is a livestock grazing area. There are plenty of sheep pebbles to back up my assumptions. I play a little game of hopscotch to avoid crushing the droppings beneath my step. Scraping sheep shit from the treads of hiking boots at the end of the day is a royal buzzkill.

I walk the lonely trail through the center of Villavante and out the other end without meeting another human being. I probably could avoid humans altogether this morning, but I need coffee and a bite of breakfast. I stop at a café before the medieval bridge crossing the río *Órbigo*. The proprietor is opening for the day as I stumble through his door.

I sit at the bar, and he makes me a café con leche. His dark hair is slicked back, and olive-green eyes shine behind tortoiseshell glasses. He wears a white apron, and the sleeves of his form-fitting t-shirt are rolled to his shoulders. I'm treated to the full layout of his tattooed arms as he works the espresso machine. I don't need conversation or a shared language. This is more than enough. The coffee is rich and dark, and the fresh milk is steamed into a froth of tiny bubbles. I sit alone and savor the experience.

I can hear my handsome barista in the back kitchen. He is frying my eggs and toasting a baguette. And the idea of it thrills me. There is something intimate going on between the two of us. Of course, it is only in my mind, but I'm enjoying it. I imagine coming up behind him while he is working over a hot stove. I pull the clean dishrag from his apron strings and dab his forehead before wrapping my arms around his fit torso. I read his abs like braille, working my fingers up and over each perfect cut until I find the spread of his broad chest. He inhales deeply and releases a long sigh. And then he clears his throat. He is standing in front of me with a plate of eggs. My face flushes under his gaze. The heat only intensifies as he pops a knowing wink and says, "Buen provecho, Guapa!"

Those had to be the best damn eggs I've ever tasted. Not to mention, the meal was a real bargain. Coffee, breakfast, fantasy, and floorshow only set me back three euros. Totally worth it. You can't buy that kind of experience in the United States, at least not in the cafés I frequent. Clearly, I've been away from my hubby too long. I'm feeling silly and giddy from the flirty experience, which again, played out mostly in my mind. But he's the one who winked. He's the one who called me *Guapa*. That means something, for sure.

I catch myself skipping. It is miraculous how a hearty breakfast and a little attention puts such pep in my step. I toss a sugar-free version of Chiclets in my mouth and hear a louder than usual crunching and feel the candy coating splinter on my tongue. It is oddly sharp, but the gum smooths out. And then the crunching and sharpness appear again. I spit the gum into my hand and examine shards of pearly white. Damn! The crunchy bits are my tooth enamel.

It doesn't take long to find the source. A crown positioned on the upper, left side of my jaw is loose. I wiggle it first between my thumb and forefinger, and then I wiggle it again with my tongue for the next few minutes. I can't believe I broke my damn tooth on gum. I chew gum all the time. Why now? And why here, thousands of miles from my dentist?

On the bright side, I'm stopping in Astorga today, a major town. Surely, I'll find a dentist; although, visiting the dentist is the last thing I want to do, especially after hiking over 30K. I was hoping to have enough energy left in the tank to visit Astorga's chocolate museum. Astorga has a long history of chocolate and is claimed to be the first location on the European continent to manufacture chocolate. I've been dreaming of checking it out. Chocolate and a dentist is an odd pairing, but perhaps, I'll have time for both. I quicken my pace, and I try to ignore the tooth. Fiddling with the loose crown is not going to help matters, but the tip of my tongue finds the wiggle irresistible.

The incredible bridge spanning the río *Órbigo* serves as an excellent distraction, even for my insatiable tongue. In the summer of 1434, a jousting tournament played out on these very stones beneath my step. Legend tells of a knight from León who, after being scorned by a beautiful maiden, threw down the gauntlet and defended the passage against all

challengers. Knights from all over Europe arrived to face
him. After a month of jousting and three hundred broken
lances, the scorned knight's honor was restored. This knight
from León was named Don Suero de Quiñones, and his
name sounds oddly familiar.

My imagination summons *Don Quixote* and *Sancho Panza*.
The pair is crossing before me. I hum a few bars from *Man of
La Mancha* as I enter the town. I picture my egg-frying
bartender playing the lead while I play his lady, *Dulcinea*. I sing
softly to myself, "To dream the impossible dream…" This is
my impossible dream. I'll fight my unbeatable foes. And I'll
reach that unreachable star. Broken tooth and all, I will be
victorious.

Hospital de *Órbigo* is quaint, but the magnificent bridge at
the entry set my expectations too high. I move in and out of
town without giving much pause. I pick up an earth track
cutting through beautiful woodland and dumping me back
out into scrubby, grazing lands. The dirt trail climbs up and
down small hills and is gentle beneath my tired feet. Although
I do love hiking through the tiny hamlets, accumulating
asphalt free miles is always a welcome change.

I'm climbing the last peak before reaching Astorga. My
legs are tree trunks, and each step is a ridiculous effort. The
hill isn't all that steep, and I take comfort in knowing I am
not the only one struggling. For about five minutes or so, I've
listened to a labored wheeze coming up from behind. I
haven't glanced back because I don't have that kind of energy
to waste feeding my curiosity. Instead, I listen and wait as the
wheeze grows louder and threatens to overtake me.

The wheeze is now dangerously close, coming up on my
left side and level with my shoulder. I keep my head and eyes
directed forward and try to mind my business. And then the
wheeze speaks, "Gidday." My heart drops a little in
disappointment. I know that voice. And I was hoping for
someone new. It's Luke, the Australian guy who pretended
not to recognize me. Despite sounding as if he is near an
asthmatic attack, he wants to chitchat.

"Seattle, right?" he remembers me by my home city.

"Yup. And you're Luke, right?" He wheezes in affirmation.

"Awfully good tucker last night, that paella."

"Yup, awfully good tucker," I mimic his accent. "So, what happened to Juni?" I feel like such a trifling bitch for meddling, but I need a little amusement to get me up the hill.

"Oh, well she ah…" He is stammering. I'd love to turn and stare at him right in the eyes, but I've got to focus on the uneven trail. "Um, she met up with some of her own kind."

"You mean ladies?" I try to sound as unassuming as possible.

"No. Um. Orientals. She found some other Orientals."

"Koreans." I correct.

"What's that?"

"Koreans. You mean she found other Koreans, like South Koreans."

"Yes. Yes, Koreans. People who speak the same language. That's important out here."

"That's true, Luke. A common language is helpful. I guess that is why I make fast friends with Americans and Canadians."

"And Aussies," he pipes. I keep my mouth shut, not wanting to lead him on and make him think we might become trail buddies. I find his demeanor mildly caustic.

I don't want to walk with Luke, but I can't out walk him, and he slows down every time I slow down. I haven't the time to play cat and mouse and attempt a reset by diving into a café or pretending I am going to nap beneath a shady tree. I've got to get to Astorga and find a dentist. And then after the dentist, maybe I'll have time to spare a visit to the chocolate museum.

"My wife left me," Luke blurts. "God. Why did I just say that?" I have no idea how I'm supposed to respond. "Well," he backtracks. "She hasn't left yet, but she is leaving me." I still don't know how to reply. "She's taking the kids and moving to Holland."

"Holland?" I'm truly curious. Of all the places to run off, why Holland? Levi and Elke are the only two people I've met from Holland. Both were terribly kind, and now I'd quite like to visit Holland. While I'm sure there is more to Holland than flowers, I absolutely adore tulips. I plant hundreds of bulbs each year, but the squirrels devour my efforts all winter long. Faithfully, I replant and try again.

"Yes. She's a smart bird, my wife. Got a job offer and is bent on taking it."

"Can't you go with her?"

"No. She doesn't want me to. Says she needs time alone."

"Maybe she does."

"What's that even mean?"

"Well, she's not suggesting a divorce. Maybe she needs space."

"She won't have sex with me," he says flatly.

I try to ignore his comment. "Did you hear me?" He says. "My own wife won't have sex with me."

"Well... I damn sure wouldn't have sex with you either." I'm sorry as soon as the words leave my mouth.

"Pardon me?" He sounds astonished.

"Forgive me. That was a stupid thing to say. It's really none of my business."

"No. Really," He demands. "Why won't you have sex with me?" A couple of peregrinos pass on our left with raised eyebrows, and I can't help but wonder how I got myself into this mess. Luke thinks he is quite a catch. He is textbook handsome – tall, dark, and rugged. But he carries a smarminess I cannot overcome.

"To start with, what was the deal with Juni? Does your real wife wash your laundry and kiss your ass? Chauvinist pigs are unsexy, second only to cheaters."

"I don't cheat on my wife," he says in a huff.

"Like I said, it's not my business." I expect him to drop back or step out ahead. I've undoubtedly offended him, and I don't plan on continuing down this line of rhetoric. Nothing enlightening can come of it.

Luke skulks beside me the whole way into Astorga. I ditch him at the farmacia, agreeing to meet him later in the square. I don't declare an actual promise, but I keep my fingers crossed behind my back all the same.

Unsure of how to go about finding a dentist, I figure a pharmacy might be a wise place to start. Pharmacists should know local physicians and dentists. Right? My Spanish comes out all choked up like I am ready to cry. I supplement with hand gestures and point to the offending tooth. Success! She understands me and gives directions to the nearest emergency dentist, but there are too many details for my road-weary mind to track.

Anxiety perks and the lump in my throat grows. It's true, I am vain when it comes to my smile and general appearance, but I didn't expect to get emotional about a loose tooth. Noticing my discomfort, the pharmacist comes around the counter and takes my arm. She escorts me out to the plaza and stops a woman passing by. I catch almost none of their exchange as it fires over my head like the rattle of machine guns. Before I realize what has transpired, the pharmacist heads back into her shop, and the lady passerby has me by the arm. My new escort leads me through a maze of narrow, cobblestoned streets and to the façade of what appears to be an ordinary apartment building. She rings a buzzer and speaks into the receiver.

My lady delivers me to the dental receptionist and leaves me with a hug and a kiss on each cheek. I'm confused and touched by the care I've received. The kindness shown to me, by not only my escort but also by the pharmacist, is so foreign. This would never happen at home. I scan the reception area and am relieved to see Visa and Mastercard placards. Thank heavens for credit cards. I'm not carrying enough cash to cover the cost of a dental visit.

The receptionist shows me to the waiting area and hands me a clipboard with a form to fill out. She apologizes she does not have one printed in English, but I assure her I can manage. As I work my way through decoding the form, a soft-spoken lady comes and sits beside me. I shift a little uncomfortably, trying to create space between the two of us. After 30K in the hot sun, dusty streaks of sweat line the creases of my elbows and knees, and I'm sure I smell horrid.

She introduces herself as my dentist. She is terribly beautiful and reminds me of one of my favorite actresses, Penelope Cruz. She gathers a few clinical details before switching to the personal. "You are all alone?" I blink back the tears. "Peregrina, where are your friends? Where is your family?" She is genuinely concerned, and it's all I can take. Huge crocodile tears roll down my cheeks, and I'm so embarrassed. "No. No. Don't cry, peregrina. Everything is okay."

She wraps an arm around my filthy shoulder and leads me to an exam chair. She takes a quick set of digital x-rays and projects the tooth in question up on a movie screen. To my untrained eye, everything appears to be in order. "Can you glue it?"

"No. It must fall out first. If I pull, it could break. And then you have a big problem."

"What should I do?" I feel the tears welling up again.

"You should not cry. Be happy. Eat ice cream. Fix later. After you go home."

"Ice cream, huh?"

"Yes. Lots of ice cream."

"I can do that."

The dentist gives me another hug and escorts me toward the door. I inquire about the bill, but she waves me on, wishing me a "Buen Camino." I stumble down the stairs and back out into the busy plaza. I'm stunned. That should have been a least a hundred bucks or more. She took x-rays and performed an exam.

I walk in somewhat of a daze until coming to an abrupt halt in front of a gelato stand. I've never been prescribed ice cream before, but I intend to heed the advice of my lovely dentist. I order two scoops – dark chocolate and mandarin orange.

The chocolate gelato reminds me of the chocolate museum I had hoped to visit, but I'm feeling emotionally drained and in desperate need of a shower. I ramble along in the pedestrian zone, admiring storefronts and looking for a place to stay. It doesn't take long for my aimless jaunt to cross paths with the Camino again.

Scallop shells lead me to the neo-medieval *Palacio Episcopal de Astorga*, designed by Antoni Gaudi in 1889. I stand on the sidewalk and gawk, totally star-struck. Conveniently, there is a small pension directly across from the palace. I duck in and secure a room for the night with not only a bathtub, but a balcony in full view of this architectural marvel.

Room service delivers more ice cream, and I take a long bath, wash clothes, and contemplate the day's beautiful acts of kindness. Luke will have to get along without me tonight. I am spending the rest of the evening on the balcony, staring at my first *Gaudi*.

Astorga to Rabanal del Camino

Yesterday's goodwill has me in such a happy and hopeful mood. My heart is wide open and full of love. I want to hug every peregrino who passes me, but no one will make eye contact. Everyone is in a hurry this morning.

The massive edifice of the *Catedral de Astorga*, built and rehabbed in stages starting in 1471, provides the final photo-op before leaving the old town. My eyes are not trained in art and architecture history. However; the elements of Gothic, Baroque, and Renaissance detailing are clear and easy for me to pick out. The *way* is expanding my art appreciation skills and knowledge.

While the cathedral is impressive, nothing about it invites me in for morning meditation. I feel pressured to fall into step and join the march of peregrinos exiting Astorga. I'll save my meditation for something less imposing.

Outside of Astorga, in the hamlet of Valdeviejas, the humble 16th century *La Ermita del Ecce Homo* catches my eye. *Ecce Homo* is the scourged depiction of Jesus Christ, bound and crowned with thorns just before his crucifixion. A lovely, older woman stands outside the shaded entrance of the chapel with a sello in hand. She waits patiently to stamp the passport credentials of peregrinos passing by. There is a flood of us this morning, a mass exodus from the bowels of Astorga. Busy in yappy conversations or concerned with making it to the day's destination, everyone walks on. I'm in a wave of peregrinos crashing by, but I can't resist her grandmotherly presence. She is smiling and waving to me.

I make a beeline for her and produce my pilgrim passport. But she is a clever recruiter and withholds the sello until I step inside and view the church she dearly loves. She hands me a story, printed in English, on half a sheet of paper. She beckons me to sit a moment and read, and I obey.

I'm not one to disappoint little, old ladies. I was raised to respect elders. This is an attribute I hope transferred to my own children. This is also a feature I find most attractive about my husband. While we were dating, he conversed so kindly and respectfully with my grandmother. After that, it was obvious he was the one. You can tell a lot about a man by the way he treats grandmothers.

My eyes adjust to the dimly lit church, and I read the paper. The story tells of a mother and her young son on a pilgrimage to Santiago. They stop at the church, originally dedicated to *San Pedro*, to pray. The boy tries to fetch water but tragically falls into the well. The mother prays to Ecce Homo for her son's salvation, and the water begins to rise. The well bubbles over and spits the boy out. After such a miracle, the shrine was rededicated to Ecce Homo.

The story makes me think of my own sons and stepsons. Keeping them safe was my life's work. I light five candles and pray to Ecce Homo for the continued safety of my boys.

As I prepare to leave the church, the little lady stamps my pilgrim passport and hands it back to me. She nods her head in approval, apparently pleased with the scope of my visit. She follows me outside, and on the stoop, she holds my face in her cold and boney hands and wishes me, "Buen Camino."

What a beautiful moment of human interaction. The old woman's touch was such a gift, and so early in the day's journey. I'll remember *the boy-in-the-well* story and Ecce Homo's little recruiter for as long as I live. She is a treasure. And all I had to do was slow down, slow down for a moment and make contact. How hard was that? Teary-eyed, I hike on toward Rabanal and wonder how many of life's treasures I miss because I refuse to slow down.

I feel fresh today, as in nothing hurts yet. My spirits are lifted, and my pace is steady. I share the trail with more pilgrims than usual. This is often the situation when leaving larger towns and cities. I find myself jockeying for position on the narrow path flanking a moderately busy thoroughfare. Typically, I'm not one who needs to pass others, but several sets of peregrinos walk double-breasted and at a snail's pace.

Trying not to abandon the day's earlier lesson about slowing down, I focus on honing my practice of patience.

Despite my best efforts, I'm growing frustrated with the crowd. Bodies clog the narrow path ahead, and the idle chitchat drives me bonkers. I can't hear myself think. *Rose*, a lady from Brazil walking ahead of me, unfolds the gory details of her latest bout with liposuction. I can't lie. I'm interested. I first saw Rose in Burgos. We've never actually met, but she is part of a collective wave of familiar faces. Typically, I avoid her because she's loud. But now, she holds me hostage behind her beautiful, *Brazilian butt-lift*. Apart from liposuction, she also weighs the pros and cons of her new boob job.

The path finally widens, and I make a break for it. I work my way alongside Rose and her equally chatty girlfriend. No matter how hard I try not to stare, I perform a thorough inspection of Rose's new rack. Amazing.

I stop in Santa Catalina for a café con leche and a bit of breakfast. Outside in the warm sun, I soak in a cacophony of church bells. I sit to the right of the tower, close enough to feel the vibrations in my core. The bells feel better than they sound. A megaphoned voice, blasting from the bell tower, calls villagers and peregrinos to mass. I ignore the call, close my eyes, and lean against the building. The sun shines pink through my eyelids and for several relaxing moments, the world is rosy. I'm almost asleep when a shadow passes before me and blackens out the rose-colored sunshine. I open my eyes and see Luke, the Australian.

I smile, and he takes this as an invitation. He drops his pack and slumps down into a patio chair. He bitches about pilgrims walking side by side, blocking the trail. He complains of an onslaught of idle conversations. "Shopping," he says. "Two fat birds were talking about shopping. Is that all you women talk about these days?" I don't tell Luke about Rose's boobs. Luke is my mirror, reflecting ugly thoughts right back in my face.

I get up to leave, and Luke follows. "Wait," I stop and turn to him. "We can only walk together if you can be kind. I don't want to hear any ugly words out of you, and I don't want to speak any either." I straighten myself and stare him down. "Do you understand me?" I'm proud of how I set up the boundaries with Luke. I'm generally not skilled at this sort of thing.

"Perhaps you'd prefer I shut the fuck up," he sounds wounded.

"If that's what it takes, then so be it." I offer a smile. I don't want to be mean to him or to anyone else out here. But I do need to protect my space, my peace. I can't control crowded trails or runaway conversations, but I should be allowed to set the tone for anyone wanting to walk within my bubble. This is my bubble, my experience, and I insist on peace.

Luke follows at my heels like a dejected toddler. We walk this way for 5K until we come to El Ganso, a ghost town of a place complete with a cowboy bar. I use the setting to lighten the mood. "Comm'n, pardner. Lemme buy you a beer." It takes two beers before Luke lightens up. He tells me about his kids and his job as a junior high history teacher. I quiz him about the Camino, hoping for an impromptu history lesson, but he comes up empty. I assumed a history teacher would do his research before taking on such an adventure.

As it turns out, this was a spur of the moment trip for Luke. He planned on his regular summer vacation with his family, at a timeshare along the Gold Coast of Australia, like they do every year. However, his wife declined, blaming it on the children's extracurricular activities. "Since when should sport and piano lessons interfere with family vacation? The kids are not the real reason. The real reason is that she is a selfish, little..." I cut him off, patting his arm and reminding him of our agreement. He nods and motions for another beer.

We are three beers in before Luke chills out. We get back on the road, but he is in no hurry because he already reserved a bed at what he describes as an upscale albergue, operated by the *London Ladies Confraternity of Saint James*. "They serve afternoon tea!" He nearly giggles. This is so out of character. Luke is either super excited about afternoon tea, or he has had too much beer. Either way, I like this relaxed version of Luke better.

He invites me to join him at the boutique albergue. I agree to check it out; even though I sent a bag ahead to *Albergue Pilar*, a 72-bed facility. I'm not looking forward to bunking with masses. Hopefully, I can collect my belongings and move on.

When we arrive at Luke's albergue, he is delighted. His joy overflows even in the absence of beer. The albergue is truly lovely and certainly a boutique of albergues, but the icing on Luke's cupcake rains down on him as he learns the Australian chapter has replaced the London ladies. Luke is surrounded by his *own kind*, and they are throwing down the mother-hen treatment. He is lapping it up.

According to a posted list of house rules, I cannot stay. I nudge Luke and point out my offense. Peregrinos using backpack transport services are not welcome. "Technically, you carried your backpack," he whispers. "Besides, cyclists are welcome. They didn't even carry themselves. Biking is the easy way out." After my short career as a cycling peregrina, I cannot agree with him. My ass is still chapped from the ride.

I'm not riding the bad-karma train to Santiago. I'm not ashamed of sending a bag forward, and I'm not going to lie about it. Luke lets out a whine as I get up to leave. I thank the ladies and inform them of my disqualification. I half expect them to tell me not to worry about it, that I am welcome anyway. But they don't. Instead, the ladies lower their gaze and shake their heads, muttering something I'm happy not to overhear. I'm not in the mood for injury or scorn, and I won't justify my actions to these broads. I try to thank them graciously, but it comes out a little forced. Half expecting Luke to be at my heels, I turn and walk out. Luke doesn't budge, and I'm cool with that.

The *Albergue Nuestra Señora del Pilar* has an energetic vibe. The enclosed courtyard is sunny and alive with the buzzing of peregrinos doing laundry and socializing at the in-house bar. Inside the front stoop, my blue go-ahead bag stands out like a buoy in a sea of backpacks. I head over and snatch it up.

A hospitalera greets me warmly and leads me to the registration table. She requests my travel passport and my pilgrim credentials. She inspects one and stamps the other. The seventy-six beds are dispersed into two dorms, and that doesn't sound appealing. Although I like the communal vibe, I inquire about a private room. She leaves me for a moment to investigate, and I take advantage of the free WIFI to research the meaning of the albergue's translated name, *Our Lady of Pillar.*

It is believed while James the Apostle was spreading the word in pagan lands near Zaragoza, he was met by an apparition of Mary. The downhearted James had only converted a handful of souls and was somewhat frustrated. One night, while he was praying beside a river bank, Mary came to him. She appeared atop a pillar and in the company of angels. She encouraged James to continue teaching the gospel and assured him his peregrination efforts would be fruitful. She promised Christianity would spread throughout Spain and be as strong as the pillar she stood upon.

Engrossed in my reading, I'm startled when a Santa Claus of a man joins me at the registration table and strikes up a conversation. He is kindly, and I admire his South African accent, but he smells terrible – like an old goat or a whole herd of old goats. I have no natural poker face. I'm careful not to grimace or lean away. His stench is powerful, and I resort to mouth breathing. *I will greet each pilgrim with love and kindness in my heart.*

When the hostess returns, she confirms the availability of a private room with two double beds. The cost is forty euros, and I thank her but politely decline. I don't want to spend that much tonight, not in Rabanal. Last night's splurge with the Gaudi view only set me back thirty-five euros. She nods in understanding and scans her charts for a vacant bed in the dorms.

"One moment," The Santa Claus man interjects. "Do you wish to share a room with me?" His proposition startles me, and my negative response comes out more forcefully than intended. He apologizes profusely, but I'm too shocked and humiliated at my own behavior to gracefully accept.

After I settle into my bunk and take care of my washing, I head out to find food. There are a handful of options, and I select a handsome pension atop the hill. Unfortunately, the pilgrim meal isn't served in the inviting bar or the lovely courtyard. It is served in cafeteria-ambiance, down in the basement.

Luke sees me enter the cafeteria and waves me over. He is sitting with none other than my Mr. Santa Claus. I'm thankful. Although awkward, I need a shot at redemption. Before I sit, the poor man begins his apology. He assures he meant nothing inappropriate. I wave my hands to cut him off, but he doesn't settle. I step it up a notch and pat up his forearm, hoping to console him. "No, please. I'm the one who should apologize. I was frazzled, tired from the road, and hot. Crazy hot. I didn't think before I spoke…" I am truly sorry I hurt this dear man's feelings, and I wish I could take it back. Had I slowed down, given my brain a chance to catch up with my mouth, I would have never assumed he was some creepy pervert. Not every man in my life is a creepy pervert, but I do tend to think the worst. But this is the Camino. Narrow cultural norms do not apply. If it isn't weird or sexual to sleep next to a strange man in an open dorm, then why should it be different in a room for two? I would have thought nothing of it had the proposal came from a Mrs. Claus. But it didn't, and unfortunately, it is different, at least for me. Poor Mr. Claus is not at fault for failing to understand my self-imposed limitations.

Rabanal to Molinaseca

Location, location, location. It's all about location. This real-estate golden rule rings true in all types of property ventures, including a rented bunk. Last night, my bed was located next to the swinging bathroom door. And the door swung alright, from about midnight to 0400, when I finally gave up and moved out into the courtyard to prepare Agnus and the bag I'll send forward to Molinaseca.

I unload as much as I dare from Agnus and fill the water bladder with only one liter. I usually carry two, but I've got to save my legs today. I roll the top of the blue bag down and clip it closed. I write the address of the municipal albergue in Molinaseca on the delivery envelope and slip in a few coins before sealing and attaching it to my belongings. With a bit of Camino magic, my bag and I will meet again tonight.

Today's hike promises to be brutal. There was nervous energy at dinner last night and in the courtyard of the albergue. Everybody was talking about it. It is an important day on the Camino and a turning point for some. We will climb up and over the highest point along the French Way, reaching an elevation of 1,505 meters at *Cruz de Ferro*, or the Iron Cross. Contrary to widespread belief, today's hike is higher than the ascent over the Pyrenees between St. Jean Pied de Port and Roncesvalles at 1,450 meters.

Today is about lightening the load, and I don't mean by using a backpack delivery system, although that certainly does help. I'm talking about emotional load, the weight of a burden. Traditionally, peregrinos along the French way carry a stone to symbolize a burden or many burdens they wish to unload. A tall, iron cross at the highest elevation of the journey marks the spot. For some, including me, leaving the stone is a cleansing ritual. It's a chance to shake off emotional deadweights like regret, guilt, shame, fear, sorrow, rage, and boogiemen.

I remove the burden stone from the secret pocket in Agnus' lid and slip it inside my bra over my heart. Its smooth coolness makes me shiver. I want to keep it pressed close to me today, so I notice the absence when I drop it and my boogiemen at the base of the cross.

I hike through the village and up the hill where Luke, Mr. Claus, and I had dinner last night. I regret stuffing my headlamp in the blue bag to send forward. I desperately need it as I leave the blacktopped road and take up a dirt track pocked with jagged rocks, tractor ruts, and mud puddles. The path is peppered with sheep shit and cow flops. I can't see poop, but I can smell it. There's nothing I can do to avoid squishing the dung between the treads of my boots. But with any luck, I'll walk through a creek and a stretch of graveled road to remedy the problem. I detest scraping poop from my boots at the end of the day.

I try to activate my night eyes, pressing gently over closed lids until I see a burst of blue and yellow, like fireworks and chrysanthemums. It doesn't take the first time, so I try another round. There is no science to my method, but after a third try, I swear I can see more clearly. A fence line leads me up a scramble of rocks, and I pick my way through a boggy pasture.

I rest on a rock wall amidst a pile of rubble on the outskirts of Foncebadón. I sit perfectly still as the sky lightens, and I listen for the stirring of the morning's first peregrinos creeping out of the albergues. Where there are pilgrims, there will be coffee. The sky shifts from indigo to violet. I hear the faint scuffing of boots and the clacking of poles. It's time to move on in.

I remember the town, Foncebadón, from Shirly McClain's book, *The Camino: A Journey of the Spirit*. According to McClain, the village is abandoned except for a pack of ferocious, wild dogs. Her book is fifteen years old, and things have changed. The place is in various stages of ruin and still fast asleep, but it is anything but abandoned. I haven't seen a dog yet, let alone a whole pack.

I follow a dim light leading me to the back of a bar and work my way around to the front and find the entrance. I am the first peregrina to arrive. I use the self-service sello to stamp my credentials and order a café con leche and a side of toast. I am ready for eggs, but the bartender is not.

Fully caffeinated and carb-loaded, I'm off to tackle the highest point of my journey. The physical challenges of the day are substantial, but the emotional charge is what's spurring me on. It is purely symbolic, but I believe in the power of proclamation and throwing out wants and needs and gratitude into the universe. Asking for what I want and need, expressing thanks for all I have, and proclaiming my intentions are prayers as well as exercises in the law of attraction. *Like attracts like.* I will proclaim my bravery, and I will be brave. I will proclaim freedom from fear and guilt and boogeymen, and I shall be free. In a couple of kilometers, I will manifest change and redirect my life. This is powerful stuff.

I walk the 2K deep in thought, trying to pound at the specifics of my proclamation. I do not have a religious education beyond Sunday school sessions at a country Methodist Church, but I have witnessed the power and the windfall of a well-organized and detailed prayer.

It was a Friday afternoon in the summer of 1993. I lived in Seattle and was seven-months pregnant with my second child. I was also unmarried. That day, my car overheated when I was collecting my six-year-old, Nicholas, from the sitter. The car was on its last leg, and the sitter encouraged me to pray for another one. She was one of those born-again types. "Praise, Jesus," for this and "Praise, Jesus," for that. But I couldn't do it. I hadn't been raised that way. My childhood Jesus did not give cars or designer jeans or new puppies. I thought it was greedy and rude to pray for personal gains, especially ones of monetary value.

After the car cooled down, I went on my way. While crossing a nightmare of an intersection in Seattle, the water pump froze, and the car was dead. No one offered to help. I sat in the driver's seat for a while, thinking somebody would save me, but no one did. Finally, with a child in the back seat and one in the belly, I pushed that shitty Datsun B210 across three lanes and into a gas station parking lot. The onsite mechanic called the time of death, and that was that.

Nicholas and I dug beneath floor mats and between seats and emptied cup holders to scrounge enough change to catch the bus home. I had enough to get us within two miles of our flat. Nick walked the first mile, but I piggybacked him the rest of the way. With one kid on my back and one in my belly, all I could do was pray. And I prayed the whole mile. I prayed for a new car, a Subaru wagon. Red. Four-wheel drive would be a useful feature, so I prayed for that too.

Later that night, I scoured the paper for a car I could buy on shaky credit. There was a listing for an older model, 4x4 Subaru wagon. *Make an offer.* I circled it with a crayon and repeated my prayer.

On Saturday afternoon, the postman delivered an unexpected check from my Army reserve unit. Evidently, there had been a mix up in my recent promotion, and I hadn't been paid correctly. The makeup check was only $800, but I called the circled telephone number anyway.

The owner drove the car into the city for me to inspect. It was perfect, a red 4x4 wagon. It was a little rougher than I had visualized but just right for my needs. It was his late wife's car. She passed away from breast cancer five years earlier, and he had finally built up the strength to rehome her belongings. The car was worth more than I had to offer, but it didn't matter. We both got what we needed that day.

I wait my turn at the bottom of an enormous pile of stones. A young cyclist bows his head and leans against the iron cross. He is up there for a while, and I divert my eyes to give him privacy. More peregrinos are coming up the trail, and I grow impatient. I want time alone with my thoughts, time without idle banter and selfies. I have visualized this moment for nearly a year. It's a turning point in my life.

When it is my turn, I climb the pile of rocks, watching where I put my feet. I don't want to tread on photographs of grandmas and grandpas, and I don't want to disturb makeshift shrines of wildflowers, stacked rocks, and woven crosses made from grass. Like the cyclist before me, I rest my head on the pole to meditate and pray. I flip the smooth, white stone through my fingers and focus on the constructs of bravery and freedom.

When I drop this stone, I drop my burdens. When I drop this stone, I drop my shame and my guilt and my fear and my rage. When I drop this stone, I drop my boogieman – I drop Sergeant Kenny Walker and all the other assholes who have harassed me, stalked me, intimidated me, and abused my body and my mind. When I drop this stone, the Boogieman dies! When I drop this stone, I pick up my freedom and restart my life.

Against the base of the pole, I find a tiny Virgin Mary made of plastic. She is the color of glow-in-the-dark green, and I'm so tempted to scoop her up and peer at her through cupped hands to see if she really does glow. But she is not mine to disturb. She is the prayer of another. Instead, I place my stone on the ground next to her, leaving it and my proclamations under her compassionate watch.

The stone, symbolically loaded with my fear and angst, weighed less than a hundred grams. When tucked into the shelf-lining of my tank top, it was barely noticeable. However, in its absence, I feel a difference. I am lighter. And I am crying with joy and relief.

I get it. I'm not naïve. I made proclamations and prayed for strength to see them through, but it won't be easy. Fear and shame and guilt and rage have been my companions for thirty years. These emotions will die hard, but I'm not worried. Somehow, I just know from this moment forward, I will be brave. And I will be free.

Hiking the ridge between *Cruz de Ferro* and *Punto Alto* is a feast for the senses. The sun is bright and warm on my back. The sky is a cloudless blue, and I smell the fragrant sage bushes and taste the clay dust kicked up from the rocky path. I listen for the cuckoo bird, but I do not hear her this morning. Instead, I hear a distant cowbell. The ringing is consistent and in peals of threes and fours. I imagine a nut-brown beauty with sidewinding horns grazing in the pasture below. At her side is a blonde calf, shiny and new. She pulls up a tuft of grass and chews for a bit, walks a few steps, and then pulls up another tuft. The calf suckles between her steps, and the two will repeat this dance until the sun sets.

The trail drops and briefly parallels with the roadway. Conveniently, the meeting of ways coincides with a gravel clearing. And even more convenient, a snack trailer and umbrella tables spring up out of nowhere. It's a roadside oasis, and I make myself comfortable. I take off my boots, change my socks, and put up my feet. I also enjoy another delicious *zitrone-Aquarius*. While not typically keen on sports drinks, this one hits the spot.

The mentally taxing parts of my day are complete, and I made it through unscathed. Now, it's time to focus on the physical. Like most mature peregrinos, I'm fonder of hiking uphill rather than down. In my youth, I complained when hiking up switchbacks but loved the thrill of running back down. Now, the opposite is true. I'd rather walk uphill all-day long. My lungs may burn, and my quads might catch fire, but I can lean into the incline and keep going. Plus, the risk of injury is dramatically reduced when falling uphill.

After a long break, I lace my boots and lengthen my hiking poles. The idea is to rely heavily on the poles to save the knees. The first bit of downhill is the worst. The decomposing shale flakes beneath my feet, and I slide on loose gravel. A dull ache in my temples tells me I'm gritting my teeth. This isn't helpful for migraines or a loose tooth. I take a short rest and stretch my shoulders and neck, trying to relax.

I drop three hundred meters in three kilometers before walking into Acebo. My knees and thighs are pools of jelly, but adorable Acebo helps me forget the pain. This place is like something out of a movie set, maybe a spaghetti-western set in colonial Mexico. I pass a café lousy with peregrinos and walk beneath cantilevered patios threatening to collapse at any moment. A rusty screen door hangs on one hinge and sways in the breeze. I admire clay pots filled with red geraniums and white impatiens. Dilapidated buildings along the main street appear abandoned, but somebody is home to water the flowers.

A scruffy old dog with a terrible underbite wanders into the street to greet me. He doesn't beg food or affection. He's been rejected too many times. Instead, he is content to walk by my side to the edge of town. He stops and sits just before the smooth blacktop begins. This is as far as he goes. I reach down with thoughts of patting his matted head, but he juts out a row of bottom teeth and warns me with a low growl. Slowly, I retract my hand. "Alrighty. No touching. I get it. Well, I guess this is goodbye."

On the outskirts of Molinaseca, the sky opens, and sheets of rain hammer the blacktop. The roadway becomes a swift and shallow stream. Again, I'm too late to put on my rain jacket or my pack cover. Thunder rolls and I see a flash of lightning. Jelly-legs and all, I make a run for it and dive beneath the arched entrance of the *Ermita de Nuestra Señora de las Angustias* or *Our Lady of the Sorrows*.

I take advantage of the opportunity and seek shelter inside the chapel. An old man greets me, stamps my credential, and gives me a tour. He pulls me by my wet sleeve from one piece of iconography to the next. He is very old, and his frail voice cannot compete with the pounding rain. I don't hear a word, but I nod and pretend I do. He keeps on for a full fifteen minutes before getting distracted by a batch of fresh peregrinos seeking shelter.

Once the old gentleman releases my sleeve, I take a seat to ride out the rain and contemplate my sorrows. After all, this is the perfect place for conducting such inventory. After a few moments of reflective deliberation, I catalog no present sorrows. I am happy.

My sons are healthy and at various stages of dream fulfillment. I am financially secure, and despite my health struggles, I am here and well enough to walk. My marriage is repairable. It's been a good marriage, not spectacular, but I'm not disappointed. As a couple, we achieved wonderful things, and if we've reached the end of our useful road together, I will still be happy – happy to go it alone or happy to work it out. I can't lose.

My future is bright. Perhaps departing the military was the *best worst thing* that ever happened to me. I never fit in any way, no matter how hard I tried. But I am a natural in the classroom. I am my very best when helping others learn. Teaching is my true calling, and it's not too late to answer the call. I've tried not to focus too much on my upcoming professorship, but now with my heaviest burdens deposited in the care of a glow-in-the-dark Virgin Mary, I am free to sort things out.

Three weeks sans sofa, I am completely unstuck. There is no returning. I'm not exactly sure what that means regarding my homestead and marriage. Much relies on Jim's willingness to overcome and adapt. But until I find my equilibrium, it's all or nothing. I've got to stay all out, or I'll fall all the way back in. I must keep moving and exploring and learning and meeting new people. My pilgrimage will not end in Santiago. It may never end.

The rain lets up, and I head back outside and make my way across a medieval peregrino bridge and into the heart of Molinaseca. Nestled at the base of the hills I climbed up and over today is the picture-perfect pilgrim halt. The río Meruelo provides a romantic backdrop to enjoy a pitcher of sangría or eat a plate of pasta at the patio table with fellow peregrinos. My heart is set on doing both. Unfortunately, the municipal albergue is all the way through the charming village and out the other side. I must first get a bed and claim my blue bag before I can return and enjoy the river.

To my delight, I run into Mimi and McKinley. We are roommates, sharing a 12-bed dorm. I dump my stuff and invite both ladies to join me for supper. Mimi accepts, but McKinley declines because she has a date with the washing machine and the dryer. Mik pulls up her t-shirt and shows off several red welts. "Bedbugs," she says with disgust. "I must have picked them up in Mazarife." My skin crawls as I recall our night in the albergue together. Perhaps it wasn't my imagination after all. I want to hug Mik, but she holds both hands out in protest. "Stay back! I'm literally crawling with them." Mimi screams dramatically. I roll my eyes at Mik and apologize for Mimi's overreaction. Sometimes, I want to punch Mimi in the face. It's not nice, I know. But no matter how many times I recite my positive peregrina mantra, the girl gets under my skin.

I dump all my change on Mik's bed. She is going to need it for the coin-operated laundry. To kill the bedbugs, everything she owns must be washed in hot water and detergent and dried at the highest setting for at least two hours. She has a long night ahead of her, and she'll finally have to wash her hair.

Mimi and I make our way into town. I'm happy to see her again, but I'm irritated by her lack of grace with Mik. Nobody deserves bedbugs, and Mik is already humiliated. Bedbugs are an equal opportunity pest, feasting on the flesh of the rich and poor and the clean and the unwashed. The real problem is Mik didn't know she had them until last night. The welts from bedbug bites can take a few days to materialize. This means she probably transported them into two other albergues before bringing them along to Molinaseca. Fortunately, our albergue maintains modern laundry facilities. This is a rare luxury.

Mimi and I walk to the riverside and sit at the end of a long table. We split a pitcher of sangría and welcome fellow peregrinos as they fill the seats. It's what I had envisioned. We are joined by Luke and Bernard and Santa Claus from South Africa. Luke introduces Heidi from Switzerland and Keith, a history teacher from Connecticut. Keith introduces Rose, the very loud Brazilian lady I followed out of Astorga. I can't tell if Rose and Keith are a *Camino thing*. If they are, they won't be for long because Mimi is gaga over Keith, and she wastes no time getting back into cheerleader character. In moments, she is twirling her hair and dumping her boobs on the table. Poor Rose fades into the backdrop like a wallflower.

Heidi from Switzerland speaks only a little English, but her cocked eyebrow speaks volumes. She winks at me and grins as we are treated to the courtship of Mimi. Luke, Keith, and Bernard jockey for position. It's a silly-ass display of testosterone and peregrino horniness. For once, I'm more than pleased to join Rose as a wallflower. I drink my wine and eat my spaghetti and watch the race.

As it turns out, I am the night's winner. Arm in arm, Mimi and I return to our dorm to sleep side by side. Those silly men did not stand a chance. And Luke bought her dinner. Now, that miffed me a little. I've had to put up with him for days, and he hasn't ponied up for a lousy beer or glass of wine.

My legs ache all night, and I find it hard to sleep. Eight hundred milligrams of ibuprofen should do the trick, but it doesn't help. The steep drop from *Cruz de Ferro* was too much for my knees and thighs. Surprisingly, my toes and heels remain blister free. I saw an awful lot of bandaged feet at dinner, and poor Heidi lost her big toenail. All in all, I'm thankful.

Molinaseca to Villafranca del Bierzo

In the sideways rain, the girls and I push on toward
Ponferrada. None of us slept well, mostly because our legs
were cramping all night. Mimi suffered an additional trauma,
"Like, Oh-My-God. I kept feeling them tiny bugs all over my
body." Mik grits her teeth. If Mimi gets a punch in the face
today, it won't be from me.

Our trek into Ponferrada is six unattractive kilometers
spent staring down at the sidewalk. The rain falls so hard we
cannot see more than a few feet in front of our faces. We
stop at a café adjacent to the enchanting *Castillo de los
Templarios* to regroup. Over thick pots of hot chocolate and
churros, we hatch a plan. Together, we will tour the castle,
and then Mik and Mimi will take a day off in Ponferrada. I
will push on once the rain lets up.

The 12th century Templar castle is storybook-stunning.
In a torrential downpour, we climb through the ruins, and
eventually, I make my way to the castle library. Of course,
nothing is original, but the display of replicated documents
and antiquated books is impressive. I've lost track of the girls,
but I don't mind. Our group dynamic is caustic, and I'm not
willing to entertain that kind of energy today. I'm too tired to
compromise and too tired to fight.

The rain is annoyingly persistent, and I don't feel like
fighting Mother Nature either. Once outside the castle walls, I
flag down a taxi. The driver pops the lid of his trunk, and I
toss Agnus and my wet rain jacket inside and jump in the
front seat. "Villafranca. El Parador!" The driver blinks at me
with a confused look on his face. I try again, "El Parador, por
favor."

"Si, Señora. El Parador!" He peels out as if he is
transporting the most important fare of his life. My driver is
young. In fact, he is probably too young to have a license, let
alone operate a cab. He is driving erratically and takes both
hands off the wheel to gesticulate while he practices his

English skills on me. Since the whole Meniere's problem, carsickness is an issue; therefore, I hopped into the front seat of the cab, but this intervention is not helping. I am nauseous and white-knuckling the dashboard within the first few moments. I also consider borrowing the rainbow set of rosary beads swinging from his rearview mirror.

My driver is proud of his English, but he doesn't know the phrase, "slow down." I know this is true because I've yelled it three times already. And for the life of me, I cannot remember how to say it in Spanish. I finally come up with, "Tranquilo! Tranquilo!" Basically, I've told him to relax or be tranquil. It's not exactly what I mean, but he grasps the concept.

He apologizes for scaring me, and between his English and my Spanish, I'm able to piece together a charming little story. In fact, I am the most important fare of his life because I am the only fare of his life. He is old enough to drive, but he is not a cab driver. This is his father's cab. And his father is *enfermo*. He suffers from the flu or some other ailment accompanied by, "mucha diarrhea." It's an overshare, but it makes me laugh.

"Rule number one of cab driving: Never admit you are not a cab driver." The boy has no clue what I am saying to him, so he shrugs and smiles. "Rule number two of cab driving: Never talk about diarrhea!" At this last comment, he bursts into laughter and nearly drives us off the road. I switch back to shouting, "Tranquilo! Tranquilo!"

By the grace of God, the boy delivers me to the front door of the Parador. He jumps out and retrieves Agnus and my raincoat from the trunk. I pay and tip handsomely because I am thankful to be alive. His eyes shine as he unfolds the cash in his hand. "Muchas gracias, Señora!" He hugs me tightly and then offers a calmer, "Buen Camino!"

The Villafranca Parador was Luke's recommendation. He booked a room for tonight too. I read reviews and knew it wasn't anything like León or Santo Domingo, but I had no idea it would be so blah, so modern. As a consolation prize, it's cheap. Besides, a 4-star hotel with an outdoor pool is still a total treat under any circumstance. I have nothing to complain about.

I enjoy dinner with Luke, Heidi from Switzerland, and Bernard from Germany. They all walked together from Molinaseca, and Luke convinced them both to stay here, at the Parador. He should receive a commission. Luke speaks German and is thrilled to hang out with Heidi and Bernard. He practices his rusty language skills and enjoys the challenge.

Dinner conversation is mostly in German. I am left out, but I don't mind much. However, I am a little miffed when Luke buys dinner for Heidi. First, it was Mimi, and now it is Heidi. Not that I need him to buy me a meal, but we have a history. Luke is smarmy and trying hard to get lucky. After all, he didn't buy Bernard's dinner.

Over a dessert of apple tart and ice cream, I try to convince the group to join me in a ride up O'Cebreiro on horseback. I read about horse rentals in my Brierly guide and hatched a perfect plan to depart Villafranca before sunrise, hike 25K to Herrerias stables, rent the horses, and enjoy a leisurely ride together up the steep trail to O'Cebreiro. It is a perfect plan, but something is lacking in my sales pitch. Nobody is interested.

Villafranca del Bierzo to Herrerias

The sun has risen, but I have not. Tucked beneath the thread-count of deliciously crisp linen, I could stay here all day, but I need to eat. This is the latest I've slept since Pamplona. I linger a little longer before throwing off the covers and slipping into the luxury of a warm bubble bath. This time, I even shave my legs with the complimentary razor. This is my first shave since leaving Seattle. There is something about freshly shaven legs that makes me feel high maintenance like I've forgotten where I am and what I am doing here.

I dump out my backpack and sort through my sparse toiletries, wishing I had tinted sunscreen and frosted lip balm. What would have been the harm in packing a few luxuries? I'm sick to death of the same two tank tops, and despite my best efforts with bleach, my once-white sun shirt is still stained and streaked with blues and grays. It's a bruise to remind me of the rough treatment I received many kilometers ago.

Normally, I avoid a big breakfast, but the breakfast buffet included in the full board rate is stunning. There are croissants and baked goods, fresh squeezed orange juice, rich café con leche, and champagne. While it's not as impressive as the buffet at the Parador in León, it is far better than the *huevos fritos con tostada* or bland wedge of egg and potato tortilla I may or may not find up the road.

So far, I'm not tired of eggs and toast. But this morning, I'm taking a new direction because I can't resist the trays mounded with sliced melons, strawberries, and pineapple wedges. There are jars of amber honey and bins of nuts, dried fruit, muesli, and pumpkin seeds to serve as toppings for a bowl of locally made, natural yogurt. I'm sure I could eat Spanish yogurt with wild honey every morning for the rest of my life. And this is odd because I used to hate plain yogurt.

I loiter in the breakfast room longer than planned. I'm becoming an expert at slowing down and enjoying the

moment. I read over my guidebook, sip my coffee, and try to
make room for one more strawberry. But it's no use. I've
eaten all I can. It is nearly noon before I check out. Heidi,
Luke, and Bernard are probably long gone by now.

The afternoon's hike is gentle, as Brierley promised. The
bubbling gush of the río Valcarce cools the roadside path,
and the foliage skirting the river is a lush ruckus of birdsong.
I listen for the cuckoo, but she's done working for the day.
My revised plan is to make the easy hike to Herrerías and rent
the horse in the morning. It's a setback I do not regret.

I give in to the hypnotic tap-tap-tap of my hiking poles
and grow nostalgic with the leisurely pace. I am excited to
meet my rental horse. I grew up with horses, but I haven't
ridden in at least twenty years. As a kid, I owned a horse
named Niki. She was a beautiful chestnut with a cinnamon
mane and three white socks. I could never get enough of her
musky scent, a brackish mix of leather, cedar, sweat, and
aromatic alfalfa. She should have been every little girl's
dream. But she owned a mean streak, and I lacked equestrian
skills.

I delivered her foal on a dewy Spring morning. I was an
old hand at midwifery. By the time I was twelve, I was well
on my way to mastering the art of animal husbandry. I
observed the birthing of cats, dogs, and cows. I waited,
incubator-side, for exhausted chicks to work free from the
confines of eggshell orbs. I played midwife to uncountable
piglets and served as surrogate mother to bottle-fed lambs,
goat kids, and calves. I knew all about animal babies and the
birthing process, but the size and scale of horse labor caught
me off guard. I had not prepared for the violent thrashing
and horse-sized groans of pain. After about six hours in,
Niki's efforts had only produced a gummy little hoof.
Reaching my hand inside her, I followed the hoof up a fragile
limb.

Armpit deep in amniotic muck, I poked around and tried
to grab him, but his body parts slipped from my hand. I slid
my other hand inside, wondering what to do if Niki jumped

to her feet. Contemplating her bad temper, I was afraid she'd kick the hell out of me. Or worse, the school bus would arrive in time to see me dragged around the pasture with my arms stuck in a horse's ass. But I braved on and was dearly rewarded. And I named him Nicholas.

My love for the colt was more than any teenage heart could bear. I touched his soft hooves, stroked his fuzzy coat, and brushed my face against his whiskered muzzle. I slept in the field with him for the first few nights, taking shelter under a canopy of Douglas fir trees. I hated to leave his side, but eventually, Mom made me go back to school.

It didn't take long before Nicholas was halter broke, but he didn't like being led. Instead, he followed me around the farm, nipping gently at my shoulders, stealing my hat, or grabbing my ponytail. Nicholas was a little pest, but I let him do as he pleased. When I rode Niki, he trotted along beside. He grew up beautifully, a thumbprint of his mother but without all the attitude.

My parents sold Niki and Nicholas while I was on a trip during my junior year of high school. When I returned, I tried to find him but to no avail. Nicholas was out of my life but not out of my heart. For years, I thought I'd never love another being as much as I adored that colt. Then along came my first son. And I named him *Nicholas*.

I'm almost to Herrerias when I spot Bernard drinking a beer beneath the shade of a café umbrella. I've never seen anyone appear so miserable while drinking beer. It's like he is sipping a goblet of poison. I take it upon myself to cheer him up, that is of course if he needs cheering. It is always hard to tell when it comes to Bernard. The bubbles and the lemon in his beer tell me he is drinking a *radler*. This is one of my favorite German beer concoctions. I sidle up, flop down in an empty chair next to him, and order up a radler of my own. The radler, a lively mixture of beer and lemonade, lifts my spirits.

"To blister-free days and cold beer." I hold my glass up in a toast.

"You like this shit?" He squints at me in suspicion and does not clink my glass.

"Yes, I love it," I confirm. "In fact, it's the first beer I learned to drink, way back in my Army days when I was stationed in Germany."

"Well. It is shit," he says flatly.

I don't know how to respond, so I shut up and drink my beer. I don't care what Bernard thinks, because my radler is delicious and cold in my hands, and it hits the spot. I decide to stay awhile and slip out of my boots and peel away my sweaty socks. I expect Bernard to protest my lack of table manners, but he does not. Removing one's shoes and socks while at the table is probably poor manners in most countries, but this is the Camino. Different rules apply.

The first few gulps of beer go straight to my head. This always happens when I'm dehydrated. The alcohol presses down on me like two strong arms and goes to work on my shoulders. A few shrugs and head rolls release the tension in my neck. And just like magic, I'm all tingly and loose. I smile as the warm glow of beer-euphoria trickles down through my scalp and makes its way to my fingertips and toes. I choke on a giggle of pure pleasure.

Bernard knits his shaggy, white eyebrows. "What is funny?"

"Nothing. I'm just super happy."

"You are happy for no reason."

"I know. I've been told that my whole life."

"Look," he points to the chair where I've plopped my abused feet. "Your feet are shit." He's not wrong. There are no fresh blisters, but the poor feet are beaten.

"Don't care. I'm happy anyway." And I really am. I want to hug Bernard in celebration, but I don't dare. I love this day and this beer, and in my little bubble of impromptu bliss, I love Bitchy-Bernard. He is only fronting, or at least that is my gut feeling. Despite the crabby face and folded arms, there is something gentle and kind radiating from him. I feel it when I lean in close. It's a vibration of good energy that even his most stoic German expression cannot mask.

Way back in Logroño, I decided to befriend Bernard. And so far, I'm one of the few. I rarely see him walking or talking with anyone. Bernard is *Camino-Eeyore,* a surly version of the depressed little donkey in A. A. Milne's tales of *The Hundred Acre Wood.* I suppose that makes me Winnie-the-Pooh, because I have pulled him into our temporary tribe, and I have loved him anyway.

Bernard recommends we stay put, right here in this lovely pension for the night. Thankfully, he doesn't suggest we share a room. I was planning to find an inexpensive option after my night at the Villafranca Parador, but I don't have the heart to seek out an albergue. I'll need to ease back into the wall to wall companionship.

Part 5
Galicia

Herrerias to Triacastela

The charming trail into Herrerias, complete with rustic footbridge and babbling brook, leads to the entrance of the stable. The ride isn't scheduled to depart until 0900. However, there are several of us, anxious to get up the mountain before the rain, already gathered.

Viktor, the stable owner, and his son methodically saddle and prepare eight sturdy and reliable mountain horses for our climb. Viktor's lack of urgency is killing me, but I keep reminding myself the ride will ultimately save time and energy. Two hours tick by and more pilgrims stop to inquire. By 1100, ten pilgrims stand by eight mounts. The son runs to an adjacent pasture and calls over an older mare. Once she is saddled, Viktor addresses the pilgrims. "Who has experience with horses?" He speaks perfect English, but no one raises a hand. My experience is antiquated and not all that positive, so I keep quiet. Viktor tries again, "Who has ridden a horse before." Like a big dummy, I raise my hand. "Bravo!" exclaims Viktor.

He speaks in Spanish to his son and points to the paddock. His son's eyes are wild in disbelief, and he shakes his head. "No, no," stammers the boy. "No, la Luna Loca!"

What's in a name? Luna is a silver-dappled Appaloosa, younger and greener than her fellows. Viktor gives me a wink. "She's going to give you a very fun ride." I smile, but I don't want fun. I want safe and leisurely. Moments later, protected only by a bicycle helmet and a set of rusty horsemanship skills, I hoist my ample butt atop a horse named Crazy Moon. She immediately starts fussing and sidestepping and grinding into the hitching post to wipe me off. A loud thwack makes Luna and me jump. I glance behind just in time to prepare for the second thwack as Viktor swings a wooden pizza paddle at Luna's backside. I brace myself, and she gives a halfhearted buck. After the second swat, she settles down. But it won't last.

About two kilometers into the ride, the clouds looming above break free. At first, I am thankful because I forgot how sweaty my legs get when pressed against saddle leather. Before long, I am soaked and shivering, gritting my teeth to stop the chatter. Steam rising from Luna is my heat source, and in the steam, I smell every bit of her *horsiness*. She doesn't have the musky scent I remember from Niki. No. Luna smells of moldy straw and old pee.

As it turns out, my horse is aptly named. Luna is totally *Loca*. In many ways, we are the same. She is overly competitive, pushing forward to the head of the pack, jockeying for position by nipping and kicking at the others. She has a personality conflict with every other horse. She can't stand to be in the rear or in the middle. Luna must be first; however, once she is in the lead, she doesn't know where to go, and neither do I. This is a fresh experience for the both of us. Viktor's kid accompanies us up the hill, but the poor boy is on foot. Right now, he is in the rear with the older mare, twisting her tail to make her move.

Visibility is diminished by a blanket of fog, and the sideways rain makes it impossible to keep my glasses clear. This is supposed to be one of the prettiest stretches of trail, but I can barely see. Every now and again, I glance down to catch a glimpse of Luna's hooves dangerously close to the edge of a steep ravine. Luna instinctively wants to live. She will not purposefully roll down into the rocky gully below and deliver us to our sudden deaths. She is spiteful, but not suicidal.

Luna and I push blindly on until the trail opens wider. The plan is to stop and let the others pass, but she won't cooperate. Animal cruelty is not my thing, but I reef back on the reins. She almost sits down. Stunned, she stops and shakes her head while the pack moves forward. Of course, she has just enough spunk in reserve to reach out and bite the older mare's ass.

I stay as far back from the pack as I can but remain close enough to make out the old mare and the kid before they disappear into the mist. Mostly, I follow by sound and Luna's urge to take the lead. The kid is diligent and works overtime, twisting the tail of the old mare and then falling back to check on me.

Eventually, Luna settles down, and I relax a bit and enjoy the experience. I coo words of encouragement to Luna, as I had years ago with Niki. "Easy, now. Up the hill. Such a good girl." She likes it, snorting and nodding her head in reply. Her attitude shifts, and for the first time, her ears flip forward, and her head bows down. She accepts me as her rider and gets on with the laborious chore of hauling me up the mountain.

Luna is trying her best, but I still don't feel out of danger. Her hooves slip and slide on the wet rocks causing bone-jolting stumbles. She hits a patch of mud and slides backward, nearly falling to her knees. I keep up the kind words to help her along. "Easy, Girl. Come on. Up the hill. Such a good girl."

We reach the asphalted road outside the walls of O'Cebreiro, and I can see Viktor's kid ahead in the fog. He is helping riders dismount, but I'm not waiting for him to come to me. I slide down and walk her toward the boy. She leads easily, trailing behind. I am about to hand her over when she reaches forward and bites my shoulder. It isn't a playful nip, nor is it horribly painful. This is Luna's little way of saying goodbye.

A tingling sensation comes over my neck and shoulders. It spreads down through my torso and shoots out my fingertips. I feel light and refreshed and oddly young. It takes me a moment to figure out what is happening. It is fear and tension leaving my body. I let out a long exhale and dislodge the knot I carried up the mountain from deep in the pit of my stomach. The vacated knot leaves a gaping hole, and I'm left with a rumbling ache. I have survived a ride on hell's favorite horse and am standing unscathed atop O'Cebreiro. And I am starving!

Apart from being hungry, I'm freezing. Luna and I rode through a downpour, and while I am wearing my rain jacket, I'm soaked from hips to toes. I need clean socks and dry bottoms and something warm in my tummy. But first, I need to find Agnus. To spare Luna the extra weight, Agnus hitched a ride up the mountain in a shuttle with the other riders' backpacks. She is waiting in a pub somewhere, high and dry.

I cross the road and head toward a break in the stone wall. I glance over my shoulder to take one last gaze at the silvery lady who carried me here, but Luna and the stablemaster's son have vanished. I blink a couple of times, straining to make out their figures, but they are swallowed up in the gray cloak of mist shrouding the village.

I enter the time warp of O'Cebreiro and deeply inhale aromas of damp stone, wet grass, wood burning fires, and cow poop. It is true much of the way smells of livestock dung, but the addition of wood smoke adds an intensity to the earthy profile. I love the smell up here, even the manure undertones. I wish I could bottle it to take home and make shampoo.

Through the mist, I admire a round hut made of stone with a peaked thatched roof. The hut, or *palloza,* sheltered villagers in Celtic times a thousand years ago and right up until the 1960s. The dwelling is so stinking quaint I want to scream. I snap photos, but the viewfinder doesn't capture the scene in all its cuteness-overload.

An old, stocky beagle approaches me while I fumble with the settings on my phone. The hound circles me twice, sniffs my hiking boots and moves on. The dog waddles over to an old man sitting on a rock wall, eating a *bocadillo.* The beagle scores a long shred of *jamón* and a scratch behind the ears. Satisfied, he meanders back toward the stone hut.

Standing in the middle of the square, I am transported to another century, but everything is familiar like I've been here in a dream. I sing a little tune in my head, a song from the musical, *Brigadoon.* But, no. It's not *Brigadoon.* That would be

Scottish. O'Cebreiro is oddly Irish but more storybook, more fantastical, like a Gaelic fairyland.

I catch a glimpse of myself in the warped window glass. The bow of the glass makes me appear extra squatty, like the mirrors in a carnival funhouse. I laugh at tree trunk legs beneath the pleats of my hiking skirt. My hair, heavy with mist, hangs in corkscrews, and my cheeks are round and rosy from the chilly ride. That's it! I've turned into a hobbit. I'm a fat, little hobbit from the *Shire!* I have seen this place before in my Tolkien-infused imagination.

I find the medieval bar where the shuttle dumped my pack. The front door is split in half, with the upper half open. Mouthwatering wafts of onion and cabbage and fried potato drift into the street. My tummy growls and churns. I grab the handle and open the lower half of the door to enter the dimly lit dining hall. In the back, bright orange and blue flames crackle and lick at a hanging pot in an open fireplace. Rustic wooden tables dot the slate floor, and cozy peregrinos sip coffee and wine and ladle spoons of hearty soup into their mouths.

There are no vacant tables, but a friendly wave invites me to a 4-top, occupied by only two. The welcoming occupants, Ronan and Nora, are Irish. I thank them for their kindness, order a glass of wine and a bowl of soup, and then I search Agnus for dry clothes.

Now dry and warm and in good company, I devour a steaming bowl of *Caldo Gallego,* a traditional *Galician* soup of cabbage, potatoes, and onions. Ronan enjoys a bowl as well, and Nora buries her nose in her wine glass. She hates the smell of the greens. The green bits are from some sort of single-leafed cabbage relative. It reminds me of kale, but not as bitter. The leaves grow on tall stalks, like the stalks of brussels sprouts. All along the riverside gardens from Villafranca on, I admired garden patches growing only potatoes, onions, and tall greens. Apparently, these are soup gardens.

Ronan reads my Brierley guide over my shoulder. The mountain albergues and pensions are completo. Although he and Nora are exhausted from the morning's climb, they have no choice but to push on. Thanks to Luna, I have fresh legs and set my sites on Triacastela. It's more than 20K, but mostly flat until the last five. I can make it down before dark.

My tooth is dangerously loose. I'm afraid it will fall out of my head any day now. My plan is to make Triacastela tonight and catch a cab to a dentist in Sarria tomorrow. I hate to hop another cab because the hike into Sarria, coupled with a visit to the impressive monastery of Samos, shouldn't be missed. But this tooth desperately needs attention.

Luke enters the hall. He is red-faced and angry, so I stare down at my guide and pretend to be deep in contemplation. Maybe he won't see me. It's against my mantra to *greet each peregrino with love and kindness in my heart,* but Luke has used up more than his ration of love and kindness from me. When he is irritated, he is a total energy drain.

It's no use. Luke hovers over me. Not only do I feel his presence, I hear his labored mouth-breathing and smell his body odor. But I can't be a bitch, not now, not after coming this far. I muster a hefty wallop of goodwill and jump up to greet him. "Hey, Luke! You made it! Welcome to O'Cebreiro." My greeting is forced, but not fake. There is a difference. I'm mastering the nanosecond attitude adjustment.

Luke plops down like a wet mop. I pass my guidebook to Ronan, so I am free to make conversation. As usual, Luke is angry. Luke is angry at the rain. Luke is angry at the steep climb and at the throbbing beneath his kneecap. Luke is angry at God and Spain and this mountain and how he chose to spend his summer vacation. He was not lulled into luxury at the Parador, even though he spent an extra night, and he is not charmed by the enchanted O'Cebreiro. He cannot see the beauty waiting just beyond his own misery.

"I'm getting out of this hellhole once the rain stops," Luke says.

"You have to," Ronan says. "O'Cebreiro is completo."

"Fine by me," seethes Luke. "Where are you headed?" he asks me.

"Triacastela, and then cabbing to Sarria in the morning to fix this tooth."

"I'll go with you."

"You sure? It's 20K, and you look like hell."

"I'll be fine. I need to get out of here."

Before leaving, I make a pitstop at the pre-Romanesque *Santa Maria la Real*, founded in 836 and thought to be the oldest church along the Camino de Santiago. The church is noted as the site of a Eucharistic miracle in the 1300s. During a poorly attended mass delivered by a halfhearted priest, the host and wine transformed into actual flesh and blood. This miracle nourished what little faith was left in the mountain hamlet.

Luke waits outside the church, still fuming at God and the weather. I collect a sello for my passport and light a candle for the survival of my marriage. The candle ritual is important to me. The process of converting inner-turmoil to an outward act of faith is empowering. Instead of fretting, I am doing something.

For the most part, Luke suffers in silence, and the walk is peaceful. The scenery along the route to Triacastela is by far my favorite. I hate that we must hurry, but it was already so late in the day to attempt another twenty 20K.

We run into a bit of a cow-jam in Fonfria. A cow-jam is like a traffic jam, but with – well, cows. A whole herd of huge, black and white dairy cows share the trail and move down the road in the same direction. I show off my farmgirl moxie by naming that breed, "Holstein," I say proudly. But Luke couldn't give two shits about bovine identification. He kicks at one who comes a little too close for his comfort. Cow karma is a bitch, and Luke slips in a cow flop and hits the asphalted road. I help him to his feet, but not without laughing my ass off.

We arrive in Triacastela, named for three castles that no longer exist. We stop at a café to figure out where we want to stay. I rifle through Agnus for my guidebook, but it is gone. I must have left it with Ronan, the Irish kid, on top of O'Cebreiro!

How can I continue without my trusty guide? John Brierley is my lifeline, my guru, my one constant companion. The book holds my future and my past. I circled places and annotated the margins and filled in the comment sections with memories and names and emails of peregrinos I want to keep in touch with. The loss is shattering.

Luke is pleased to come to my rescue, but a little too pleased for my taste. He steps in, replacing John Brierly as my guide. He pulls out a map and a printout of albergues and pensions. And we set out to find a home for the night.

Much to our unpleasant surprise, the albergues are completo. With less than a week's walk to Santiago de Compostela, the crowds are thickening and securing a bed for the night is becoming a challenge. Sarria, the next town forward and where I pray to find a dentist, is supposed to be overrun with pilgrims clamoring for lodging and resources. This is because the majority of peregrinos begins in Sarria. Just beyond town marks the 100-kilometer minimum. Walking peregrinos must complete this minimum without bus or taxi or private car to earn the Compostela, or in my case, to collect a get-out-of-hell-free-card.

I've heard rumors of tour buses dumping mobs at the 100K marker in the morning and then collecting them further down the trail in the afternoon. I'm not looking forward to the din of the mobs or the crowded pathways, but I know I'll overcome. Negotiating physical and mental obstacles has become second nature to me.

There are close to 200 bunks in a half dozen albergues in Triacastela, but there is no room for Luke and me. I consider jumping a cab to Sarria and getting a head start on my search for a dentist, but I don't. I can't leave this quaint village. I want to attend pilgrim mass and enjoy supper in the sunshine with fellow peregrinos. We left the misty gray and the rain of

O'Cebreiro and replaced it with rainbows and ancient chestnut trees and pitchers of sangría.

Fortunately, we get lucky and nab the last two rooms in a pension at the end of town. We pay dearly, at least three times more than expected. This makes an already angry Luke angrier. "Well, that's Camino capitalism for you," he snarls. Honestly, I couldn't care less about the price. I'm thankful to have a place to sleep. I climb the narrow stairs and turn the marble knob. My room in the pension reminds me of my makeshift bedroom in the storage closet atop the stairs at my grandmother's house. The walls are paneled in the same imitation birch, and the floor is old hardwood. There is also a collection of dead flies on the windowsill. I strip out of my clothes and flop on the threadbare chenille coverlet. I close my eyes and drift off to sleep beneath the velvet tapestry of a technicolor Jesus.

Triacastela to Sarria

Luke and I sit together in the café below our bedrooms. I slept beautifully, and Luke appears genuinely refreshed. He is smiling, and the furl of his brow is smoother. Breakfast is included in the room rate, but it's just coffee, orange juice, and toast. My tooth is so wiggly, I forego the bread and enjoy my coffee.

Luke has convinced me to skip the cab into Sarria and walk with him today. It didn't take much persuading on his part because it's what I wanted to do anyway. The route is hilly but short, and I'm feeling energetic. In the absence of my trusty Brierley guide, I depend on Luke. This is out of the ordinary for me, as I rarely proxy control. It's foreign and constricting – like new underwear that does not fit properly. He studies his map and decides we should take the lower and shorter route. Unfortunately, this route bypasses an impressive monastery in Samos, but it will get me into Sarria before siesta to hunt for a dentist.

I am midsentence, describing the velvet tapestry of technicolor Jesus when my tooth falls out of my head and plinks across the table to the floor. Luke is gobsmacked. He has no idea how to respond. I drop under the table, partly out of sheer humiliation, but mostly out of desperation to retrieve my crown.

In a moment of uncharacteristic chivalry, Luke joins me on all fours, and the hunt is on. I'm mortified. Unabashed, Luke climbs underneath tables and between the legs of locals and peregrinos alike and comes up victorious. He holds my pearly white crown in the air by the plastic post that is supposed to be anchored into the tooth socket.

He returns to our table, where I am covering my mouth with one hand. He bows deeply, "My queen, it appears you have lost your crown!" English speaking patrons cheer and the rest gawk in bemusement.

I lower the crown into my hot coffee as a means of sterilization. Of course, I know coffee is not sterile, but it makes me feel better to at least wash it off. And then like an earring stud, I slip the post back into the socket and click the tooth into place. To my delight, it holds – at least for a little while.

Our newly made plans are broken as Luke asks the waitress to call me a cab. When the taxi arrives, I hug Luke goodbye and wish him a "Buen Camino." We don't make plans to hook up again because we assume it will happen anyway.

The cab driver, a dark-haired lady in her sixties, does not speak English. I jump in the passenger seat and explain in Spanish where I need to go. She understands I want to go into Sarria, but she doesn't understand the part about the dental emergency. Finally, I reach into my mouth and pop out my tooth. The message and mission are crystal clear.

It's a perfect day for a walk. The morning sun lights up the shady trail. We pass a few peregrinos, and I feel sorry for myself. I hang my head like the sick kid sent home from camp just as the real fun begins. It feels odd to be flying by fellow peregrinos at such speed. I glance at the speedometer, thinking we must be doing at least 100kph, but we are putting along at 60kph. But it feels fast, especially on this narrow road.

My driver follows a river for several miles before I realize she is driving the upper route, cutting through Samos. When we arrive at the monastery, she pulls over and motions for me to get out and explore. I am thrilled! The day is not a total loss.

Once in Sarria, she parks the cab in front of a dental clinic and helps me with Agnus. I pay my fare, and I'm surprised when she takes my arm and leads me to the door. Like my last dental escort in Astorga, she rings the bell, comes inside to explain the situation to the receptionist, and leaves me with a hug and a kiss on each cheek. And just like in Astorga, a lump grows in my throat and my eyes water.

This time, I fill out no paperwork and am led directly to an exam chair. My dentist doesn't speak English, and neither does his assistant. I plunk out my tooth and hold it up for inspection. Again, no words are needed. When the procedure is finished, I pull out a fistful of cash for payment. The dentist bashfully plucks out a single twenty-euro bill.

It's unbelievable. In less than fifteen minutes after hugging my cab driver, I walk out the clinic door with the crown glued back into place and tears streaming down my face. I do not normally get emotional over dental repair, but my Camino dentists, along with the kind delivery ladies, have deeply moved me with their compassion and care.

Sarria is a much busier town than I am comfortable navigating. Without WIFI or Brierley, it takes a long time and a bit of panic before I find the first yellow shell directing me back to the route. Between the dental visit and my temporary disorientation, I am mentally spent. I drag myself through town and up a long hill and contemplate my next move. It's too early in the day to find an albergue, but I'm tired and weepy. I plop down outside an Italian restaurant to soak in the sun. It's noon and five o'clock somewhere, so I order prosecco.

I am feeling a touch melancholy. I'm solo again, which is what I thought I wanted, but I have no one to help me celebrate the reuniting of my tooth and me. Gretchen, Jana, Mimi, and Mik would have loved the café scene this morning. It would be wonderful to laugh with them again. I can still see Luke down on all fours, ass in the air, hunting for something white against a backdrop of white tile. When I replay it in my head, it's funny as hell, but wasn't funny at the time. This is partly because crowns are expensive, but mostly because I am terribly vain. I cannot get over how vulnerable I felt and how much I relied on Luke. All I could do was hold my hand over my mouth with my tongue stuck into the empty socket.

My pre-Camino unfamiliarity to the kindness of strangers makes me wonder if the locals are angels on earth. While most do seem genuinely kinder than my neighbors at home, I have a feeling my stranger-danger anxiety is a *Pavlovian* case of classical conditioning leftover from my formative years in the military. Instead of reaching out when I really needed help, I hid my vulnerability. I shut myself in and strapped myself to a sinking sofa in the dark waters of my living room. My only tethers to reality were invisible lifelines to the television and laptop. Ironically, it's through these lifelines I first learned about the pilgrimage and then feverishly researched, planned, and executed my peregrina coming-out party. Perhaps pre-Camino me couldn't receive kindness. Maybe my heart was shut. But now, my heart is wide open and bleeding all over the place. There is no turning back, and I'm so grateful.

A bob of blonde hair bounces up the hill toward me. The wind flips it up and whips it out to the side. A hand comes up and smooths it back into place. Beneath the thatch of corn silk, I see the red face of a young woman. She is working hard to get up the hill, and it shows. As she draws closer, I greet her. "Buen Camino."

I'm surprised as she passes by without returning the customary exchange, but I'm more surprised when she turns around and comes back. "Wait! I'm sorry. Buen Camino."

"No worries," I assure her. "You are tired, and your mind is in another world."

"It is," she says. "I'm quitting and taking a bus back to León in the morning."

I don't offer opinion or condolence, but I point to a chair and motion for her to sit. She drops her pack on the sidewalk next to me and sits down. I signal the waiter to bring a round of prosecco. Her name is Stine, and she is from Denmark.

"I'm sick of it! Every day, I walk alone. Every night, I eat by myself. This is not fun, walking and walking and being alone. And now I have bugs!"

I focus on my poker face, "How long have you had bugs?"

"A couple of days." She takes a long swig of prosecco.

"Wash everything you own and dry it for at least two hours. This place has an albergue in the back with a proper washer and dryer."

"I was walking to the albergue at the monastery. It's cheap, but no laundry machines. Is this where you are staying?"

"I haven't decided. The service is good. And the Italian hospitaleros are *muy guapo!*"

Finally, Stine smiles. We take our glasses inside and get to work. She strips and jumps in the shower, while I dump her pack in an empty stall and stuff everything not washable, including her backpack, into a garbage bag supplied by the hospitalero. He sprays insecticide inside the bag, seals it up, and carries it outside to bake in the hot sun.

I loan Stine my green dress while her belongings are being debugged. We move back outside and order a pitcher of sangría and a pizza Margherita. Stine is a college student on her first summer vacation away from home. And it's been a disaster. "I started in Logroño and haven't met one nice person!" She dabs her eyes and blows her nose. "Until now," she corrects herself. "Everyone is so closed-off, you know?" She looks to me for verification, but I don't give it.

I want to explain my earlier epiphany about the outpouring of compassion I've received. I want to explain how we must walk with open hearts, but this is not a subject suitable for vicarious learning. Life's most important lessons must be lived. Instead, I keep her company and let her vent. She is frustrated and hurt and needs to talk it out.

We share photos of family and pets, and she comments on my handsome boy, Garret. He is my middle son and the same age as Stine. "I'll come to America and marry your Garret," she muses. "I've had no luck finding a boyfriend this summer."

"Is that what you were hoping for? Love?"

"Secretly, yes. But maybe I am too ugly." Her comment is ridiculous, and she realizes this too. I do not indulge her; instead, I ask about her certainty to quit.

"Yes. I'm done. Absolutely," Stine confirms. "I booked a flight out of León, already."

The idea of quitting after enduring so many kilometers is hard to fathom. Stine will regret her decision, not in a day or two, but later, after the bedbug bites and blisters have healed. I'm tempted to invite her to tag along with me, but I do not have the power to gift a meaningful Camino experience. I have plenty of experience handcrafting Christmas magic, orchestrating Easter egg hunts, cooking Thanksgiving dinners, playing Tooth Fairy, and hosting birthday parties. But this is different. Pilgrimage is a gift we give ourselves.

Luke is walking up the sidewalk, and I wave him over. He has reserved a room at a new albergue another 3K ahead. Evidently, it's a terrific place, complete with a swimming pool. He invites me to come along, but I've already committed to hanging out with Stine. He pokes his head inside and sniffs, "a little rundown, don't you think?" He is referring to the graffiti-covered walls and the mishmash of café tables and chairs, but he couldn't be more wrong. The albergue is spacious, artistic, and well-furnished. Plus, the bartender makes the best sangría on the route.

I invite him to a slice of our pizza and a glass of sangría. I expect him to decline and push on to his destination, but he takes a seat instead. He keeps the conversation light after Stine announces her decision to quit. "Ah, that's too bad," is his only comment.

Luke is uncharacteristically animated. The sangría is helping him along. He recounts the morning's dental misadventure to the waiters and Stine, and everyone enjoys his story. Our waiter is young and handsome and overly-attentive. He moves in close to examine my newly replaced crown, and I can smell the fresh shave on his handsome face.

Stine and I are the only ladies in the company of several Italian men and Luke. We are sponges, soaking up the attention and the bottomless pitcher of sangría. The hospitaleros speak to us in Italian, calling us "Bella," and we respond in trills of girlish giggles. Stine is in her element, and

I suppose I'm acting foolish. The flirty banter is refreshing. My body is comfortable, and I am exactly where I'm supposed to be, here at this table enjoying the warm Spanish sun. My smile is intact. My feet remain blister-free, and I'm overflowing with gratitude and joy. I cannot remember ever feeling this content.

The night wears on, and I lose track of Luke. When I'm finally ready to call it a night, Stine and the waiter are sitting across the table from each other. They are holding hands and staring intently into each other's eyes. The young man is desperately trying to convince Stine to stay in Sarria for the summer and volunteer at the albergue. I'm happy she found what she secretly wanted, a little love.

I work my way through the maze, cross the albergue, and head up the back stairs to my room. When I open the door, I'm startled to find a man snoring in one of the two single beds. At first, I'm confused, and then I'm angry.

"Luke! What the hell?"

"I didn't want to be alone," he whines.

"How did you get a key?"

"I told the bartender we were together, that you're my wife."

"Oh, my holy shit…"

I'm disgusted, but there's nothing to do about it. There are two beds, and he is harmless. If it came down to it, I'm sure I could knock the shit out him. So, there is no real reason to kick him out. Besides, it's too late for either of us to find another place to sleep.

While Luke may be harmless, he snores like a freight train, and I feel awkward and guilty. My hubby would not approve nor understand this arrangement. It was hard enough to ease his mind about the safety and normality of co-ed dorms and bathrooms. This feels all wrong, like something I can't be honest about in the future.

I toss and turn for a couple of hours before tiptoeing back down the steps and making my way through the albergue. I grab my green dress from the rail of Stine's bunk and bend down to whisper my goodbye, but her bed is empty. I nod and smile knowingly and make my way through the dining room and out the front door. I'll never know if Stine stayed on in Sarria with her dreamy, Italian waiter, but I'd want to believe she finally opened her heart to love and to the Camino.

Sarria to Portomarín

I fill up my water bladder at a peregrino fountain before leaving Sarria. This will be my first full day without a guidebook. I'm finally doing what the grumpy hospitalero in Viloria suggested, "Just walk. You'll find your true path." He told us to throw out our guidebooks, and I've accidentally complied. He recommended we stop following yellow arrows and shells. I'm not entirely there yet. I spy a splash of yellow and follow it out of town.

The urge to check my guidebook to see how many kilometers I've walked or how many kilometers to the next stop or the gains and losses in elevation is overwhelming. There is nothing to check, so I keep walking. I average 5K an hour. Portomarín is about 20K. With rest breaks, it should take me five hours to reach the village, but I forgot to check the time before leaving Sarria. I try to gauge it by my hunger. I walk about an hour before I build up an appetite. Surely an hour has lapsed because I'm hungry as hell.

The morning sun shines down on me, and it feels lovely. My muscles are loose and warm, and I'll bet I've covered at least 10K. While part of me is anxious to quantify my hourly progress, I try to ignore the markers counting down the kilometers to Santiago de Compostela. The markers sprang up like weeds once I entered the region of Galicia. They tick down the final steps of my newfound freedom. I know I'm just shy of the 100-kilometer mark, so I stop for breakfast to buy some time.

Although I do miss my husband and my dog, I don't want to go home. I'm also excited about my new job, but I don't want to go back to work. It's hard to imagine trading in my hiking boots and the beauty of Mother Nature for business-casual and the fluorescent lights of a classroom. I don't like the fact my journey is almost over. Now fully acclimated, this is my new normal. Is it foolish to want to remain a peregrina forever? No. I don't think so.

Thanks to the dentist in Sarria, I eat my eggs and toast with renewed gusto. It is liberating to chew on both sides again. I'm about to order another café con leche when I witness the tour bus phenomenon. Rumors are true. I pay my bill and try to escape before the silence is shattered, but I'm too late. A tide of shiny, new pilgrims demanding service swallows me whole. The din makes me dizzy, and the crowd chokes the exit. I desperately need out. There are too many people touching me, but I keep calm. Sliding sideways around bodies, I gently push my way outside. I'm sweaty and frazzled but emotionally and physically stable.

I step up the pace to outrun the noise, but the faster I go, the more I trip. I must be God's clumsiest pilgrim. Stumbling aside, I'm rather pleased with myself. I handled the crowded café well. I didn't like it, but I didn't panic, and I didn't need to hide out in the bathroom either. How far I have come since my agoraphobia-fueled panic attack at the Madrid airport!

I will greet each pilgrim with love and kindness in my heart – even the shiny, new ones. I need an attitude reset. This is not my Camino. This is not my country, and I am not a Catholic. I am a visitor, a pilgrim; I have no more rights to this trail than the next busload coming up behind me. No matter how many times I remind myself of these things, the day feels combative. I fight for a bubble of peace and race to stay ahead of the wave.

The day's effort to outrun the crowd earns me two tender blisters, one on the ball of each foot. I rest at a café in Mercadoiro, enjoy a lemon *Aquarius*, and apply *Compeed* patches. I have not met with a familiar face today. I haven't seen Bernard or Heidi or Mimi or Mik or Luke. The absence of my tribe makes me uneasy. I enjoy walking alone, but I also like to run into a friend every now and again. It's like I've spent the entire day dodging strangers.

I limp the next few kilometers and cross the swollen *río Miño* to Portomarín, my stopping place for the night. To my dismay, a monstrous stair climb stands between me and the village. Ahead, a British pilgrim exclaims to her girlfriend, "Oh, you've got to be fucking kidding me!" Yes. That sums up my sentiments, exactly.

I climb the stairs, muttering profanity under my breath, and then follow the blacktop until it turns to cobblestone. I duck into the shade of an impressive stone colonnade, thankful to be out of the hot sun. The colonnade leads to a lively plaza dotted with café tables and occupied by peregrinos and locals. Despite my blisters, I feel solid, like I've got another 10K in the tank. I poke my head into the 12th-century church of *San Nicolas* to check on pilgrim mass. I haven't attended mass since Sahagun, and I'm long overdue.

San Nicolas appears unusual to me. It is Romanesque but doesn't look at all churchy. It is more like a fortress. I bone up on my Portomarín history and learn the building was designed to multitask. It is both a church and a defensive fortress. The original church foundation is submerged beneath the river I crossed to get into town. The church was dismantled brick by brick, hauled up the hill, and carefully reconstructed. This was done to create a reservoir to serve the areas agricultural and household demands for water. Fascinating!

Portomarín is an attractive pilgrim halt, but it is missing familiar faces. The square is chocked full of peregrinos I do not recognize. I've time-warped ahead or fallen behind. I'm not sure which. For the past few weeks, there has been a set of faces – a flow. This doesn't mean I socialize with these faces or know names, but they are still part of my tribe. We nod to each other upon meeting. We are a peregrino-amoeba inching toward Santiago de Compostela. I am comfy in our unspoken solidarity, but now I feel displaced and unsure.

I contemplate walking on in hopes of meeting my tribe ahead at the next albergue. But then, out of the corner of my eye, I spy a hot-pink sports bra. It's Mimi! She is limping toward me along the colonnade and flanked by two men. I'm ecstatic to see her. I wave, but she doesn't return the salutation because her arms are flung over the shoulders of the men beside her.

Worried she is injured, I rush to meet her. But she isn't thrilled to see me. I try to remember our last departure, wondering if we had a tiff. It was in Ponferrada, and I did get a little annoyed with her bedbug theatrics, but there wasn't an argument.

Reluctantly, Mimi introduces me to Klaus and Wilhelm, two obviously German dudes. I suggest we grab a beer and catch up. Mimi declines, but the boys are game. I buy a round for the table and listen to their adventures. The boys have carried Mimi and Mimi's backpack off and on for the last 60K. According to Wilhelm, they found her alone and crying on the steep trail up O'Cebreiro. They have been inseparable ever since. Klaus points to the jagged scratch on Mimi's leg, "She fell on the rocks. She's lucky we found her." I examine the scratch. It still looks bad. I make out the teeth and comb-like pattern of metal foot grips from her bicycle pedal. Mimi's secret is safe with me.

Two is company, and three is a crowd. But this is not the case with Mimi and her boys. Four is a crowd. I'm the fourth, wobbly wheel nobody wants. This only becomes apparent after the first round runs dry, and I fail to fetch another. I'm not desperate enough for company, so I excuse myself, find a bed, and get ready for mass.

Portomarín to Palas de Rei

I went to bed before dinner last night and accidentally slept later than usual. This is a sign. My body is forcing me to slow down, and I plan to listen. I take a moment before getting out of bed to stretch and frame my thoughts. I will be a kinder pilgrim today, now that I've had a full night of rest. I'm all chilled out and happy with the world again. My personal goal for today is to shine my peregrina lovelight on new and road-weary peregrinos alike.

Some may call me a new peregrina. I started in Pamplona, not in Holland like Levi or Elke, and not in Paris like Bernard and a few others I have met. Compared to many, I am green. But I'm not fresh. The fresh ones smell better. When the newbies pass by, I catch a whiff of fabric softener and real laundry detergent. Yesterday, I picked up the scent of *Channel No. 5*. It was heavenly!

I make my way to the café downstairs and order breakfast. It's just eggs and toast again, but it is so much fun to eat worry free. I hadn't realized how much the loose crown was crushing on my gastronomical joy.

I leave Portomarín at a relaxed pace. My *Compeed* covered blisters are not-so-gentle reminders of what happens when I overstep. I am disappointed about the blisters. I suffered so much during the first two weeks of my journey, and I thought I had made it beyond that phase. What I find most galling is I could have avoided the pain if I had not lost control of my emotions. Again, I failed to listen to my body. I am a slow learning peregrina, but I will learn.

The route is full of smells, most agricultural and mildly unpleasant. However, nothing compares to the olfactory assault of the fertilizer plant in *Toxibo*. The town is aptly named. This place smells toxic. I used to play this odor identification game, *name-that-shit*, on the school bus with my friends. On the ride home in rural Oregon, there was always shit in need of identification. I play a solo game now, as I walk the length of the massive fertilizer plant. I am fortunate, or rather unfortunate, to be downwind. Conditions are ripe for play. At first, I smell run-of-the-mill cow shit, but within a few steps, I change my mind to dairy cow poo. Dairy is less grassy with higher notes of rotting corn cobs. As I progress, I absolutely smell hog shit. Not the free-range pigs I befriended as a child, but the kind kept in long sheds and out of sunlight and fed a diet of dried corn and soybean meal. It's the soybean that gives off the sour smell. As I'm nearing the end of my trip down *Olfactory Lane*, I am assaulted by the rankest one of all. Chicken!

My gag reflex hits, and I taste a bit of the orange marmalade from my breakfast toast. It was better the first time. Chicken shit is the only shit that makes me puke. Tender blisters and all, I break into a jog. I've got to clear out of this shit-wonderland.

It takes me awhile to outrun the smell, and I find myself at a roadside bar in Gonzar. Every table is occupied, inside and out, so I squeeze in on a threesome of Spanish kids. Sonia speaks the most English, so she serves as group translator. The kids are *Galacian* teens, locals, walking in celebration of their graduation from high school. I feel a dull ache in my mother-bones and think of Jaden, my most recent graduate.

I miss the baby Jaden. It's cliché, but he was a toddler yesterday, and now he is a high school graduate. His final years of school were murder. I was the helicopter mom hovering over him, checking in with teachers, and proofreading homework. I couldn't let him fail, and we fought every day over his lack of effort. All he wanted was to move out and move in with his dad. He wore me down, but I didn't want him to leave. I still don't. What I want is to bring him to Europe with me. He could attend my university, and we could explore between semesters. It's a great idea, but he disagrees. I'm trying to understand, but it still stings.

The Galacian kids are ready to take off. They invite me to walk with them, and I'm pleased to join their happy troupe.

It's kind of funny, but these kids are the same kind of peregrinos that usually annoy the hell out of me. They are loud. They play grab-ass in the middle of the trail, pushing and shoving and knocking off each other's hats. And they sing. They sing at the top of their lungs. And it's not good. Their lack of seriousness is oddly refreshing. I'll admit, I probably would not feel this way had they not welcomed me in as their fourth wheel. And now, I am what annoys me. Isn't that something?

New peregrinos revive the old question: *Why are you walking the* Camino*?* No one has asked me this question in weeks. An inquisitive Korean man sits across the table and awaits my answer. Our coffee cups separate us from the truth. "I'm searching for equilibrium." It comes out in a voice so smooth and sure. I glance over my shoulder to see where it came from. But it was me!

Searching for equilibrium is the true and perfect answer. It's all about finding a balance, sorting things out, and coming to terms with the past and the future. The response leaves me free to go deep or only wade in up to my ankles. I don't know this friendly and curious man, and I don't have all day to explain the shit-show that has been my life. So, I stick with physical equilibrium. "I have Meniere's disease, a balance disorder. It is hard to enjoy nature like I used to do, so I'm challenging myself by getting back outside." He nods his head appreciatively, and then in return, I pose the question to him.

"I have a walking problem too. My hip is brand new. Titanium!" He raps his right hip two times with this fist and makes a knocking sound by clicking his tongue against his palate. "I'm taking it for a test drive!" He laughs like he's told the best joke ever. I am polite and laugh with him. The exchange is precisely what he had hoped for. He wants a selfie with me. As instructed, I make a peace sign to match his peace sign, and he immortalizes the moment forever.

After lunch, Sonia, my young Spanish companion, asks the question again. I reply, "I'm searching for equilibrium, life's balance. My children are grown, and I want to go off

and have adventures, but my husband wants to stay home.
We must find a way to balance our desires."

She smiles knowingly and tells me about her mother.
"She wants me to go university. So, I applied. I leave for
Madrid next month, and now all she can do is cry. She
doesn't know how to balance her life without me. She needs
what you need – Equilibrium."

The teenagers and I walk together shoulder to shoulder.
My tribe of youthful Spaniards is tranquil now. They ran out
of steam a few kilometers back. They scuff their sneakers
along the path and kick up dust. I should scold them and
make them pick up their feet, but the scuffing sound is
familiar and comforting. I listen to their breathing and
footfalls, and I contemplate what it means to find
equilibrium. If this is what I'm searching for, I need to know
when I've found it.

Finding equilibrium is very much about the physical,
especially out here on the trail. I must strike the right balance
in pace and step. Too fast? And I rub hotspots on the balls of
my feet. Overextend? And I blister beneath my toes. I
balance the weight in Agnus and pay attention to my
footwear and sleep cycle and nutrition and booze
consumption and alone time. *Peregrina-homeostasis* is in
perpetual flux. Too much or too little of any element throws
me out of equilibrium. Learning to maintain physical stability
is easier because the deficit is partnered with visible
consequences.

It's the mental game, on and off the Camino, that
perplexes me. How do I get what I want without bulldozing
and taking from others? And how do I go where I want to go
without leaving loved ones behind? How do I compromise
without being a doormat? Where do I draw the line between
inattentive and vigilant? Or hypervigilant and paranoid? Who
should I trust and who should I suspect? I don't want to be in
harm's way, but I don't want to close myself off from the
world again.

My vertigo is as much emotional as it is physical. Life has
been a dizzying ride, and the only cure is to hop off and walk.
Walking combats my crazy. *Interesting.* Perhaps I should ask
for a yearly prescription to the Camino. All expenses, except a
modest co-pay, would be covered by my health insurance
plan. Now that's my kind of healthcare reform!

Walking is good medicine, and it's the perfect medium for
finding and maintaining equilibrium. I'm tested every
kilometer of every day, and the results are immediate and easy
to interpret. When I achieve a balanced physical state, I am
free from pain and able to walk in a relaxed manner for
longer distances. When I've struck a mental balance, I feel
safe and happy and grateful. The Camino de Santiago is my
proving grounds.

The *Galacian* teens lag several meters behind as we enter
an ancient hamlet. Ahead, a father and son walk side by side.
They are wearing the coveralls and rubber boots of local dairy
farmers. The son bends down and picks up something
rectangular. A book? Yes. He is flipping the pages. He passes
it to his dad, and it hits me. It's a *Brierley guidebook*! Some poor
peregrino dropped it. I quicken my pace to close the gap, but
the dad heads toward a dumpster. I wrack my brain for
words. I want to holler, "Wait!" or "Stop!" I know these
Spanish words, but I can't find them. I turn to call out to
Sonia, but she's wearing earbuds and singing softly to herself.

The man lifts the lid of the dumpster as I shout, "¡Espere!
Por favor. ¡Espere!" But he does not wait. The book plops
and the lid clangs shut. When the teens catch up, I explain
the tragedy. Marco, the only boy in our troupe, peers into the
dumpster and laughs. He fishes out the book with a hiking
pole. It is a Brierley guide, written in German and covered in
horse shit! Who puts horse shit in a dumpster?

I'm downhearted about the book, and the kids cannot
understand why. They travel sans map and sans guidebook.
"What's the problem?" says Sonja. I try to explain the book is
a lifeline. They have each other and smartphones with
roaming data and mothers to call in the event of an

emergency or loneliness. I have a phone that doubles as a brick, and I'm alone and motherless and without direction. Marco and Sonia and Olivia form a circle around me and give me a group hug. It's partly sarcastic, of course, and they take it too far. The embrace ends in a dogpile, and I find myself on the ground gazing up at my three young friends. My vertigo is no match for teenage roughhousing.

I'm helped to my feet by Sonia and Olivia, as Marco flings the shitty guidebook back into the dumpster. We continue along our way, and I am closer to my new band of peregrinos than before the tussle. There's nothing like a hug and horseplay to strengthen bonds. When we enter Palas de Rei, they don't invite me to join them for the night. They don't need to. There is an unspoken expectation. I take up the bottom bunk below Marco. Sonia selects the one across from me and below Olivia. And just like that, I am the Camino mother of three.

Palas de Rei to Salceda

Like most teenagers, these kids are not early risers. I pack Agnus and wait around for as long as I can stand it, but they still won't get out of bed. My body wants to move, so I kiss each forehead goodbye. We make a pact to meet back up in Melide for lunch. Reluctantly, I leave the albergue, and I can't help but worry I may never see these cutie pies again.

The morning walk is easy. Agnus is light, and my legs are strong. I cross a postcard-worthy medieval bridge into Furelos and stop for a coffee at a bar on the other side. Conveniently located across from the bar is the church of *San Juan*. After my coffee, I take advantage of my position and pop inside the church to collect a sello, light a couple of candles, and pray.

The day wears on, and my spirits remain high. I've walked the entire morning solo, but I don't feel alone. The gentle trail, woodlands, and river valleys are my companions. Gone are the choking crowds that bottlenecked the narrow paths beyond Sarria. I assumed the bus tours and swarms of new peregrinos would be the new normal. Thankfully, I was wrong. As it turns out, there is plenty of trail for everyone.

I walk into Melide, watching for the Galacian teens and searching for the perfect place to eat octopus. Octopus is a big deal around here. I've eaten it in Hawaii and Mexico and wasn't crazy about it, but I'm interested in sampling the local interpretation.

I'm checking out an octo-bar when I hear my name. Up ahead, two people are waving their hands and yelling my name. It is my name, but it sounds lovelier than I have ever heard it hollered. Ah, the Irish accent. That's it! I lean my poles against a brick wall and ready myself for the running embraces of Ronan and Nora, the Irish couple I met in O'Cebreiro. Our encounter on the mountain was brief, so their enthusiasm catches me off guard.

Ronan reaches me first and wraps his arms around me. He lets go so Nora can take a turn. We are hugging on the street, but I'm not exactly sure why. "My God, Lass!" says Nora. "We've been hunting all over for you!"

"You have?" I'm stunned by my popularity.

"You are a hard lady to catch!" Ronan rifles through his pack as he speaks. "Here it is!" You forgot your book. We've been trying like hell to get it back to you." He holds up a tattered and dogeared Brierley guide. It's only been out of my possession for four days, but it looks foreign. I scrutinize it to be sure it is mine.

"Remember? I borrowed it," he says. "And then your grumpy friend came by. And you left. It's yours. Really!"

They look disappointed with the anticlimactic reunion of woman and book, so I step it up a notch. "Yes! Of course! I'm lost without this thing. I can't thank you enough." I motion to the bar. "Come on. Let me buy you a beer!" We file into the bar and slip into a booth. I order a round of San Miguel, a plate of octopus, and a side of little green peppers.

Octopus, regardless of continent, is not my favorite. It's a terrific source of low-fat protein, and while I find it edible, it's nothing I'd ever crave. Besides, I kind of have this thing for octopi. It's not extreme, not like my love for pigs, but I am fond of the creatures. The *Pacific Red Octopus* was the mascot of my last Coast Guard gig, a Maritime Force Protection Unit. I've often thought about getting an octopi tattoo to commemorate my Coast Guard service, but I haven't worked up the motivation or courage, yet.

For culinary purposes, I can take or leave the octopus; however, the peppers are a different story. These little green lanterns are pan-fried in olive oil, without batter, and then sprinkled with coarse sea salt. I've never eaten a better accompaniment to beer. My only question is, why am I just discovering these? I am about 50K from the finish line. Where have these been my whole trek?

We order a second round of San Miguel and another plate of peppers. I connect to the bar's free WIFI and check my messages. There's one from Sonia, and it's unwelcome news. Marco was bitten by a dog outside of Palas de Rei. He is okay, but they are off the trail for a couple of days. He needs stitches in his thigh and a tetanus shot in his ass. She also writes it was his fault. He lunged at the dog, a German Shephard, trying to get it to play.

I tell Nora and Ronan about the kids and their plight. "Stupid fecking brats," says Ronan. His reaction surprises me until he tells me about his work at an animal shelter, and how so many dogs are abandoned or euthanized because human children behave worse than animals. He rehabilitates the gentle, larger dogs to become emotional support companions and service animals. My heart leaps, and I scramble to show him photos of Jasper. What luck! What are the chances to find such an uncommon common bond?

We leave the bar, and Ronan and I dive into a stimulating conversation about service dogs and service dog training. I could talk about this all the way to Santiago. Unfortunately, the pads of both feet are heating up, right where the *Compeed* patches are covering old blisters. My body needs to slow down, and I need to listen. Nora is short and struggling to keep up. She is only too happy to let Ronan step off on his own and hang back with me.

Nora is a charming schoolteacher from Kilkenny. We strike up an in-depth conversation about kids and teaching and national education standards. I love to discuss my passion for teaching but talking about dogs involves less energy. We both tire and slip into a comfortable silence. Like my friend McKinley, Nora's stride is exceptionally short but quick. I lope along next to her at a relaxed pace while she takes choppy steps. We are well-matched.

Nora leads me through a freeway underpass, and we are accosted by a group of young women holding clipboards. Having read multiple warnings in online forums, I half expected to meet up with this scam as early as Burgos. These girls pose as deaf mutes collecting donations. They are said to be persistent and sometimes hostile. I am prepared. My preplanned strategy is to offer a couple of bucks and move on, saving the drama for another cause. I don't care if it is a scam or not. My goal is to avoid confrontation.

A hulk of a girl shoves a clipboard into my chest. Nora steps forward and closes the gap between us. The girl is tapping the clipboard and pointing out names of donators and amounts collected. I keep one hand firmly on the flap of my shoulder bag and reach into my skirt pocket for a two-euro coin. I smile and make the offering, but the girl gets frustrated and beats on the clipboard. She points to the donation amounts. Each annotated donation is over thirty euros. I will happily be taken for two euro, but not thirty. I close my fist around my coin. "No. No tengo dinero para ti!" And that is true. I have no money for her. Nora grabs my arm, and together we step around the pack. We are within earshot when one calls me a bitch, in English!

My legs are shaking, and the tick-tick-ticking in my chest has returned. It's my old friend, *Panic*. He's back. Damn, and I thought for sure I had shaken him. I was solid at the underpass, but now I'm a bowl of jelly.

Nora is unfazed and surprised at my reaction. She pats my arm and reassures me, "They were harmless, Lass! Gypsies. You can't let them intimidate you."

"Gypsies?"

"Yes. Yes. It's an old scam. Seen it a million times. The secret is to keep walking."

Nora is right. It was a bunch of girls. All I had to do was walk away. They weren't blocking the path. They didn't have clubs or knives or guns. They had clipboards, for God sakes.

Nora and I enter a Eucalyptus forest. She is unfamiliar with these trees, but I recognize them from thirty years ago when I was an exchange student in Australia. For nostalgia's sake, I scan the treetops for Koala bears, but of course, I find none. I was such a brave girl back then, boarding my first airplane, leaving family and friends for the first time, and taking off to a new country. I had never moved as a child, and apart from elementary graduation to high school, I had never switched schools. By the time my year in Australia was over, *change* was my new normal. I couldn't sit still. Returning to the same old school and the same old house with the same old rules killed me. I couldn't wait to finish my senior year and get the hell out of there. That's part of what made me such an easy target for the military. I wanted to go, but I had nowhere to go. I was low hanging fruit. Easy pickings.

For a split second, I let my mind flash to Sergeant Walker. But I catch myself. *No way, Asshole. You're dead to me. Remember? I dropped you at the Cruz de Ferro.*

Nora and I happen upon the strangest sight. It's a group of little kids, ranging from about eight to twelve years old. They wear matching blue t-shirts and ride bikes. They are supervised by teenagers wearing red t-shirts. I point to two young men in red shirts, "Camp counselors?" We stand behind a traffic jam of bikes sorting out the scene and watching the counselors untangle the mess.

"Church group?" suggests Nora.

"They're *peregrinitos*, pilgrims-in-training. Maybe they are headed to Santiago too."

"No bloody way!" Nora cringes. "I can't imagine taking all these kids that many miles…" She points to a chubby, little girl struggling to stay upright. "Look at the little lassie! She needs stabilizers." And just then, the little lass tips over. Her name is Gladys. We know this because it's printed on the back of her t-shirt. A teenage boy scoops her up, bike and all, and gives her a push. Within a few revolutions of her pedals, she is back on her side with both legs still straddling her bike. She stays still until uprighted again by the same young man. Undaunted, she restarts, and this time, she does rather well.

The teens are cheering, and Nora and I are cheering. The other children have already gone up and over the hill. Gladys makes it about halfway up, and her bike begins to totter. She stands on the peddles and pushes with all her might. She's almost to the top, when Nora screams out, "Come on, Gladys! Put your calves into it!" And then Gladys disappears over the top. The teens high-five each other and extend the high-fiving to us.

After the revelry in the eucalyptus forest dies down, Nora and I follow the youthful bicyclists and counselors up and over Gladys' victory hill. Nora walks with a grin plastered across her face, and I'll bet she is thinking of an early rite of passage, the day the stabilizers came off her bike.

I remember my first bike. It was a present from Santa Claus. It was dark blue with a banana seat flecked with silver glitter. I received it on Christmas morning, complete with training wheels. After a couple of weeks and rather unceremoniously, the extra wheels disappeared. It was Irv, my late brother, who held the handlebars steady. He gave a push and then ran behind me, as I took my first trip down the dirt road.

Nicholas, my oldest, was born on a bike. His first ride down a grassy hill without his training wheels worried me sick, but the kid was a natural. He boldly took the hill and let out a "Yahoo!" as he gained speed. My step boys were twelve and thirteen and already competent bike riders when they came into my life. But I cannot remember the training wheel rite of passage for Garret or Jaden. I catalog back through Christmases and birthdays, trying to remember the first bikes. I can see the little red trike Garret rode all over the military housing compound in Hawaii, and the plastic John Deere tractor pushcart Jaden dearly loved, but nothing beyond.

Where was I for Garret and Jaden? It's a small thing in the big picture of childrearing, but my lack of recall is haunting. Did I miss it? And how did I stay so busy all this time, that I am only just now realizing I missed it? Granted, I was a working mom and fulltime student for most of their younger lives, but I should remember more.

I feel sad. Guilty is probably the better word. I can't help but wonder if my sons feel jilted. I had so much going on when they were growing up. I tried to be a good mom, to always be there. But who took the damn training wheels off Garret and Jaden's bikes?

The trail cutting through the eucalyptus forest is damp
and deliciously soft. Shreds of bark composting underfoot
create a layer of spongy carpet. I inhale the cleansing air and
try to put aside motherhood woes. *You did your best.* Everyone
is happy and healthy. Each boy owned a bike, and more
importantly, no one still rides with training wheels. What
more can I ask?

We come around a bend in the forest and see a mountain
of a man sitting on a picnic table. The table is covered with all
sorts of foodstuffs. There are a couple of oranges, an apple,
and a stack of single bananas. There are bags of chips and
granola bars and bottles of water. I assume he is offering
these items donativo, for hungry pilgrims. I've seen this set
up all along the route. Entrepreneurial locals set up a snack
bar, and hungry pilgrims select items and donate money. Back
in Logroño, I traded a few euros for a thick slice of
homemade bread and a cold beer. And I bought cherries near
Molinaseca.

Naturally, we drift toward his table. We are surprised to
learn he is not in the selling business. He is in the receiving
business. "I'm hungry!" he barks at us in English. I don't
have any snacks to give, so I keep walking as Nora told me I
should have done with the pretend-mute girls. "I'm hungry!"
He barks again. I glance over my shoulder and expect to see
Nora right next to me, but she is still back at the table. He is
towering over her like a forest ogre. "Give me money," he
shouts and reaches for the small satchel strapped around her
waist.

I don't know exactly how it happened, but I love Nora's
retelling of the story. "Suddenly, there she was, like a bloody
ninja! She appeared out of nowhere – a fecking apparition.
And she's all up in this ogre's face. And she shoves him! Yes,
this fierce kitten nearly knocks him on his ass. She tells him
off, all right - to smartly go feck himself."

I enjoy the retelling when we meet up with Ronan in
Ribadiso, and then several times after. No one has ever called

me a *fierce kitten* before, and it cracks me up. I have no idea what I thought when I shoved the man. I don't remember feeling frightened. In fact, my legs didn't turn to jelly.

A pack of girls sent me spiraling into a panic attack, but I was pumped up and ready to rumble with the forest ogre. I can't lie. The drama in the forest has energized me. The adrenaline and confidence invigorate my body. Being Nora's hero is fun. I must feign humility, but I'm secretly thrilled.

I planned to walk only to Ribadiso, a manageable 25K on natural paths and isolated roadway. However, after meeting back up with Ronan, Nora has encouraged me to continue into Arzúa, where she has a reserved bed. My adrenaline is still flushing through my veins. It would be a shame to waste it, so I tag along.

Ronan walks with us but plans to continue beyond Arzúa. He met a Spanish girl on the trail a week ago, and her family lives in the next hamlet. Ronan's romantic prospects with a local girl are confusing. For some reason, I assumed Ronan and Nora were a thing.

"Because we are both Irish? Because we walk together?" Nora sounds exasperated. This obviously isn't the first time the terms of their relationship are questioned. "I suppose you and that grumpy fellow, Luke, are sweethearts?"

"Oh, hell no!"

"Could've fooled me," Nora huffs. "You two quarrel like old, married folk."

The distance from Ribadiso to Arzúa is about 3K, and Nora ribs me all the way. The transition from an idyllic and sleepy hamlet to a stark and commercialized pilgrim halt is unnerving. I love Nora's company, but I am not digging Arzúa. To make matters worse, there are no empty beds in Nora's albergue. In fact, the town is completo! I'm not worried. I have enough energy to walk on. Surely, I'll find something along the outskirts.

We sit and enjoy a beer together before splitting up for the night. There are several familiar faces around sidewalk tables flanking the busy street. My old tribe, with a sprinkle of new, has regrouped. With less than 40K to the finish line, it's possible we may not run into each other before entering Santiago de Compostela. Each kilometer and each face become more precious as I near the end.

The need for solitude has lessened, and my desire for camaraderie has grown. I feel like I've lost a ton of weight, physically and mentally. Unfortunately, my clothes fit the same, but I am lighter and happier. I'm also having a lot of fun. Lately, it's been more like a party than a penance. And I'm cool with that.

Nora elbows me in the ribs and raises her eyebrows. I give her a daft stare, but then she points to Luke coming up the street. She gets in a little more of her gentle ribbing until he is within earshot. I have not seen Luke since Sarria after getting pissed off at him for crashing my private room. I expect him to act sheepishly, but he does not. He plops down like nothing happened. *Nothing did happen*, but I feel awkward about the situation.

With great animation and creative license, Nora retells the ogre story to Luke. Ronan has heard it twice already, but nearly laughs himself out of his chair. Nora can really spin a yarn. Luke is not amused. In fact, he scolds my reckless behavior. But reckless is the last thing I felt.

"You should have run for help," he chastises. "You could have been hurt!"

Luke's harsh critic catches me by surprise. It's not his business, and I'm not his wife. I keep it light by not reminding him of these facts, but he's killed the mood, and I prepare to move on for the night.

Newly concerned for my safety, Luke tries to convince me to share his private room instead of walking out of town with Ronan. He argues he owes me one, and he does. But I decline. Apart from his snoring, I'm not comfortable sleeping next to him. I didn't like it in Sarria, and I don't want it now.

Ronan and I bid our group farewell, and we head out of town. We walk in silence until we are out of the nerve-shattering din of traffic. My shoulders relax beneath Agnus.

My gait stretches out, and my pace slows. Ronan tells me a little about Isabella, the Spanish girl he plans to visit tonight. When the Isabella conversation runs dry, Ronan switches to dogs. We talk about Jasper, training and exercise, feeding and grooming, and breed temperament. Clearly, my dear Ronan is more comfortable with Labradors than ladies.

It's dark when Ronan must turn off our path to make his way into his girlfriend's hamlet. Unfortunately, I did not find a bed on the outskirts of Arzúa, and there has been nothing since. He encourages me to join him. "I'm sure it will be okay. She'll understand."

"Are you crazy, Ronan? You don't bring another woman along to meet your sweetheart's parents, even if the other woman is old enough to be your mother."

"She's not really my sweetheart."

"And she never will be if you keep this up." I give him a long hug before sending him on his way. I know I will not see this lovely young man again. Isabella is a lucky girl.

I dig out my headlamp before continuing. I walk through another eucalyptus forest. Although brave, my aloneness weighs on my mind. I startle at every twig snapping in the woods, jerking my head toward the sound and scanning the forest with my beam of light. I am comfortable with Mother Nature. Wild animals lurking in the woods do not scare me; however, I'm skittish as hell when it comes to ogres.

About an hour goes by before I see the light. Excited, I quicken my pace. It must be an albergue. The glow leads me to a lovely patio and into a nearly deserted bar. There isn't a peregrino on site. The bartender tells me the unfortunate news. This is not an albergue. The next albergue isn't for another three and a half kilometers. In the dark, it will take me the better part of an hour to reach it, and then what? What if they don't have space?

The bartender kindly offers me a lift, but he knows I cannot accept. Fast forwarding, even this short distance, will disqualify me from receiving the coveted Compostela. Instead, he calls ahead and ensures there is space. The

albergue beds are sold out, but there is one private room left.
I don't hesitate.

I hotfoot it through the forest, making better time than
predicted. The pension host greets me warmly, and his wife
offers a late seating for supper and expedited laundry service.
I'm so grateful to be out of the dark forest and into the warm
glow of their beautiful pension. I drop off Agnus in my well-
appointed room and head out to the patio to eat.

My tardy arrival limits the menu choices. The hostess
suggests the trout or the trout. I go with the trout. She pours
me a glass of red wine and leaves the bottle on my table.
Besides me, there are only three other diners. A pair of ladies
occupy a table in the center, and a man sits alone against the
back wall. I make eye contact and smile at the ladies and then
at the man. He raises his glass, and I lift mine. It's a friendly
exchange.

The gentleman, who is already enjoying his food, gets up
and walks across the dining room to my table. "Pardon me,"
he speaks to me in English, but it is obviously not his first
language. "I do not like eating alone. Won't you join me?"
Honestly, I'd rather not, but it feels incredibly rude to decline.
I grab my glass and bottle and follow him back to his table.

Raul lives in Madrid. He began his journey in Sarria and is
overly impressed I started in Pamplona, and equally
impressed I walked 40K today. I can't lie; I'm impressed too.
Forty is my record. Apart from getting a little frazzled in the
dark woods, I feel surprisingly robust. My feet and legs are
no worse for the added distance.

Raul asks me the *big question*, and I reply with a vague
version of my equilibrium answer. I plan to follow up with
something about finding my feet after a couple of life
changes, but Raul cuts me off. He has waited all day to share
his answer to the *big question* nobody has bothered to ask him.
He jumps right on it without my prompting. His job is
complicated. His love life is complicated. His living situation
is complicated. His relationship with God is complicated…
Raul is complicated.

I listen patiently and enjoy my wine. To show I'm actively participating, I give the occasional head nod. Raul's complications are familiar, but he is boring the hell out of me. Many kilometers ago, I too was complicated and would have appreciated the opportunity to obsess over our mutually complicated lives. But the simplified peregrina in me sees things differently now. I don't want to roll around in indulgent, self-imposed chaos. I'm cleaner, lighter, and mostly unencumbered by all the crap I carried with me at the beginning of the journey. It is remarkable what a long walk can do for an overstimulated soul.

Raul is late to the peregrino game, and I can tell he desperately wants a meaningful experience, even if he must fabricate one. When my food arrives, a beautifully pan-fried trout, he pauses his dissertation only long enough for me to thank my server. He continues a one-sided discussion about the "magical happenstance" of meeting each other and the "deep, spiritual connection" we share. He is picking up vibes I am not laying down.

Raul poses a question, but before I'm able to decode and send a response, he asks again. The second request rings with a tone of irritation. "Well, won't you walk into Santiago with me tomorrow?" It's a simple question, but I'm flabbergasted. It's too soon for that kind of commitment. Raul is not part of my tribe. And up until now, I hadn't given my arrival much thought. Regardless of kilometer count, the finish line is far away and unreal. I assumed I would arrive with my wave of peregrinos, but I may have outwalked a few. Suddenly, I feel very alone.

I stammer for an answer. I don't want to commit, but I don't want to be rude. "I had not intended to finish tomorrow." This is true. I hadn't planned on it. I had expected to stay back in Ribadiso tonight and then Lavacolla tomorrow night. This would leave about 11K and an easy jaunt to the Cathedral for the next day.

"It's less than thirty kilometers to Santiago," he argues. "You walked forty today."

"I know, but I planned to meet up with friends at the Parador, but not tomorrow." This is not true, but it is not exactly a lie. Luke, Bernard, and Heidi from Switzerland all plan to stay at the Parador, but I have no clue when. I held no Parador plans, until this very moment.

"The Parador?" Raul sounds impressed. "Very expensive."

"It's not too bad with a roommate."

"Perfecto! I will be your roommate."

Well, shit. This took a turn for the worse. "That won't work for me, Raul."

"Why not?"

"Because I am married and sharing a room with a man makes me uncomfortable."

"That is very stupid."

"I suppose it is. But maybe we can walk together instead."

He is placated but pushes for my social media information, so he can message me in the morning. I recommend we meet for breakfast, but he won't let me off the hook. The guy is persistent. He desperately wants a Camino friend, and I'm his last chance.

Raul has worn me down. I cannot continue negotiations about how far and with whom I will walk tomorrow. He pesters me for contact information, and I give in. He sends me a test-message, while I'm sitting right in front of him. And he isn't satisfied until I post a reply. I respond with a smiley face, and he is thrilled. We are now best-friends-forever. I excuse myself, offer a half hug, and slip off to my room.

My room is charming. There are rustic stone walls, a queen-size bed, and a slanted roof with a skylight. The bathroom is modern and stocked with fluffy towels, lots of hot water, and real shampoo. There are bars of sweet smelling soap, bottles of lotion and conditioner, and a razor. But best of all, there is a shower seat, so I can safely shave my legs. All the essentials are here to perform my final peregrina cleansing.

I had intended to perform a cleansing ritual tomorrow night in Lavacolla. According to my guidebook, the place gets its name from the Spanish root word *lavar,* which means *to wash.* Medieval pilgrims stopped in Lavacolla to purify themselves before entering the city. The place is popular with modern pilgrims because of its international airport. I'll fly home from Lavacolla in a few days, but I'm not ready to think about that yet.

I turn on the hot water and am about to slide on to the shower seat when my phone pings. It's a message from Nora. She and Luke are worried. I reply, letting her know my location and status. I also promise to follow up on my whereabouts tomorrow. I hear the phone ping three more times while I wash my hair, but I ignore it and reach for the razor instead.

After a long and luxurious shower, I wrap in a towel, flop on the bed, and check my messages. I assume the pings are from Nora, but they are not. It's Raul: *I am happy to meet you! I need a foot massage. I want to massage your body!* I send Raul a firm decline and wish him goodnight.

Just before I tuck into bed, I notice a remote control on my nightstand. There is no television in the room, so I examine it closer. To my delight, it controls the skylight. I hit the buttons and invite in the night sky. I'm so excited to sleep under a blanket of stars on what is potentially my final evening on the Camino. How fitting.

I receive another three messages from Raul. He certainly doesn't waste time. He writes: *I want to see you naked! I am touching myself! Please come to room 110.*

I eye the key on my nightstand. I am in 111. Raul is right next door! I feel the choke of panic settle high in my chest. It's stupid. I know. I try and reason with myself and talk the panic down. Raul has no idea I'm next door. He did not plan this. It's a coincidence. Besides, my door is locked. I get up to recheck the lock. And then I remember the canister of pepper spray. I haven't seen it in weeks. I dig through my pack and find it stuffed in a side compartment, long forgotten – until now.

I place the canister on the nightstand within arm's reach. It pisses me off that I feel the need to have it near. I had forgotten all about it. I tangled with a forest ogre and survived a dark walk in the woods. Neither event frightened me enough to remind me of the pepper-spray. I have come so far since the airport bathroom back in Pamplona. And now? Now I'm going to let some little dickhead scare me? I'm furious. I get up and recheck the lock on the door.

My phone pings two more times. Of course, it is Raul: *I know you want to fuck me. You are a dirty whore!*

I feel the electric pulse of the boogieman trying to ride a flash of rage back into my head. "Go away, Dickhead. You are dead to me!" I make this proclamation aloud and turn off the phone. It's not enough to flip the switch, so I bury the phone in the bottom of Agnus and carry her into the bathroom. I don't need to read or respond to this trash, but I don't trust myself not to look at the next ping. Sometimes, I am my own worst enemy.

I recheck the lock on the door and listen for any movement in the hallway. An hour passes. And I get up and recheck the lock on the door. I will check five more times before sleep finds me.

Salceda to Santiago de Compostela

I hoped to get a jump on Raul and walk before dawn, but with my phone stuffed in the bottom of my rucksack, there was no wake-up alarm. After shampooing and shaving, and reburying the boogieman last night, I am ready to make my way to the *Cathedral of Santiago de Compostela*. I stuff all nonessentials in the blue bag to fast-forward to Santiago. With thirty hilly kilometers on mostly hardscape, I need to be gentle on my legs and feet.

Panic almost stops me from sending the bag to the Parador because I told Raul about it. While I don't want to be harassed, I won't be intimidated. I address the tag, slip a few coins in the envelope, seal it up, and attach it to my belongings. That little dickhead, Raul, is not going to cheat me out of 5-star luxury and a final farewell with my tribe. He can go screw himself.

I head downstairs to the breakfast room and spot Raul before he spots me. Forgoing breakfast, I dump my blue bag at the front desk and pay my bill. Part of me is angry about not confronting him, for not pouring hot coffee right into his lap, but I reassure myself I am not running like the scared little rabbit I used to be. Avoiding confrontation and harassment is not the same as running away. Whatever I want to say to Raul will not change last night, and it will not change his future behavior. I am nobody to Raul. But more importantly, he is nobody to me. He is a total douchebag, and he will not define my final day.

For safety's sake, I tell the host my troubles. Someone ought to know, just in case. The host takes me around the back of his property and shows me a shortcut to shave three kilometers. He also promises to buy me time by playing games with Raul's bill.

Agnus, who is now ridiculously light, rides high on my back. I feel inside my shoulder bag for the canister of pepper spray. At first, I was reluctant to put it back within arm's reach. It was refreshing to lose it in my backpack and in my mind. Erring on the side of caution is not the same thing as paranoia. Raul is creepy and behaved in a way I did not predict or provoke. His desires are not under my command. I can only control actions within my bubble. He will not act upon me in my bubble. That's for damn sure.

I work my way through the shortcut and back on to the main route. The forest trail flanks a busy road and crisscrosses a few times. It's easy underfoot with only a slight incline. I soften my shoulders and focus on maintaining a relaxed gait. This is my last day on the Camino. I'm not going to rush, and I'm not going to be afraid. I'm going to take in the scenery and enjoy the friendly company of my fellow peregrinos. *I will greet each peregrino with love and kindness in my heart* – Each one except for Raul. Raul will be greeted with pepper spray.

After a few kilometers, I'm back on the main trail, and my body shifts into a higher gear. I am a horse headed back to the barn after a long ride. I loosen the reins and let it rip. Relaxed and at a comfortable pace, I complete the first 10K in record time. I follow a tunnel under the roadway and pop out next to a café. The café is buzzing with peregrinos. I consider walking on to avoid the crowd, but I'm long overdue for breakfast.

I'm thrilled to run into some of the old gang. I take a seat next to Bernard. Within moments, we are joined by Keith, the American history teacher I have not seen since Molinaseca. He is walking with Mimi. Sans Wilhelm and Klaus, she is happy to see me. Apparently, Bernard and Keith are poor substitutes for her German fanboys. We catch each other up on the latest trail-gossip, but I don't talk about Raul or retell the pretend-mute or ogre stories. The storytelling is flat without an Irish accent.

We are all anxious to finish no matter how calm and relaxed we pretend to be. Keith contemplates overnighting in Lavacolla. Bernard threatens to cab right on through, bypassing Santiago and walking to Finisterre. We beg him to reconsider, and we know he will. Only Mimi is completely honest. "I just want to be done with this stupid thing!" Her eyes brim with tears. I can't help but hug her. She has struggled with many of the same physical and emotional elements I have, but we've processed differently.

We leave the café together, but we do not stay together. Mimi and I cannot match Bernard and Keith's pace. It isn't long until the two are out of site. Mimi walks beside me, but not with me. She is still angry about bicycles in Sahagun or bedbugs in Molinaseca or whatever I did or didn't do in Portomarín. She is sulking and punishing me with her silence. Punishment has never felt so good.

With only eighteen kilometers remaining, I am nostalgic. I am ready to finish, but I am also sad. My emotions are getting the best of me. My eyes brim with tears at the smallest of things. This happens when I'm operating on little sleep, and I slept very little last night. The situation with Raul left me with insomnia, but I didn't waste the whole night fretting. Instead, I occupied my mind and filled the sleepless hours by replaying my entire journey. I revisited Madrid and my agoraphobic moment crossing the passenger terminal to the train station. And then I examined Pamplona and how frightened I was in the deserted airport. I don't recognize that girl anymore. Things could have turned out way worse had it not been for the kindness of the security guard and the cab driver.

I thought about the curious woman carrying a blue-green bird in a gilded cage. She was my guide, leading me toward Santiago. Like an apparition, she appeared and disappeared until I forgot to watch for her. *Nuestra, del Periquito.* Our Lady of the Parakeet.

I thought about Gretchen and Jonny, my first set of Camino kids. How my heart broke when Drew performed a Camino reset and banished me from his family. But the very next day, I met the lovely Jana. She taught me to slow down and treat myself gently. I thought about McKinley and her birthday at the Parador. And bedbugs. I will always think of bedbugs. I thought about Burgos and bicycles. And my ass still remembers riding with Mimi across the Meseta.

I thought about Luke and how earlier on, he reflected some of my ugly behaviors and inner conversations. But then later, I saw him as a metaphor, a window inside and a way to understand how my husband might be feeling. Like Luke's wife, I am moving to another country for work. I now know this for sure. While I am not taking away his children, I am taking Jasper. The loss of a dog can't compare to that of a child, but Jim will still suffer. Like Luke, Jim is staying behind. But unlike Luke, Jim is invited. I've begged him to join me. What I offer Jim is much greater than what he must give up. We are at a standoff, and all I can do is reassure my love for him. He must wrestle with his own foolish pride.

I revisited the *Cruz de Ferro*. And my skin prickled in excitement. I did what I came to do. I dropped my rock of burdens and claimed my bravery and freedom. I will never ever be the same.

I inventoried blisters and a bashed-up knee and marveled at how my body has become so very strong. I can't remember my last bout with vertigo or my last migraine. I am in such fantastic health, so much better than when I was at home on the sofa. I've mastered the state of physical equilibrium.

Over the past few days, I've been running the gauntlet, testing my ability to balance the emotional load. I rode a horse named *Luna Loca*. I've lost and found a crown. I panicked over a pack of not-so-mute, mute girls. But rebounded and faced a forest ogre. I braved a scary walk in a dark forest and out-foxed a total hound.

My emotional balance is in a state of constant flux, and I must fight like hell for equilibrium. But I fight. And I survive. I move forward. I keep walking. The walking helps me keep my shit together. I can't help but wonder what the trail will throw my way next.

Mimi and I stop in San Paio for a break, but she decides she is done for the day. We agree to meet for mass and dinner tomorrow night, and then we hug goodbye. It feels weird to walk this final stretch alone, having shared more than 700 kilometers with so many hearts.

I pop down into a tunnel and walk beneath a busy thoroughfare. The cars and trucks rumble overhead. When I pop back out, I'm surprised to see three men walking ahead of me. These men are not typical peregrinos. They walk slow and are without backpacks. Each is dressed in a long, white, cotton robe with matching cap. One man is so tiny, about chest high to me. The second man is of average size, and the third is huge. He is at least seven feet tall.

Curiosity wins, and I speed up to check them out. The very tall man and the tiny man turn around to greet me. The other man keeps walking. The tallest one is a boy, a teenager. His baby face glows in a dark copper brown. He closes heavily lashed, almond-shaped eyes and bows his head. He is soft and beautiful, like a giant baby. The tiny man's face is covered with a wiry, black beard. He smiles warmly and outstretches his arms as he speaks, "One love, one God! One God, one love!"

I'm not exactly sure the appropriate response, but I put my hand on my heart, bow slightly, and I wish him a *Buen Camino*. Evidently, I'm right on the money, because he is thrilled. He praises *Allah* and continues his mantra. "One love, one God! One God, one love!"

Our exchange is fruitful, and the men walk on. I follow but drop back a bit to widen the distance between us. I can't help but wonder why three Muslim men are walking the Camino de Santiago. The tiny man said they walk to promote unity. *One love. One God.* But I'm hesitant. I haven't questioned the motivations of any other peregrinos. So why now? Obviously, I'm guilty of profiling. I catalog according to ethnicity, skin color, religion… It's such bullshit. I hate that I do this, but I know much of the tendency stems from my long, military history. I came of age in a culture of war. I'm trained to observe differences and to analyze. This training assists in maintaining a level of vigilance, but my overactive imagination gives way to paranoia. Paranoia robs me of living wholly and experiencing the beauty of Earth and her people.

I stop in Lavacolla for an *Aquarius*, the last one of my hike. I must give them up, partly because of the sugar, but mostly because I won't be able to find them again. Before enjoying my beverage, I swing open the door to the ladies' restroom and am surprised to see the big boy in the long robe standing before the mirror. Wide-eyed, he acts even more shocked to see me. I point to the symbol on the door, the round head atop a triangle body. He responds with a hand gesture panning down his robe to his high-top sneakers. Yes. It is true. With my bare legs showing, the robed-boy resembles the symbol more than me.

I want to hug this kid, but I don't. I nod my head in understanding and raise a hand to my mouth to conceal a smile. Once he figures out his error, he's going to need privacy. I don't want him to feel embarrassed or awkward by my presence. I let the door swing closed and take my drink to go.

I stop in *Monte del Gozo*, but I don't climb to the monument commemorating the visit of Pope John Luke II. There's a herd of pilgrims at the top, taking selfies and trying to spot the Cathedral of Santiago from up high. I'm not in a selfie mood. Instead, I bathe beneath a water faucet. I have made it within the city limits of Santiago de Compostela, but I still have a long way to go. I rinse my hair, wash my face, and splash away dust from my arms and legs. Before hitting the pavement, I duck into the humble chapel of *San Marcos* for a private moment. I have no words to express my gratitude, but I send up my thanks. I am healthy, and I cannot begin to catalog all the simple joys and life lessons along this pilgrimage. Nothing will ever undo the beauty and grace I have witnessed along the way.

I make my way toward the old quarter, following pairs and trios and groups and other single peregrinos. As I enter the pedestrian zone, I hear my name. I scan the patio tables and spot a man with a shock of white hair. He is wildly waving his hands. It's Bernard! Waving much less wildly is Keith, the American history teacher. They are drinking beers in the sunshine, and Bernard cajoles me to "Have a pint before meeting your maker." It's an offer I cannot refuse.

I was so ready to make my entrance into the cathedral square and cross the finish line. I imagined a flood of tears and a few heartfelt hallelujahs. But now, just two blocks away, I'm drinking beers with a couple of atheists. How's that for a twist of fate?

This is my last moment with Bernard, so I sit and make time. Keith will go on to the *Official Peregrino Office*, surrender his pilgrim credentials, and collect the Compostela awarded to those who walk for cultural or other reasons. I will apply for the version intended for spiritual or religious purposes. Bernard will receive neither. He didn't bother to gather the stamps because he never meant to come this far. Bernard started hiking south of Paris with the original goal to walk over the Pyrenees, but he kept walking, and he will continue until he runs out of earth in Finisterre.

I drain the last of my beer as Rose, the Brazilian woman I tend to avoid, rushes our table. She is part of Keith's inner circle, not mine. But Keith is not excited to see her. I'm sure she is a ton of fun, but she is too loud for me, and she never stops talking. Several times, I've walked in front or behind Rose, and all I could hear was *Rose*. She speaks of handbags, shoes that are not for hiking, plastic surgery, and cosmetic treatments. She has endured breast implants, a butt lift, collagen injections, and liposuction. I don't want to know these things, but I was within earshot. A time or two, I was tempted to tell her to shut-the-hell-up, but I never did. While I didn't want to be unkind, I never went out of my way to show her kindness.

She gesticulates passionately. Her hands try to keep time with her mouth, but they don't stand a chance. English is not Rose's first language, but she sure knows a lot of words. Her group ditched her. They snuck out of the albergue while she was in the shower. "Stupid bitches. They are jealous. You know. Jealous bitches!" And now, Rose is alone but doesn't want to be alone. She begs Keith to walk in with her, but he flatly refuses.

"How did this happen to me?" Rose is now jumping up and down, waving her hands and doing the *white-lady-crying* thing. But her version is not nearly as convincing as Mimi's. "Why am I alone? Why does everybody hate me?" Poor Rose. I've asked myself these questions too, but I've never shouted them in a crowded plaza in Spain.

I stand and hug Bernard and Keith goodbye. "Come on, Rose. We can walk in together." I reach out and take hold of her hand. Without losing a beat, Rose stops crying and starts yapping. I cannot stand it.

I make it about a half of a block before I stop. "Rose, shh!" I speak gently and hold a finger to my lips. "You're okay now, Honey. You made it. You are safe. It's time to shut up, already – to be at peace." I hold her hand as we walk in silence through the final stone corridor. A busker plays *Amazing Grace* on the *Galician* bagpipes, and a lump grows in my throat. I drop a few coins into his music case. Rose empties her pockets.

Tears stream down Rose's face as we gaze up at the Cathedral. Restoration scaffolding interferes with the view, but the true beauty cannot be hidden. Rose hugs me tightly and calls me her Camino angel. "God sat you at the table drinking beer to wait for me," she claims. It wasn't God who ordered another round for the table. It was Bernard. Regardless, I'm happy I was there for her. I'm also grateful for the one last lesson in kindness. After our hug in front of the scaffolded cathedral, I never see Rose again.

I meet up with Luke and Nora at the Parador, but Nora rushes off with her own tribe. Luke and I enjoy the best gin and tonic of my life at the patio bar. He is disappointed at the anticlimactic finish and refuses my invite to attend a pilgrim mass tonight. "What a letdown," he says. "I walked all this way for nothing." Luke expected more, a parade or perhaps a banner written in God's hand with life instructions. I'm not sure what Luke wants, but his negativity is killing the good vibrations. Without ceremony or exchange of social media information, I wish him luck and hug him goodbye.

After a hot bath, I slip into my worn-out silk dress and walk to the cathedral to attend mass and venerate the bones of dear old *Santiago*. As promised, I say a prayer for *Rafael*, my cab driver back in Pamplona. As usual, I light candles for my boys and for the survival of my marriage. I also light a candle for *Levi*, the recovering heroin addict from Holland. Levi and I walked only a few miles together, but I carried his story and his tiny tick-puller the whole *Way*. I pray he finds peace and his way home from addiction.

The Pilgrim mass is lovely but overcrowded. The music is angelic. And the swinging *Botafumeiro* is a fragrant and visually stunning delight. Everything is as described by Brierly in my guidebook. Surprisingly, I feel no closure. Unlike many of my fellow peregrinos, I did not walk into Santiago today to end my pilgrimage. I am not attending mass to check the last box on my peregrino-to-do list. For me, there is no end. And for this, I am profoundly grateful.

A pilgrimage along the Camino de Santiago de Compostela is not to be confused with a jaunt down the yellow brick road. If a seeker arrives at the *Oficina del Peregrino* as part of the procession and expects a bequeathment of wisdom, matters of the heart, and bravery, he or she will be sorely disappointed. This is not the land of *Oz*. Unquestionably, these rewards and more are out there but must be dearly earned along the journey and beyond.

Before I leave Santiago de Compostela, I already know I will return. I know I will walk the Camino again and again. The *Way* has wiggled into my heart. I have become a seeker and a source of light, a *true peregrina*.

Santiago de Compostela and Beyond

I walked my second Camino two years after my first, but this time I was brave and healthy enough to tackle the Pyrenees. Although I practiced and reinforced the lessons of my first pilgrimage, I could not replicate the relationships or the profound, emotional journey of self-discovery and healing. You only get one first-Camino.

I walked the third time with my husband, Jim. It is said a love affair awaits beneath a blanket of stars along the *Camino de Santiago*. It waits for peregrinos with open hearts. After living apart while I held a professorship abroad, our hearts were battered and bruised. But we tightly laced up our boots, and we pulled our hearts wide open. And now, Jim and I share a Camino love affair.

I have walked this same path three times, and each time I see it differently. This is true even though the medieval churches and villages are right where I left them. The mountains are just as high, the path is unaltered, and cows still graze atop hilly pastures. Red poppies dance in the wind and the sleepy heads of giant sunflowers turn to greet me as I bathe in the morning light. Grapes still grow in the vineyards, and the same crops occupy the same fields and are tended by the same farmers. But I see it differently with each evolution because I am renewed in each peregrination.

I was reborn beneath a blanket of stars along the Camino de Santiago de Compostela. I am once again a perfect bundle of energy and light. I am brave and intuitively connected to nature. I've rekindled faith in God and in human kindness. My peregrina heart bursts with a wanderlust and a desire to embrace Mother Earth and her people. I am again who I was born to be.

Acknowledgments

This book is possible only through shared relationships with fellow peregrinos along the way to Santiago de Compostela.

Thank you, Gretchen and Jonny and Drew and Grandpa for adopting me into my first Camino family. Thank you, Jana, for demonstrating grace under pressure and teaching me the fine art of slowing down. Thank you, McKinley, for sharing your champagne and not your bedbugs.

Thank you, Levi, for trusting me. I've used the tick-puller you gifted once on Jasper. As promised, I thought of you.

Thank you, Casey and Angela, for encouragement, friendship, and creative input.

And thank you, Jim, for love, support, and on-the-spot readiness with a brown handkerchief. I no longer take you or these attributes for granted.

About the Author

C.W. Lockhart is a traveling collegiate professor at the University of Maryland University College. Following two decades of military service in the US Army and Coast Guard, she now pursues lifelong passions for education and travel. An award-winning professor, Lockhart has taught writing, literature, art history, management, and organizational leadership courses in the United States, England, Germany, Ireland, Scotland, Italy, and Japan. She works and wanders the world with Jasper, her globetrotting Labrador. Lockhart makes her permanent home in Seabeck, Washington.

CPSIA information can be obtained
at www.ICGtesting.com
Printed in the USA
LVHW080944251118
598141LV00016B/706/P